THE FUTURE OF AMERICAN OIL

THE EXPERTS TESTIFY

THE FUTURE OF AMERICAN OIL

THE EXPERTS TESTIFY

Testimony before the Congress of the United States by
Peter A. Bator, Edward W. Erickson, Barry Friedman,
Raymond B. Gary, Neil H. Jacoby, Thomas E. Kauper,
Richard B. Mancke, Edward J. Mitchell, Thomas Gale
Moore, Reed Moyer, Stewart C. Myers, Dixy Lee Ray,
Gary L. Swenson, and Wallace W. Wilson.

Compiled by
Hastings Wyman, Jr.

Patricia Maloney Markun
Editor

American Petroleum Institute

Copyright © 1976 by
American Petroleum Institute
Printed in the United States of America
FIRST PRINTING

International Standard Book Number 0-89364-000-x
Library of Congress Catalog Card Number 76-14550

For information address:

American Petroleum Institute
2101 L Street, Northwest
Washington, D.C. 20037

iv

CONTENTS

INTRODUCTION

VERTICAL DIVESTITURE/DISMEMBERMENT

HORIZONTAL DIVESTITURE/DISMEMBERMENT

LIST OF TABLES
AND GRAPHS

FOREWORD

Arguments on the great issues of our times are presented in the testimony given before committees of the Congress of the United States. Frequently, these arguments are cogent and well documented.

Unfortunately, interested citizens and scholars do not have easy and timely access to this valuable evidence.

In this volume, the American Petroleum Institute has gathered from the record the testimony of 14 authorities on one issue that deeply affects all Americans. The issue is whether the nation's largest oil companies are to be dismembered.

One set of Congressional proponents would force these companies to split up into smaller, single-function firms. The other set of proposals would prevent the oil companies, the nation's most experienced energy producers, from working on the development of other sources of energy for the Nation's future.

These witnesses—professors, economists, and financial experts—represent leading universities and other institutions in this country. Their views and data cover all aspects of the issue, and their testimony is published here in complete, unabridged form.

Proposals to dismember the American oil industry and to restrict its healthy growth should be studied carefully, for in the outcome of such legislative proposals rests the future of American oil. On that subject, the experts testify.

Frank N. Ikard
President

The Bator testimony examines the legal consequences of the vertical divestiture of petroleum firms. Bator estimates that such dismemberment likely would result in massive litigation of ten or more years duration involving the Federal administrative agencies, the Federal judiciary and the private sector. Such considerations raise serious difficulty with the suggestion that legislative dismemberment is an appropriate short cut to antitrust litigation.

LEGAL CONSEQUENCES OF DISMEMBERMENT

STATEMENT OF PETER A. BATOR,* DAVIS POLK & WARDWELL BEFORE THE SUBCOMMITTEE ON ANTITRUST AND MONOPOLY, COMMITTEE ON THE JUDICIARY, UNITED STATES SENATE — JANUARY 27, 1976

Mr. Chairman, I want to thank the Subcommittee for the opportunity granted me to testify today regarding the legal consequences of Senator Bayh's bill, S. 2387, mandating divestiture by certain vertically integrated oil companies. My name is Peter A. Bator and I am a partner in the New York City law firm of Davis Polk & Wardell. My firm consists of approximately 180 lawyers and carries on a diversified general practice, although our work is to some degree concentrated in the corporate financial area, together with litigation, antitrust advice and tax work. My own practice has been largely in the area of corporate financial work, including representation of banks, investment banking firms and corporate clients in connection with securities issues, project financings, acquisitions and so forth.

The firm does not generally represent—that is, we do not act as general counsel or principal outside counsel for—any of the major integrated oil companies as defined in S. 2387. We do act as principal outside counsel for

---

*Partner, Davis Polk & Wardwell.

some medium sized or smaller oil companies, and we do represent from time to time certain of the major integrated oil companies on specific projects, usually on a specific piece of financing or a specific litigation matter. We also advise one of the major integrated companies on a continuing basis on certain tax matters. In addition, through commercial and investment banking clients, my firm and I individually have had substantial experience in advising on the legal aspects of many financing transactions of the major oil companies.

The research on which this statement is based has been done at the request of the American Petroleum Institute, a trade association which has not heretofore been a client of our firm.

I. Introduction

The purpose of my testimony today is not to discuss the wisdom of divestiture legislation but to try to give the Subcommittee a lawyer's judgment of how a divestiture program would in fact work, and to analyze some of the legal difficulties and problems which would arise if a bill such as S. 2387 were adopted.

I believe such an analysis is useful for two reasons. In the first place, our review of the testimony given before this Subcommittee* and other committees indicates that no one has in fact done such an analysis of just how a divestiture program might operate. Second, I believe such an analysis is useful in light of what has been an explicit and important justification given by the proponents of the legislation—that is, that divestiture legislation could solve in a quick, relatively easy and unbureaucratic manner the many problems which are perceived by some to exist in the oil industry. The inclusion in the bill of a three year time limit for the completion of divestiture reflects this view. It is easy to say "divest yourself of these or those assets". It is also easy to assume that such a divestiture can be effected

---

*The following statements are taken from either prepared testimony or transcripts of testimony before the Subcommittee during 1975:

"But it is my conclusion that, given the incredible delay inescapably involved in the disposition on a case by case basis of actions filed under the antitrust law, that we would be better off at least selectively by legislation to specify structures that must be dismantled . . ."; "Without assigning or suggesting an improper motive or indifference to public interest to either of those agencies [the Department of Justice and the Federal Trade Commission], part of the basic problem of any kind of massive judicial procedures seeking antitrust enforcement, the complexity of the cases, the limitation on manpower, consequent limitation in areas that they can in fact move on—all of this has persuaded me that we should seek some legislative, if you will, short cut." (Senator Hart). "As you know, [the current FTC proceeding] has not even reached the hearing stage, and it is likely to drag on into the 1980's. The time and expense to the Nation can be avoided by Congressional action which can insure that competition

speedily and without complications. But the facts are otherwise. My testimony will try to outline the complicated problems that would have to be faced in connection with a divestiture program. My conclusion is that if Congress determines that a divestiture program should be mandated, it will result in a massive amount of litigation and will require 10 or more years of great effort by the Federal judiciary and by the private sector (oil companies, financial institutions and, not the least, lawyers) before divestiture can be accomplished. The process would be a lengthy, arduous and expensive one and would require an extensive revision of existing contractual arrangements underlying the financial and operational structure of the industry. I believe Congress should recognize these factors or run the risk of performing surgery of a most radical nature, and surgery which is irreversible, on the basis of erroneous premises.

In preparation for this appearance, we have reviewed certain documents of a contractual nature from what we believe to be a representative sampling of oil companies affected by the bill, particularly documents relating to the issuance of, and security for, securities issues of these companies. We have also examined the historical pattern of a number of past divestitures, including those occasioned by antitrust litigation and the Public Utility Holding Company Act of 1935. We have made an analysis of the proposed oil industry divestiture statute under the general theories that have governed antitrust enforcement in this country. And, of course, we have analyzed the bill introduced by Senator Bayh on September 23 of last year, S. 2387, as well as reviewing the bill introduced by Senator Tunney on December 9, S. 2761, and somewhat comparable amendments offered by Senators Abourezk and Kennedy to the Natural Gas Emergency Act of 1975, which were defeated in October. We also reviewed the testimony before your Subcommittee over the past year on the question of vertical integration.

---

is restored now.'' (Senator Packwood). ''Well, because of the history of this whole antitrust effort—the lack of it—does it not really mandate that the Congress set out specific statutory requirements for how these industries ought to be structured to avoid anti-competitiveness? In other words, just a statute—such as the one we propose today—saying that if you are in this kind of business, you cannot acquire other companies, to avoid all the years of judicial determination and interpretations and consent decrees and so on that slow down and hamper effective antitrust enforcement?'' (Senator Abourezk). ''I think it is fairly clear that if we are to have a petroleum industry structured in a form to respond freely and competitively to our needs within a reasonable time, it is up to Congress to take action . . . time is the critical factor'' (Mr. Kenneth Cory, Controller, State of California). ''[Divestiture legislation] by its directness and simplicity affirms Congress' clear right to legislate policy without having to delegate implementation of that policy to agencies either reluctant or unable to do the job.'' (Mr. Harry Patrick, Secretary-Treasurer of The United Mine Workers Union).

II. Analysis of S. 2387

A starting point for analysis should be a review of S. 2387. From the preamble, it is clear that this bill purports to be "antitrust" legislation, designed to foster competition in the petroleum industry, since it contains a finding that current antitrust laws have been inadequate to maintain this competition. The bill then goes on to define four affected categories of oil companies. "Major producers" are defined as those which, alone or together with affiliates, produced within the United States in the calendar year 1974, or in any succeeding calendar year, more than 36,500,000 barrels of crude petroleum or 200 billion cubic feet of natural gas. In like vein, "major refiners" are those which, alone or with their affiliates in any such calendar year, refined within the United States 75,000,000 or more barrels of product, and "major marketers" are those who alone or with their affiliates in any such calendar year distributed 110,000,000 or more barrels of refined product. Lastly, the bill defines "petroleum transporters" as those persons using a pipeline to transport any crude or refined product, without regard to volume. It is interesting to note that the test for "major marketers" appears to be worldwide whereas the test for "major producers" and "major refiners" are domestic only.

The operative section of the bill makes it illegal after a date three years from the date of enactment for any company falling within any of the four categories to own or to control directly, indirectly or through affiliates any assets used in any of the other processes—production, refining, transportation or marketing—without regard to the size of the assets affected or their location (domestic or foreign). For example, if company X is a "major producer" as defined, it must dispose of *all* refinery assets, *all* marketing assets and *all* transportation (basically pipeline) assets. The one exception is that "major marketers" are not forbidden from holding interests in refining assets, so long as the size of those refining assets does not make the "major marketer" into a "major refiner" as well. In addition, the bill provides that after the three year period, no person owning any interest in a producing, marketing or refining asset, of whatever size, will be permitted to transport either crude petroleum or refined products in which it owns an interest through any pipeline which it owns. "Control" is broadly defined to include substantial and long-term contractual arrangements, as well as stock ownership or director interlocks.

In effect, the bill will force divestiture by any company falling within any of the three "major" categories (with the one exception noted) from connection of any kind with the other segments of the oil business both at home and abroad, and will require the complete separation of pipeline assets of whatever size from ownership or substantial contractual connection with the rest of the oil industry.

The bill concludes by given enforcement authority to the Federal Trade Commission, to which the companies are required to supply, within one year of enactment, plans of divestiture for approval. The Commission's reviewing authority—which includes the power to modify plans submitted by the companies—is based on a "fair and equitable" standard, but no plan is permitted to be approved which would not substantially accomplish the divestiture required by the statute within the three year period. Wilful violations of any provision of the statute are made punishable by substantial fines and imprisonment or suspension of the right to transact business in interstate commerce.

Despite the discussion of the bill in Congress and in the press, it appears that there has not yet been published an analysis of where the strictures of S. 2387 would fall. The Subcommittee recognizes, of course, that all pipeline assets, domestic and foreign, are potentially affected, which means this bill covers more than $9 billion in domestic assets alone owned by approximately 200 oil companies. The companies covered by the provisions of the bill relating to major producers, refiners and marketers are included in the attached chart prepared by Morgan Stanley & Co. Incorporated from public sources.* Twenty oil companies appear to fall within the definition of a "major", based on their reported production, refining or marketing volume for 1974. As you can see from the chart, a good many of them are majors in more than one area, and there are no "major marketers" which are not also "major refiners", which means that the exception provided by S. 2387 is meaningless, at least as far as it affects the industry in its current form.

The chart will indicate to you the magnitude of the economic interests which are the subject of the divestiture bills. The total assets of the companies involved amount to more than $146 billion. The aggregate long-term debt of these companies is more than $21 billion. There are hundreds of thousands of people who own the shares and debt securities of these companies directly, and several million more if one counts indirect ownership through pension funds, mutual funds and similar institutions. The aggregate market value of the common stock equity of these companies amounts to more than $77 billion and the companies have some 780,000 employees. If S. 2387 becomes law, it will trigger the largest series of divestitures in history. The assets held by the public utility holding company industry, the only sector of the United States economy even slightly com-

---

*For this chart, see page 68.

parable in size that was ever faced with legislative surgery of the kind contemplated here, amounted to a total of only $17 billion in 1935.*

In light of the size of the transactions, the scope of the interests affected, and the potential effects upon United States energy policy and our relations with petroleum producing countries, Congress is under an obligation to examine most carefully and prudently the validity of the major premises which underlie the legislation, and to move cautiously if some or all of such premises are subject to serious challenge. The premise which I propose to challenge is the one that holds that a legislative divestiture program of the type contemplated can be accomplished quickly, easily, inexpensively and unbureaucratically.

III. Methods of Divestiture

Assuming legislation such as S. 2387 has been adopted, how would one proceed? How in fact would a major oil company divest itself of various groups of assets and what problems would be raised by any such program?

As a practical matter, there appear to be only two methods for accomplishing the proposed divestiture program. A company can dispose of assets by selling them, whether to another company or to a newly formed company organized and financed for the purpose of acquiring such assets, or to an existing group, such as its own shareholders. In light of the size of the assets to be disposed of, it would seem to me—although I am not in any sense a financial expert—extraordinarily unlikely that new capital could be found to finance their purchase. I come to this conclusion at least in part because the requirements of the proposed bill, or the purported aims of divestiture, would not be accomplished if a selling oil company ended up owning the equity securities, or perhaps even the debt securities, of the buyer. In other words, a disposition by way of sale would clearly involve in large part cash, and I cannot believe that a simultaneous disposition of assets of this magnitude by 20 integrated oil companies, and of all pipeline assets of approximately 200 companies, could be financed on a largely cash basis, particularly since the most obvious group of buyers, that is the oil companies themselves, would in large part be inhibited by the bill itself or by general antitrust considerations from acting as buyers.

The second and far more likely method of divestiture, and the method often followed in divestitures of major assets required under antitrust decrees, is disposition of such assets in one form or another to the shareholders of the divesting company. This is what is normally referred to as a "spin-off". In its simplest form this means that a company would transfer the assets to be disposed of—we might refer to them as prohibited

---

*See 1941 SEC Annual Report at 69-70.

assets—together with related liabilities to a subsidiary corporation, the shares of which are then distributed as a dividend on a pro rata basis to the shareholders of the company in question. Sometimes the shares, instead of being distributed as a dividend in this manner, are offered to existing shareholders in exchange for shares of the company making the distribution. Sometimes the distribution of shares of the new company owning the prohibited assets is accompanied by a simultaneous reduction in the outstanding equity capital of the distributing company. Whatever specific form a divestiture might take, it seems almost certain that an overwhelming part of the divestiture required by S. 2387 would as a practical matter have to be accomplished through some sort of spin-off of the type I have just described, because payment in cash for the divested assets is not required. Obviously divestiture could be accompanied by sales of some assets by some companies, and in fact it would seem likely that the massive restructuring required by the divestiture bills before you would be accomplished by some combination of disposals by way of sales and various types of spin-offs to existing shareholders.

Having outlined the form a divestiture program might take, let me now try to analyze briefly the contractual and other problems which would be raised by a spin-off plus sale program in the case of any of the oil companies we have under discussion.

IV. Legal Consequences of Divestiture

A. Contractual Arrangements. In an effort to determine the impact of S. 2387 upon existing contractual relationships, we have reviewed numerous documents relating to a number of oil companies which would be affected by the bill, consisting primarily of (i) indentures pursuant to which the companies have issued notes and debentures to the public, (ii) loan agreements and note purchase agreements with banks, insurance companies, and other institutional lenders, (iii) various documents, such as throughput agreements, charters and leases, which serve as security for, and are the source of payment of, outstanding indebtedness, (iv) concession agreements with foreign governments and (v) joint venture agreements with foreign governments and others. The major effects of the bill upon these documents may be summarized as follows:

1. *Violation of Covenants.* The documents under which the oil companies have indebtedness outstanding (the "financing documents") contain provisions which prohibit certain actions by the oil companies and which were determined by the respective lenders to be necessary to safeguard their interests. There are a number of types of provisions com-

monly found in the financing documents which, depending upon the manner in which divestiture is accomplished, may be expected to be violated:

(A) provisions prohibiting an oil company and/or its subsidiaries from selling, conveying or otherwise disposing of (i) particular assets or (ii) a substantial part of its assets;

(B) provisions prohibiting an oil company from selling, conveying or otherwise disposing of the stock of certain of its subsidiaries, most notably its pipeline subsidiaries;

(C) provisions restricting the amount of dividends which an oil company may pay to its shareholders (in those cases where divestiture is accomplished by spin-off, the distribution to shareholders of assets of the magnitude we are considering could be expected to violate such provisions);

(D) provisions requiring an oil company to maintain a certain net worth or a certain ratio of assets to liabilities, or to meet other financial conditions;

(E) provisions requiring an oil company to comply with, or to keep in full force and effect, certain material contracts; and

(F) provisions requiring an oil company to maintain its corporate existence and keep in full force and effect various rights, franchises and licenses.

Attached hereto as Exhibits A through F, respectively, are examples of the various types of covenants referred to above.

Of course, many financing documents contain a number of these provisions. For example, the Sohio Pipe Line Company Note Purchase Agreement dated November 1, 1975, which is one of a series of interrelated financing documents pursuant to which $1.75 billion of the funds required for the construction of the Trans-Alaska Pipeline System has been or is to be borrowed, provides that (i) The Standard Oil Company ("Sohio") will not, and will not permit any subsidiary to, dispose of any part of its net interest in the crude oil reserves in Prudhoe Bay (except under certain circumstances, none of which would include a disposition pursuant to divestiture); and (ii) Sohio will not, nor will it permit any of its subsidiaries to, sell or otherwise dispose of, or part with control of, or offer to sell, any shares of stock of any class of Sohio Pipe Line Company (which owns Sohio's interest in TAPS) to any person other than Sohio or a wholly-owned subsidiary of Sohio. Accordingly, the divestiture by Sohio of its pipeline subsidiary would be a violation of the Note Purchase Agreement, as would a decision by Sohio to divest itself of producing assets.

Violation of the types of covenants referred to above results, either immediately or after a period of time following notice of such violation, in default under the respective financing documents. Such default in turn permits the acceleration of all indebtedness issued thereunder. In addition, many financing documents contain what are called "cross-default" clauses to the effect that the acceleration of any other indebtedness of the oil company itself constitutes a default under the financing documents. Consequently, divestiture of prohibited assets would result in a very substantial portion of outstanding oil company indebtedness becoming subject to acceleration pursuant to the terms of the financing documents. The insistence upon the contractual right to accelerate under such circumstances reflects the creditors' judgments that the occurrence of such violations exposes them to unacceptable risks of nonpayment.

Should S. 2387 become law, the FTC would presumably not permit massive acceleration of oil company debt by allowing creditors to enforce the contractual provisions which they insisted upon as a condition to extending credit to the oil companies and upon which they rely for protection of their investments.* The FTC would instead require that such creditors become debtholders of some or all of the newly formed entities resulting from the divestiture. It would not, however, appear to be "fair and equitable" for the FTC to require existing creditors to accept this new indebtedness without the benefit of any contractual safeguards. As a result, the FTC will be required to determine what contractual provisions should be binding upon these entities in order to adequately protect the interests of such creditors. I will discuss in more detail later the extent of this type of involvement which S. 2387 imposes upon the FTC, and its consequences.

2. *Prohibition of Certain Contractual Relationships.* The bill makes it unlawful for an oil company which is a major producer, refiner or marketer to own or control any transportation asset. The definition of "control" extends to any "direct or indirect legal or beneficial interest in or legal power or influence over another person, directly or indirectly, arising through . . . substantial or long-term contractual relations . . . ." As a result, the bill would prohibit the continued existence of various contracts between oil companies and their pipeline subsidiaries which constitute the security for outstanding indebtedness. For example, a very substantial amount of

---

*It should be noted that S. 2387 is silent as to the ways in which the FTC might act to approve "fair and equitable" plans of divestiture. We have assumed for the purposes of this testimony that the FTC would exercise the power to rewrite contractual provisions and prohibit massive accelerations. Of course, if a court found that the FTC did not have this power, or if the FTC chose not to exercise it, it is clear that divestiture would be followed by default, acceleration and probably the bankruptcy of certain of the companies.

long-term financing has been done in reliance upon the security afforded by throughput agreements and completion agreements between pipeline companies and their parents. Such throughput agreements provide that the parents of the pipeline subsidiaries (i) agree to ship sufficient amounts of petroleum products through the subsidiary's pipeline to enable the subsidiary to satisfy all of its indebtedness and, (ii) in the event sufficient petroleum products are not shipped, agree nevertheless to make available to the subsidiary—as advance payments for future shipments—amounts sufficient to allow the subsidiary to satisfy all of its indebtedness. Under completion agreements the shareholders of a pipeline company agree to advance sufficient funds to the subsidiary (as contributions to capital, subscriptions for additional stock or subordinated advances) to allow the subsidiary to satisfy all of its indebtedness. In each case, the obligation of the parents under these agreements is the source of payment of, and is assigned to the lenders as security for, loans advanced to the pipeline subsidiary. Yet the continued existence of these contracts three years after passage of the bill could well subject the parties to criminal sanctions. Furthermore, a decision by the FTC to permit these agreements to remain in effect after the parent companies divest themselves of their pipeline subsidiaries would, in effect, require the parent companies to make their credit available to an unrelated company in unlimited amounts.* Moreover, in the case of completion agreements it would not be permissible to treat funds advanced by the former parent company as contributions to capital or as subscriptions for additional capital stock (as contemplated by the agreements), and even if one were to consider requiring the former parent company to make such advances as loans, this would still violate the "control" restrictions of the bill since the definition of "control" extends not only to "substantial or long-term contractual relations" but also to "loans".

The bill would also render unlawful the performance of certain existing contracts, including particularly concession and joint venture agreements, which require some combination of producing, refining, marketing or transportation activities. For example, if the terms of a concession agreement require that an oil company both produce and market petroleum products, then the oil company will have to own or control both production and marketing assets in order to perform. The bill, of course, prohibits such ownership or control. The FTC might determine that such an agreement should be divided into two contracts to be performed by newly constituted

---

*Throughput and completion agreements customarily define the indebtedness for which the parent is obligated to provide to mean all liabilities of the subsidiary whatsoever, including all indebtedness then existing or incurred thereafter, all taxes, assessments and other governmental charges, all operating expenses and all expenditures for capital items.

production and marketing entities. It may be, however, that such a division makes no economic sense and the other party may decide that the performance which would be received under such circumstances would not be the performance bargained for. This may be particularly true in the case of concession agreements or joint venture agreements with foreign governments or other foreign parties where it is clear that the foreign entity is looking not only to the actual party to the agreement (which is often a subsidiary formed solely for the purpose of the agreement), but rather to the consolidated group of which the contracting party is a part. Moreover, serious questions are presented as to whether, and under what circumstances, an affected party may be required to enter into separate agreements with newly constituted entities in substitution for a single agreement with one integrated entity which was originally entered into. It does seem quite certain that foreign governments or other foreign entities could not be so required.

3. *Prohibition Against Assignment.* The bill will have a very broad impact on the entire range of oil company contracts to the extent its implementation results in a violation of provisions which generally prohibit the assignment, transfer or conveyance of rights and obligations under such contracts without the approval of the other party. Such violations may be claimed, for example, either because of (i) a sale of the assets necessary for the performance of a contract to a new entity and the assumption by that entity of the obligations under the contract, or (ii) a total change in the stock ownership of the original contracting party. The likelihood of a party asserting such a violation would depend on factors such as (i) the extent to which the party views the integration of the oil company as necessary for the adequate performance of the contract, (ii) whether or not the party sees the contract as advantageous and (iii) the alternatives which the party perceives to exist. While this problem will exist throughout the entire range of contracts, for the reasons set forth above this issue may be most sensitive in the context of concession and joint venture agreements where it may reasonably be expected that it is the resources of the consolidated group which the other party is relying upon. In such cases, newly formed entities may be at a competitive disadvantage with vertically integrated foreign oil companies.

It may also be expected that the implementation of the bill will give rise to claims by some parties that they are excused from the performance of certain contracts on the ground of "commercial frustration"; that is, as a result of an unforeseen and supervening event the performance which the party will receive from newly constituted entities does not have the value bargained for.

B. *Other Problems.* The implementation of the bill will give rise to a number of other serious problems—some or all of which may be susceptible to legislative solution—which do not appear to have received adequate consideration.

Pension Plans. Employees of the oil companies will have a large stake in any divestiture, since it would result in the splitting up of currently integrated oil companies into a number of newly formed entities, each of which would carry on a part of the business formerly conducted with a part of the former employees. This would seem to require a determination as to how to split each existing qualified pension or profit sharing plan into a number of plans. Under the Employee Retirement Income Security Act of 1974 ("ERISA"), vested pension rights of employees are protected by the guarantee of the federal Pension Benefit Guaranty Corporation (the "PBGC"). ERISA also creates a contingent liability in the event that a pension plan is terminated and the value of the plan's benefit guaranteed under ERISA exceeds the value of the plan's assets allocable to such benefits; any such excess is paid by the PBGC, which then has a right to recover such payment from the employer, up to 30% of the employer's net worth. Provisions of ERISA designed to state the effect on this contingent liability arising from the sale, merger or division of the employer are ambiguous, and there has as yet been no published interpretation of these provisions by the PBGC or by any other governmental agency or department. If one of the newly formed entities after divestiture should become bankrupt and its pension plan terminated, the PBGC may well contend that the resulting contingent employer liability would be imposed upon all of the newly formed entities and not merely upon the bankrupt entity. Accordingly, even if none of the pension plans of any of these entities is ever terminated, uncertainty may exist as to the nature and extent of the contingent employer liability of each such entity and the form of disclosure to the investing public which would be required under the Federal securities laws.

Tax Consequences. Section 355 of the Internal Revenue Code of 1954, as amended, permits a "spin-off" of assets to stockholders to be done on a tax-free basis provided that certain conditions are met. In such event the stockholders do not recognize a gain or loss on the receipt of the distributed stock of the "spun off" corporation or corporations, but merely a change in their basis in the stock which they then own. It is not at all clear, however, whether any or all "spin-offs" pursuant to S. 2387 could comply with the provisions of Section 355, and, as a result, "such spin-offs" might have substantially adverse tax consequences for existing oil company stockholders. It is also not clear how much of any mandated divestiture of assets would be accomplished by means of a "spin-off", and the sale of prohibited assets would produce a taxable event for Federal income tax purposes. In addition, the transfer of shares of stock or assets may result in the imposition of state and local taxes resulting in further adverse consequences for stockholders and the newly formed entities.

Legal Investment. If the newly formed entities are to obtain necessary funds for working capital and capital expenditures, they will need ready access to the market for the issuance of securities. Various states preclude their savings banks, insurance companies and fiduciaries from investing in securities of certain issuers unless the issuer has a specific ratio of earnings to fixed charges over a specific historical period. It is not clear whether the newly formed entities would be deemed to have been in existence for the necessary historical period within the meaning of such statutes, or how the earnings and fixed charges of the predecessor integrated company would be allocated among the new entities for purposes of such statutes. Failure to satisfy the provisions of these statutes would, as a practical matter, make it difficult or impossible for a large part of the oil industry to obtain financing from institutions governed by such legal investment laws—institutions which have provided a major portion of such financing in past years.

V. FTC Involvement: Duration and Implementation

A. *Resolution of Conflicting Interests.* As the foregoing discussion clearly indicates, the divestiture program mandated by S. 2387 would result in a massive, "forced" breach by the oil companies of financing agreements and other contractual arrangements to which they are parties. In other words, forced divestiture of assets along the lines required by S. 2387 could not possibly be accommodated within existing contractual arrangements, and, therefore, such contractual arrangements would have to be "rewritten" by the divestiture plans. In particular, unless the divestiture plans restructured the financing documents of the affected oil companies, divestiture would result in the right of creditors to accelerate and to make immediately due and payable a very substantial portion of the outstanding indebtedness of the affected oil companies.

Thus, the bill will require the FTC to become embroiled in nearly all aspects of the contractual relationships existing between the oil companies and stockholders, creditors, employees and other parties. The FTC will be required to accommodate existing contractual relationships with the newly structured oil industry brought about by divestiture. As a result, the FTC will be required to review, modify and approve plans submitted by the oil companies which, among other things:

(a) allocate assets and liabilities of existing oil companies among the newly constituted entities;

(b) restructure the rights of persons holding stock in oil companies and of persons holding options or warrants to purchase such stock or securities convertible into such stock;

(c) restructure the rights of public and private creditors of the oil companies;

(d) determine the financial covenants and restrictions which will be imposed upon newly constituted entities to fairly protect the rights of such creditors;

(e) revise commercial contracts whose provisions no longer make sense under the changed circumstances resulting from divestiture;

(f) revise existing union and other labor agreements which will probably require renegotiation subsequent to divestiture (presumably "omnibus" union contracts will not be permissible after divestiture); and

(g) revise employment contracts, pension and profit-sharing plans, leases and insurance policies (or lack thereof since existing oil companies may often choose or be permitted by contract to self-insure, whereas appropriate insurance requirements will have to be determined for new entities).

The complexity of these issues which the FTC will be called upon to resolve must not be underestimated. For example, how does one determine how much of the indebtedness of an existing oil company should be allocated to each of its successor entities? Should the amount of such liabilities be based upon the amount of assets allocated to the entity, the amount of earnings which the entity may be anticipated to generate or some other standard? For purposes of determining the amount of dividends which a new entity will be entitled to declare, how much of the earnings and profits of an existing oil company should be allocated to each successor entity? How should the tax attributes of an existing oil company be allocated; which entities should get the benefits of tax carryforwards carrybacks, and how does one determine what portion of an existing oil company's previous tax liability a loss carryback may be applied against? What portion of existing pension plan liabilities should each entity assume? Should each successor entity be jointly and severally liable in respect of all outstanding litigation against an existing oil company? How does one allocate contingent liabilities, such as future litigation or tax deficiencies?

Perhaps a specific example of the issues the FTC will face would be in order. Almost all oil company indentures or loan agreements contain provisions to the effect that the company in question will not dispose of all or substantially all of its assets unless the successor company assumes all liabilities and obligations in respect of the indebtedness in question. For some of the affected oil companies, the divestiture required by S. 2387 would involve a group of assets sufficiently large to bring into play such clauses. Holders of the indebtedness in question, or trustees on their behalf, could be expected to argue that such clauses would require each of the successor companies (i.e., the companies owning the assets disposed of) to assume joint and several liability with respect to the indebtedness, so that the holders of the indebtedness could look to each of the successor entities to be responsible for 100% of such debt, in case one or more of such entities could not service its allocated portion. It is questionable, however, whether S. 2387 would permit this kind of "cross guarantee" among the entities, in view of the prohibition against control of prohibited assets by way of substantial or long-term contractual relations. On the other hand, the plans as approved by the FTC are required to be "fair and equitable" to all persons concerned, and persons concerned clearly include holders of oil company indebtedness. This is just an example of the kind of problems which the divestiture plans will have to deal with, which the FTC will have to make decisions on and which parties affected are likely to dispute both before the FTC and in the courts.

B. *Accommodation with Federal Governmental Interests.* The bill is silent on another problem facing the FTC: accommodation of other governmental interests. Pipelines, for example, are subject to ICC jurisdiction. Presumably there would have to be some consultation with ICC officials about the proper allocation of pipeline assets in the event of divestiture. A large number of governmental agencies, including the Treasury, the Interior Department and the Department of State, currently have jurisdiction in the general area of energy policy. Would the FTC have to get approval from all of these offices to insure that a particular divestiture did not interfere with general governmental policy in areas such as foreign relations? And, of course, there will be effects upon agencies like the SEC, which will have to resolve how the entities should disclose their confused and tentative status, IRS, which will have to review the plans for tax consequences, and the Defense Department, a large oil buyer and supplier of crude.

C. *Special Problems of Foreign Persons and Governments.* A further and special group of problems will undoubtedly be raised by the requirement of S. 2387 that non-United States assets of the prohibited sort will also have to be disposed of, and "substantial" or "long-term" contractual arrangements relating to foreign prohibited assets will have to be terminated.

It cannot be doubted that foreign third parties which have contractual relationships with the oil companies, including foreign holders of oil company indebtedness issued under foreign loan agreements and containing covenants of the kind described above, will seek to enforce their contractual rights in approprIate foreign forums. It can also be expected that foreign courts will support the assertions of such third party foreigners—particularly foreign governments—that their contractual rights cannot be abrogated by unilateral United States action. The result will be, in addition to the loss to the oil companies of valuable foreign contractual rights as a result of termination actions taken by foreign third parties based on "forced" breaches of contract caused by the divestiture program, acceleration of oil company debt held by foreign creditors under loan contracts not governed by U.S. law and claims by foreigners for substantial damages for breach of contract. These claims are likely to be upheld in foreign courts and enforced against the oil companies' foreign assets.

These and a host of other difficult issues must be resolved by plans which the FTC has the responsibility of approving. Moreover, it can be expected that all classes of persons affected by the plans will intervene and participate vigorously in proceedings before the FTC with respect to such plans. Given the number of companies which the bill covers, the difficulty of the issues presented, the large number and variety of classes of persons affected by the bill, the magnitude of the interests involved and the likely event that almost all plans will be submitted to the FTC just before the one year deadline for their submission, one cannot reasonably believe that the FTC will be able to perform the role contemplated for it without the establishment of a new and large bureaucratic apparatus, and even then, the job will take years.

It can also be expected that affected persons will challenge substantially all of the plans submitted to the FTC before the Commission itself and, in addition, will seek judicial review of the FTC's decisions in the Courts of Appeals and the Supreme Court. Indeed, the number and complexity of the issues to be resolved, together with the large numbers of persons whose interests will be affected, virtually insures that the implementation of S. 2387 will give rise to a decade or more of litigation during which substantial uncertainty will exist as to the nature and extent of a broad range of existing contractual arrangements and legal obligations within the oil industry.

VI. Past Divestitures

When presented with the facts as to the difficulty and far-reaching nature of the proposed oil industry divestitures, proponents sometimes point to the Public Utility Holding Company Act of 1935. The administration of the holding Company Act does provide some instructive history. Although the statute itself provided for time delays to allow for constitutional testing of various provisions, suggesting Congressional awareness of the magnitude of the task and the diversity of interests affected, it was 1946 before the constitutionality of the Act was upheld, and the work of breaking up holding companies continued through the 1960's, although most of it was concluded in the late 1940's and early 1950's. Moreover, a number of factors indicate that the divestiture mandated by the Holding Company Act was far less complex than the divestiture which S. 2387 contemplates:

(i) The magnitude of the undertaking was far smaller—the amount of assets involved and the number and variety of the classes of affected persons was substantially less than would be involved in the oil industry, and the utility industry was entirely a domestic one.

(ii) The assets of the holding companies and subholding companies were not operating assets but largely the securities of operating companies and therefore the break-up of these holding companies did not involve the formidable problem of allocating the assets and liabilities of existing operating companies among a number of newly formed companies.

(iii) The holding companies were in financial disarray in 1935, and thus reorganization was something that would have had to be faced in any event.

(iv) The Holding Company Act did not require the divestment of operating assets by operating companies. The utility industry was essentially a local industry, and viable operating companies with existing management and earnings histories were already in place. Essentially what the Act required was the lopping off of the dead branches of the holding company superstructure, the only purpose of which was to maintain control of the operating companies.

Indeed, the history of the Public Utility Holding Company Act would seem to indicate that even where you have a reasonably carefully drafted statute based on a full record, which was designed to deal with a financially insecure industry far less massive or complex or operationally integrated than the oil industry, the time for divestiture can stretch out beyond 20 years.

But divestiture always takes longer than appears at the beginning. In 1952, for example, the Government settled an antitrust suit against Loew's, Inc. (now MGM) by a consent decree that required divestiture of movie theater assets from movie production assets within two years. Yet, due to difficulties of debt allocation and debtholders' rights, the divestiture was postponed by the court several times, finally being accomplished in 1959, seven years after the date of the decree. And Loew's seemed in 1952 to be a relatively easy company to divide, with assets totalling about $218 million and long term debt, held by a few insurance companies, of less than $30 million. Other antitrust divestitures, as well as reorganizations resulting from bankruptcies, also indicate the likelihood of extensive time delays.

VII. Comments on the Bill

As I have attempted to demonstrate, the implementation of S. 2387 will give rise to a substantial number of issues of great complexity, the resolution of which will have serious consequences for large classes of persons. In such circumstances, it would not be responsible for Congress to set such events in motion without the most careful consideration and reflection as to the form of legislation which would govern any required divestiture. I respectfully submit that the bill does not evidence the consideration and reflection called for.

For example, a literal reading of the provisions of the bill would require any oil company which is a major producer, refiner and marketer, as defined in the bill, to get out of the oil business altogether. Under the bill, once a company achieves "major" status in an area, it retains such status for all time. Section 4 of the bill provides that a "major" in any one area may not own or control any assets in any other area,* but fails to provide that a company which elects to remain a "major" in only one area must only satisfy the prohibition of Section 4 with respect to a "major" in that area and is in compliance after it has divested itself of all assets in the other areas. For example, assume X Company is a major producer, refiner and marketer and seeks to remain only in the area of production, divesting itself of all other assets. Despite the fact that X Company has divested itself of all refining and marketing assets, it nevertheless remains a "major" refiner and marketer within the wording of the bill. As a consequence, X Company will violate subdivision (3) of Section 4 of the bill, which prohibits major refiners or major marketers from owning any production assets. Indeed, X Company cannot avoid violating the bill if it remains in any area of the oil business.

As discussed above, the bill prohibits a "major" in one area from owning or controlling assets in any other area, and the definition of "control" extends to "substantial" and "long-term" contracts. The bill would,

---

*Subject to the exception, previously noted and not germane to the issue under discussion, that a major marketer may own "non-major" refining assets.

therefore, explicitly outlaw any long-term contractual arrangements between independent producers, marketers, refiners or transporters. Further, any contract between such independent producers, marketers, refiners or transporters that involves more than a small amount of crude oil or other petroleum products would arguably run afoul of the bill's prohibition against "substantial contracts", thereby subjecting the contracting parties to the possibility of criminal sanctions. Despite the fact that 5.2387 is a criminal statute, it provides no definition of "long-term" or "substantial" to guide the companies subject to the bill or the FTC in enforcing the bill. The definition of control contained in the bill seems to go a long way toward prohibiting the kind of contractual relations which would be necessary to allow independent companies to function effectively.

Finally, the bill makes it unlawful for a company to own or control prohibited assets three years after its enactment, and provides no mechanism for an extension of this three-year period. Given the virtual certainty of constitutional challenge to the bill and other substantial litigation surrounding the submission of any plan of divestiture to the FTC for its approval, it seems quite likely that a company attempting in good faith to meet the requirements of the bill may nevertheless be unable to divest itself of all prohibited assets within the prescribed period. If divestiture cannot, as a practical matter, be accomplished within three years, as I believe to be the case, then a statute requiring divestiture to be accomplished within that period, and imposing criminal sanctions for its violation, would be vulnerable to an attack on procedural due process grounds. Nor does the bill make any provision for a company obtaining "major" status during the three-year period following enactment of the bill. For example, a "non-major" producer which owns marketing and refining assets might, by virtue of a substantial discovery, become a "major producer" several years after enactment of the bill and face the threat of immediate criminal prosecution unless it can instantaneously divest itself of its prohibited assets.

VIII. Conclusion

Where, then, does this study of legal consequences lead us? The drafting inadequacies of the bill itself raise questions as to whether this kind of simple-sounding legislation is a legally viable approach to disintegrating the largest, and one of the most complex, industries in the world. Moreover, the inevitability of legal challenges to the bill and to its implementation, together with the difficulty and scope of planning and implementing the break-up of all of the major oil companies in the United States, should also make it abundantly clear that any divestiture statute is not at all a simple, swift, unbureaucratic or inexpensive way of resolving what is perceived to be wrong with the oil industry today. In terms of delay, I am not quibbling about the three years in S. 2387 or the five years provided by Senator Abourezk's amendment last October; in my view, it would take at least ten or as long as twenty years to resolve all of the questions raised, from the time of initial submission of divestiture plans to the FTC by the companies, through the review and challenge of those plans and the court tests, to the final carrying out of a divestiture order. The history of the Public Utility Holding Company Act supports this view.

Recognition of these considerations should put to rest the suggestion that a bill like S. 2387 is an appropriate short cut to the perils of antitrust litigation; no matter what route is selected, the determination of such important questions will of necessity take many years to accomplish. In light of that fact, I believe Congress should recognize what it is giving up in selecting statutorily required divestiture rather than leaving the question to traditional court review and supervision.

A divestiture statute in many ways represents a sharp departure from historical American antitrust approaches. Congress has never before found that size alone, or the vertical integration structure generally, is anti-competitive. Moreover, it has traditionally approached antitrust legislation on an across-the-board rather than single-industry basis. Finally, antitrust law enforcement has been surrounded with procedural safeguards. In divestiture cases, for example, the government has the burden of showing not only that substantial anti-competitive effects have resulted from the alleged conduct and will continue to result in the industry, but also that wide scale vertical disintegration is the best—or, as a minimum, the least harsh—method for overcoming these anti-competitive effects, before the divestiture remedy will be authorized by the court. During the course of litigation bearing on these questions, the court has the benefit of adversary testimony and cross-examination on the premises of anti-competitive effects, as well as expert discussion on the appropriateness of any particular remedy. Although opposing views of witnesses have been presented to the Subcommittee and colloquies have taken place, these issues of effect and appropriateness, as they relate to S. 2387, have never been subjected to the cauldron of a true adversary proceeding.

For example, critics have asserted, and one of the proposed legislative findings in S. 2387 accepts as a premise, that the antitrust laws have been ineffective in curbing anti-competitive abuses in the petroleum industry. Yet there is pending at this very moment an FTC proceeding seeking, among other forms of relief, the vertical disintegration of the eight largest domestic oil companies. At least one source of this proceeding, and one relied on in the bringing of the action, was a 1973 report of the FTC Staff which pointed to a number of particular factors which, in the staff's judgment, had reduced competition in the oil industry, among them the oil depletion allowance, oil import quotas, federal tax credits for oil royalties paid to foreign governments and state proration procedures. But since 1973 Congress has eliminated the depletion allowance and severely curbed the use of the foreign tax credit by American petroleum companies, the President has removed the import quotas and state proration limits have become something of a dead letter. The FTC will have to determine, in light of these developments, whether there are serious anti-competitive effects in the petroleum industry, whether any such effects result in large measure from vertical integration or from other causes, and whether the divestiture asked for at the time of initiation of the suit (which, by the way, was far less extensive than the remedy set forth in S. 2387) would still be an appropriate remedy to curb the alleged abuses. Surely, Congress must ask itself whether this FTC proceeding with its built-in adversary safeguards is not a better way to resolve such questions than radical legislative surgery.

Congress should also ask whether it is best to resolve such questions by across-the-board legislation based upon its judgment, at a single time, regarding the industry structure most productive of competition. Antitrust principles have traditionally developed on a case-by-case, rule of reason basis which permits economic, political and social hypotheses to be tested not only in adversary proceedings, but, afterward, by actual experience under a court's decree. Conduct once viewed as anti-competitive may be found in later cases to be appropriate, because of changing views of the law or differing factual circumstances. Moreover, if a remedy proves ineffective or impractical, it may be discarded in subsequent cases; even in cases already decided, if the decreed remedy proves harsh a court may modify the decree. No such possibility of rectifying mistakes or adapting to changing circumstances exists to any meaningful extent when legislation replaces litigation—once divestitures pursuant to statute occur, re-integration could not take place, at least on any short-term basis.

Thus, the selection of the legislative route by Congress brings forth a deep responsibility; it is incumbent upon the legislative branch to use the greatest possible care in passing a statute that can have such extreme consequences as the break-up of all large United States oil companies. It behooves Congress itself to make a full examination of the premises behind the legislative findings backing such a bill, not in haste or in heat, but in reasoned examination of the conduct alleged, the reasonable anticipation of future conduct and the appropriateness, effectiveness and expense of any remedy. Only after such a searching determination should Congress make a legislative finding leading to so drastic a measure, because after passage the Congressional determination will be effectively final.

In addition, Congress must ask itself the question: What happens to this country's energy industry during the ten to twenty years of uncertainty and litigation which will inevitably result from passage of S. 2387? As divestiture programs are proposed by the various oil companies, reviewed and argued before the FTC, litigated by the various interests affected, this enormously complex and vital sector of our industrial economy will be in what amounts to a state of chaos. Until plans are finally approved, litigation concluded and plans put into effect, literally no one will know who owns what, what kind of companies will emerge, what their capital structure will look like or how viable and competitive, both domestically and overseas, the fragmented components will be. Congress must carefully consider whether an industry in this state of uncertainty could finance on a private basis the huge capital-intensive projects which any national energy policy for this country requires.

EXHIBIT A

Restrictions on Disposition of Assets

So long as the Production Payment remains in force and effect [Oil Company] will not, without the consent in writing of [Lender], sell, convey, assign, lease, sublease or otherwise dispose of any Subject Interest (or any portion thereof) or release, surrender or otherwise abandon any Subject Interest (or any portion thereof) . . .

If any of the following events ("Events of Default") shall occur, namely, if: the Character and/or [Oil Company] ceases or threatens to cease to carry on its business or (without the prior written consent of [Lender] . . .) disposes or threatens to dispose of a substantial part of its businesses, properties or assets or the same are seized or appropriated;

[Oil Company] covenants and agrees that from the date of this Guaranty Agreement and thereafter so long as [Lender] holds any of the Notes, [Oil Company] will not . . . sell, lease, transfer or otherwise dispose of all or a substantial part of its properties and assets, or consolidate with or merge into any other corporation or permit any other corporation to merge into it . . .

EXHIBIT B

Restrictions on Disposition of Stock of Subsidiaries

[Oil Company] will not, nor will it permit any of its subsidiaries to, sell or otherwise dispose of, or part with control of, or offer to sell, any shares of stock of any class of [subsidiary] to any Person other than [Oil Company] or a wholly-owned subsidiary of [Oil Company], or entertain any offer from any Person other than [Oil Company] or a wholly-owned subsidiary of [Oil Company] to purchase any shares of stock of any class of [subsidiary], and [Oil Company] will not permit [subsidiary] (either directly, or indirectly by the issuance of rights or options for, or securities convertible into, such shares) to issue, sell or dispose of any shares of any class of its stock except to [Oil Company] or to a wholly-owned subsidiary of [Oil Company].

[Oil Company] covenants and agrees that from the date of this Guaranty Agreement and thereafter so long as [Lender] holds any of the Notes, [Oil Company] will not . . . fail at any time to own all of the outstanding capital stock (other than directors' qualifying shares) of [subsidiary] either directly or through one or more of its wholly-owned subsidiaries . . .

[Oil Company] will not sell, transfer or otherwise dispose of any voting shares of [pipeline subsidiary] of any class to any person and will not permit [pipeline subsidiary] to issue, sell or otherwise dispose of any of its voting shares of any class to any person other than [Oil Company] . . .

EXHIBIT C

Limitation on Dividends

Oil Company will not pay any dividend (other than stock dividends) on any of its stock and Oil Company will not, and will not permit any of its Subsidiaries to, make any payment on account of the purchase, redemption or other retirement of any of the Oil Company's stock or make any other distribution in respect thereof (each such dividend, payment and distribution being herein called a "stock payment"), except that Oil Company may make any stock payment if after giving effect thereto the aggregate amount of all stock payments made after December 31, 1974 shall not exceed the sum of (1) the consolidated net profit, after taxes and extraordinary items, of Oil Company and its Consolidated Subsidiaries for the period from December 31, 1974 to the date of the making of such stock payment, such period to be taken for the purpose as one accounting period (except that consolidated net profit after taxes and extraordinary items shall be calculated exclusive of a charge estimated as of June 1, 1975 to be dollar figure, currently proposed by the Financial Accounting Standards Board, to provide deferred income taxes on capitalized intangible drilling costs incurred to January 1, 1975, which costs were previously deducted for Federal income tax purposes) plus (2) $30,000,000.

Oil Company will not declare or pay any dividends (except dividends payable in common stock of the Company) or make any other distribution on any shares of its capital stock of any class or make any payment on account of the purchase, redemption or retirement for value (other than with the proceeds of additional stock financing) of any shares of such stock, if the Net Working Capital of Oil Company (as at the end of a calendar month not more than 50 days prior to the date of such declaration, payment or distribution) shall, after giving effect to such declaration, payment or distribution, be thereby reduced below the greater of (x) the sum of $2,000,000 or (y) an amount equal to one-half of the principal amount of the Funded Debt of Oil Company that becomes due and payable . . . during the 12 months' period commencing at the end of such calendar month.

EXHIBIT D

Maintenance of Financial Requirements

[Oil Company] will, on or before   in each year beginning with the year   , deliver to the person to whom the Notes were originally issued, and lodge at the office of [Oil Company] and make available for examination purposes at said office to any other holder of the Notes, a Certificate of [Oil Company] (herein referred to as the "Annual Net Tangible Assets Certificate") stating, at the close of business December 31 (herein referred to as the "Determination Date") of the year immediately prior to the year in which said Certificate is made, the following:

that the Net Tangible Assets of [Oil Company] on the Determination Date are at least equal to 2-1/2 times the amount of Funded Debt of [Oil Company] on said date; or, in the alternative, stating that the Net Tangible Assets of [Oil Company] on the Determination Date are a specified amount less than 2-1/2 times the amount of Funded Debt of [Oil Company] on said date.

[Oil Company] will not, and will not permit any Consolidated Subsidiary to, create, assume or permit to exist any senior funded debt unless after giving effect thereto (and to the application of proceeds thereof) the consolidated senior funded debt of [Oil Company] and its Consolidated Subsidiaries shall not exceed 75% of the consolidated Tangible Net Worth of [Oil Company] and its Consolidated Subsidiaries.

[Oil Company] will continuously maintain a Net Worth of not less than $1,500,000. For purposes of this § . . . : "Net Worth" means its net worth at and as of the particular date, composed of the sum of all amounts, determined in accordance with generally accepted accounting principles, which would properly appear on its balance sheet dated such date as (A) the par or stated value of all outstanding paid-in capital stock and (B) capital, paid-in and earned surplus (a negative amount, in the case of a deficit), less the sum of (C) any surplus or write-up resulting from any reappraisal of any property or asset, (D) any amounts at which good will, patents, trademarks, copyrights and deferred charges, including but not limited to unamortized debt discount, debt expenses and organization expenses, but not prepaid expenses, appear on the asset side of such balance sheet, (E) any amounts at which shares of its capital stock appear on the asset side of such balance sheet, (F) any amounts of indebtedness not included on the liability side of such balance sheet and (G) the amount of any net worth otherwise required to be set aside or reserved by it pursuant to any law or regulation or any agreement or instrument.

EXHIBIT E

Compliance With Certain Agreements

[Oil Company] will perform and observe all agreements, covenants and undertakings of [Oil Company] contained in the Completion Agreement, the Throughput Agreement and the related . . . Assignment, and will not consent to any amendment or termination of the Completion Agreement or the Throughput Agreement except as provided therein.

[Oil Company] will promptly . . . perform or cause to be performed each and every act, matter or thing required by, each and all of the leases to which [Oil Company] is a party or in which it has any interest and will do all other things necessary to keep unimpaired [Oil Company's] rights thereunder and prevent any default thereunder or any forfeiture of any rights of [Oil Company] in respect thereof . . .

EXHIBIT F

Maintenance of Corporate Existence

[Oil Company] covenants and agrees that so long as any of the Notes shall be outstanding [Oil Company] will do or cause to be done all things necessary to preserve and keep in full force and effect its corporate existence . . .

[Oil Company] will take or cause to be taken all such action as from time to time may be necessary to maintain, preserve or renew its corporate existence.

Erickson examines the U.S. petroleum industry and finds that it consists of a diversity of vertically integrated, non-integrated and partially integrated firms. According to him, the industry is effectively competitive as demonstrated by its long-run normal rate of profitability. Because of this, there is no monopoly to be eliminated by divestiture. However, since vertical integration reduces capital cost to some firms, divestitures will add to the U.S. energy bill.

2

THE ENERGY CRISIS AND THE OIL INDUSTRY

STATEMENT OF EDWARD W. ERICKSON,* NORTH CAROLINA STATE UNIVERSITY, BEFORE THE SUBCOMMITTEE ON ANTITRUST AND MONOPOLY, COMMITTEE ON THE JUDICIARY, UNITED STATES SENATE — JANUARY 27, 1976

Introduction

These hearings are focused upon potential legislation which will involve some measure of vertical divestiture of the firms in the U.S. petroleum industry. I presume that your attention is thus focused because you believe that such divestiture will have net positive benefits for the citizens of the United States. In the popular mind, these benefits are often assumed to include rooting out monopoly and lowering energy prices to U.S. consumers. I believe that these ideas are wrong and potentially harmful. To justify so drastic a policy prescription as divestiture upon so seriously awry a misconception would be apt to compound rather than alleviate the problem we face. I appreciate very much the opportunity to dis-

---

*Professor of Economics and Business, North Carolina State University, Raleigh.

cuss with you the gap between the public perception and the economic reality concerning the effectiveness of competition in the U.S. petroleum industry.

There is monopoly power today in the world petroleum industry. But it resides in the governments of the producing companies. Divestiture of the major oil companies from their pipelines, refineries, producing properties or service stations would have no discernible effect to make the domestic petroleum industry more effectively competitive. In fact, contrary to the views of the Federal Trade Commission, the press and others, the most significant competitors of any one of the major oil companies are the other majors. And that competition is vigorous, effective and socially beneficial. It does Americans a disservice to lead them to believe that that there are some easy panaceas — such as antitrust action or legislative amputation — to our energy policy problems. The truth is that the creation of domestic resources and the purchase of security of supply is a costly and time-consuming process.

The U.S. petroleum industry is now effectively competitive. There are many firms. Concentration is low. Entry and exit are everyday phenomena. Resources are mobile. Long-run profitability indicates competitive performance. The rate of technical advance is strong and impressive. The largest companies compete vigorously with each other.

If the major benefit of divestiture is presumed to flow from the breakup of an alleged monopoly, that benefit is illusory. It is not too strong a figure of speech to say that the contribution of divestiture to the effectiveness of competition in the U.S. petroleum industry would be equivalent to the contribution of another ton of salt to the salinity of the oceans. The U.S. petroleum industry is now effectively competitive. There are many ways to gauge the effectiveness of competition. These include measures of structure, behavior and performance. Performance is the ultimate test. Competitive performance results from resource mobility in an open economy. It is possible that the initial effect of divestiture would be to inhibit resource mobility by increasing uncertainties for investment decision makers. After adjustment to the surgical trauma that would follow divestiture, the U.S. petroleum industry would still be effectively competitive. But it is likely that effective competition under divestiture would take place at a generally higher level of costs. American consumers would ultimately have to bear those costs. In this and other respects, it would be a disservice to the American public.

Just as divestiture will not create any economic miracles through elimination of a monopoly component in U.S. energy prices, neither will divestiture result in a reduction of the costs of securing energy resources for U.S. consumers. The incremental costs of energy to the U.S. economy are determined by the prices and cohesion of the OPEC cartel — a monopoly of foreign governments, *not* U.S. companies — and the facts of nature and geology and the limits of technology. Divestiture will not change the facts of nature and, I believe, cannot therefore be relied upon to reduce energy costs to the U.S. consuming public. Moreover, as I will discuss in more detail below, it is likely that divestiture would result in an increase in costs for the U.S. petroleum industry. Divestiture will not make the U.S. petroleum industry more effectively competitive. Divestiture will not work any magic to create resources out of whole cloth. Divestiture could inhibit the investment process necessary to create the domestic energy capital the U.S. requires with a consequent increase in the U.S. dependence upon energy imports. Divestiture would cost U.S. consumers money.

If there are no economic benefits from divestiture, are there any sound reasons for pursuing such a policy? Quite frankly, I do not believe so. Such a drastic policy as divestiture must have clear and convincing net benefits. Lacking such benefits, divestiture would be an ill-advised policy. I believe divestiture to be ill-advised, and I believe divestiture to be especially ill-advised if the rationale for divestiture is the creation of a more effectively competitive U.S. petroleum industry than that which now exists.

Competition in the U.S. Petroleum Industry*

The United States has traditionally relied on free market forces and decentralized decision-making for solutions to resource allocation problems. Competition in the U.S. petroleum industry is an important topic. Bigness is unfortunately confused with monopoly power. This confusion clouds the consideration of rational policy responses to the current energy crisis. The discussion of the competition issue generates a great deal of emotion on both sides of the question. It is too much to expect that we will be able to settle the issue here; it seems to be a permanent feature of political

---

*My written statement submitted previously to this Subcommittee which accompanied my letter to Senator Bayh of November 13, 1975 consisted of two chapters from a book I recently co-edited. The book is titled *The Energy Question* and it deals with the short- and long-run causes and consequences of the energy crisis. Volume 1 focuses upon the world dimensions of the problem and Volume 2 focuses upon North America. The two chapters which formed my earlier written statement are the editors' introduction to Volume 1 and the chapter I co-authored in Volume 2 which deals with the U.S. petroleum industry. The editors' introduction to Volume 1 outlines some of the interrelated policy failures which contributed to and have exacerbated the problems with which we now must cope. The chapter titled "The U.S. Petroleum Industry" from Volume 2 summarizes my views on the effectiveness of competition in the U.S. petroleum industry. This section of my current testimony is a summarization of the views presented there and earlier furnished to the Subcommittee.

economics. We do, however, hope that we can illustrate convincingly with hard facts some of the reasons why, in our analytical judgment, the U.S. petroleum industry is effectively competitive.

I here focus upon the record of long-run profitability in the U.S. petroleum industry. Profitability is an important index of the existence and exercise of market power. The petroleum industry is a large industry, and the firms within it are also large. Effective monopoly results in a divergence between long-run marginal costs and prices. Prices in excess of long-run marginal costs (including a competitive return on invested capital) result in excessive earnings. These excessive earnings are reflected in higher than normal, above average rates of return on stockholders' equity capital. Thus, the rate of return on corporate stockholders' equity capital is one measure of the presence or absence of market power in the petroleum industry.

The record of long-run profitability in the U.S. petroleum industry indicates that the firms in this industry do not enjoy substantial, systematic market power. This index of effective competition yields positive results whether the comparison is to all U.S. manufacturing, Moody's 125 Industrials, Moody's 24 Public Utilities, or a group of industrial firms known to possess market power, or the cost of equity capital for the petroleum industry.

Market power shows up as economic profits. The U.S. petroleum industry has not earned the kind of long-run returns on stockholders' equity which are to be expected for firms that enjoy substantial, systematic market power. Recent profits of the petroleum industry have been much higher than the long-run average. This is partly a result of the energy crisis and its attendant shortages. The energy crisis has been policy induced and is not a result of private market power of the U.S. petroleum industry. Long-run profitability is the appropriate measure of competitiveness. As firms have adjusted to changed circumstances, profits have, in general, been falling. This is in part a result of resource mobility in competitive markets. Were U.S. energy markets less restricted by controls and regulations, this process would work more uniformly and rapidly to the benefit of the U.S. public.

Table 1 Compares the overall average profitability of the eight major petroleum companies named in the FTC complaint with ten large industrial concerns generally conceded to possess some market power. The comparison indicates that each of the nonpetroleum firms earns more than the average for the eight major petroleum companies. The average for the ten nonpetroleum firms is 20.2 percent. The average for the eight major petroleum companies is 11.1 percent. The ten-company nonpetroleum average exceeds the average for the eight major petroleum companies by

9.1 percentage points, or 82 percent.

Table 2 compares the rate of return on stockholders' equity for the eight major petroleum companies with the average for Moody's 125 Industrials on a year-by-year basis from 1951 to 1971. In 16 of 21 years, the average for the eight major petroleum companies is less than that for the firms that make up Moody's 125 Industrials. Moreover, in eight of the ten years covering 1962-71, the rate of return for the eight major petroleum companies was less than the return for Moody's 125 Industrials. In one year, 1967, they were equal. In only one year, 1970, did the return for the eight major petroleum companies exceed that of Moody's 125 Industrials — and then by only six-tenths of one percentage point, or 5.8 percent.

Comparison to averages such as Moody's 125 Industrials and all manufacturing industry may be misleading. This is because some of the nonpetroleum firms in these averages may possess market power (see, for example, Table 1). This makes the averages themselves higher than the normal, long-run, competitive rate of return. There is a way to correct for this. A standard procedure in regulatory proceedings is to calculate the cost of equity capital for the particular firm(s) in question. Earnings on equity capital are then compared to the cost of equity capital.

Table 1
A comparison of rates of return on stockholders' equity between ten selected large firms in concentrated industries and the eight major petroleum companies.

Firm	Rate of return on stockholders' equity, 1972
General Motors	17.8
Xerox	23.4
IBM	18.7
Burroughs	15.4
Bristol-Myers	17.8
Eastman Kodak	20.4
Kellogg	22.3
Procter and Gamble	19.1
Pfizer	17.7
Eli Lilly	29.8
Ten company average	20.2
Average for eight major petroleum companies (1971)	11.1

Modern analysts typically calculate a range for the cost of equity capital. This is because a range is more reliable than a point estimate. Using standard techniques for the years 1967-71, the range for the cost of equity capital for the eight major petroleum companies is 10.3 to 12.3 percent. The midpoint of this range is 11.3 percent.

Table 2
Comparison of rates of return

Year	Moody's 125 Industrials	Eight largest petroleum firms
1971	11.2	11.1
1970	10.2	10.8
1969	12.2	10.8
1968	13.0	12.4
1967	12.4	12.4
1966	14.2	11.6
1965	13.7	12.1
1964	13.3	10.5
1963	12.4	11.5
1962	11.6	10.7
1961	10.5	10.4
1960	10.8	10.2
1959	11.6	9.8
1958	10.2	9.6
1957	13.2	13.1
1956	14.3	14.1
1955	15.4	13.7
1954	13.2	12.8
1953	13.4	13.9
1952	13.2	13.6
1951	14.6	15.3

For this same 1967-71 period, the average earnings on stockholders' equity for the eight major petroleum companies were 11.5 percent. Within the limits of the precision of such calculations, the earnings on stockholders' equity (11.5 percent) and the cost of equity capital (11.3 percent) are approximately equal. This is what we would expect in an effectively competitive industry operating in an economy with well-functioning capital markets. The rate-of-return data indicate that the eight major petroleum companies are part of a competitive industry and are themselves earning the competitive rate of return. If simple monopoly power or more complex collusive behavior were an important feature for the petroleum industry, one would expect it to show up in the rate-of-return data. It does not.

The conclusion that I draw from these long-run profitability data is that the U.S. petroleum industry is effectively competitive. But long-run profitability data are not the only data and analyses which support the conclusion of an effectively competitive U.S. petroleum industry. This conclusion is also supported by the record of:

—the rate of return to offshore activity,

—the patterns of entry and bidding in competitive lease sales for offshore acreage,

—entry into refining, producing and other sectors of the industry, and

—the long-run patterns of real refinery margins and product prices net of state and federal taxes.

When all of these factors are considered together, they form a rounded whole and support a robust conclusion. That conclusion, I repeat, is that the U.S. petroleum industry is effectively competitive. Divestiture will not improve the competitive performance of the U.S. petroleum industry. But divestiture would increase the general level of costs at which this competition occurs.

The Costs of Divestiture and Disintegration

The U.S. petroleum industry is generally thought of as having four vertical stages. These are producing, refining, transportation and marketing. These four stages, however, do not tell the whole story. First of all, the transportation sector actually consists of two separate stages. The first of these two stages is the transportation of crude oil to refining centers. The second is the transportation of refined products to marketing outlets. But even this breakdown glosses over many significant details of the organization of the industry.

Consider, for example, the producing stage of the industry. There are many separate functions which contribute to the makeup of what is commonly referred to as crude oil production. These functions, in approximate temporal and vertical order, include geological and geophysical prospecting, lease acquisition, exploratory drilling, platform construction, development drilling, well logging, operation of production facilities, well workovers, flow lines, lease tanks, gathering systems and field terminals. This pattern is repeated with stage specific variations in the other sectors of the industry.

In this complicated pattern of overlapping functions and activities, the firms engaged in the U.S. petroleum industry use at various times and circumstances different combinations of company owned and purchased contract services. Within the producing sector, there is a large number of specialty firms which provide, for example, contract drilling services, pipeline construction, well workover services, geophysical work and platform construction. These specialty firms constitute sub-industries within the overall producing sector which is itself a stage of the overall U.S. petroleum industry. The companies whose primary commitment in the producing sector of the industry is to finding and producing oil also provide many of these services directly with their own company crews.

Whether or not a given company, at a given time for a given project chooses to purchase contract services or generate required services directly with its own crews depends upon the comparison of the net advantages to the company of the alternatives under the circumstances associated with that project. As it is with the specific details of the producing sector, so it is with general patterns of vertical integration for the industry at large.

No company is completely vertically integrated and self-sufficient in the sense that it provides all the services necessary to find and produce its crude oil; produces all of the crude oil required by its refineries; transports that crude oil in its own trucks, barges, tankcars and pipelines; refines only crude oil produced by itself in its own refineries; moves the refined product output of its refineries in its own transportation facilities; and sells its refined products only under its own brand name from its own market outlets.

The pattern and extent of vertical integration is different for different companies. The importance of activities at each stage of the industry relative to the total activities of a company varies from specific company to specific company. Moreover, not only large companies have found it advantageous to be vertically integrated. Many smaller companies are also integrated into several stages of the industry. The patterns of vertical integration vary across firms, and each firm pursues its own advantage as it sees it.

There is some casual evidence that the degree of vertical integration in the U.S. petroleum industry may be increasing. Examples of this trend, if it is a trend, are the merger of Hess and Amerada to form Amerada-Hess, the growth by Ashland Oil and the potential expansion of Louisiana Land and Exploration into refining. This may be evidence that at the moment the net advantages are running in the direction of increased economies of vertical integration. But the degree of vertical integration does vary across firms, and at each stage of the industry there are many firms represented that have little or no vertical integration with respect to the major stages of the industry.

This heterogeneity is at once economically and socially pleasing and methodologically distressing with respect to specifying the costs of divestiture and vertical disintegration. The observed heterogeneity is economically and socially pleasing because, together with the large numbers of firms in the industry, the low market shares of even the largest firms, and the evidence of long-run profitability and other indicia, it reinforces the conclusion of effective competition. Heterogeneity is evidence that under many circumstances a firm does not have to be fully integrated to be economically viable. Heterogeneity is methodologically distressing because it complicates the problem of estimating the costs of divestiture and vertical disintegration.

The question is as follows. If vertical integration is an important source of economies, why do not all firms have to be vertically integrated (and perhaps vertically integrated to the same degree) to be economically viable? If we observe some firms which are not, or hardly at all, vertically integrated, but which nevertheless are viable economic entities, does it not follow that we can divest and vertically disintegrate the U.S. petroleum industry with no cost to economic efficiency, U.S. society and American consumers? I believe the answer to this question is no.

The answer to this question ties back to the fact that the U.S. petroleum industry is highly and effectively competitive. In a competitive industry, small advantages are important. This is especially true in a technologically dynamic, capital-intensive industry such as the U.S. petroleum industry which operates under uncertainty and changing circumstances. Vertical integration improves the planning process, reduces uncertainty with regard to investment decisions, and broadens the earning base while improving the portfolio characteristics of asset composition.

At any given stage of the industry, or for any interface between stages, it is possible to discuss these advantages on an anecdotal basis. But it is also possible to see their impact in a more generally systematic and quantifiable way. I discussed above the importance of long-run profitability data in terms of assessing the effectiveness of competition in the U.S. petroleum industry. It is also possible to use profitability data to indicate the advantages of vertical integration and calculate a rough approximation of the cost of divestiture and vertical disintegration. In this calculation, the heterogeneity of firms in the U.S. industry becomes an advantage.

In a competitive industry, profits are a cost. They are the cost of inducing firms—as the agents of society—to allocate resources to those activities which society values. If vertical integration reduces uncertainty, facilitates planning and contributes negative covariance to the earnings of the asset structure of the firm, then those firms which are relatively more vertically integrated will have lower costs of capital than less vertically integrated firms. It is possible to test this hypothesis by examining the long-run profitability data for various classes of firms.

Consider firms which fall into three broad groups. These groups are:

—non-integrated producers,

—refiners-marketers,

—vertically integrated firms.

The average rate of return on invested capital for these classes of firms over the period 1951-1973 was as follows:

—non-integrated producers _____ 0.152

—non-integrated refiners-markerters _____ 0.099

—vertically integrated firms _____ 0.086

These return numbers, together with data on the amount of capital invested, permit a rough approximation of the cost to U.S. society of divestiture and vertical disintegration.

At the end of 1974, for the 29 firms surveyed by the Chase Manhattan Bank, the total domestic net investment of the U.S. petroleum industry in producing, transportation, refining, marketing and other assets was approximately 52 billion dollars. Gross investment was 93 billion dollars. Net income earned in the United States was 6.4 billion dollars. This is equivalent to a rate of return on net investment of 12.3 percent—a competitive rate of return on net investment. There are no hard data on what proportion of total net investment in domestic U.S. petroleum industry investment is accounted for by the 52 billion dollars which the 29 firms represent. But on a worldwide basis, these 29 companies account for 75 percent of non-communist crude oil production. The 20 largest U.S. companies accounted for 86 percent of 1970 U.S. crude oil production capacity and 87 percent of U.S. gasoline refining capacity. Of the 52 billion dollars of domestic U.S. net investment for the 29 companies, 50 percent was in production, 22 percent in refining, and 28 percent in marketing, transportation and other categories. Marketing represented 55 percent of the non-production, non-refining investment. On the basis of these figures, for the calculations at hand, I assume that the 29 companies account for about 85 percent of the total domestic net investment in the U.S. petroleum industry.

The question then is: What would be the cost to the U.S. public of divestiture and vertical disintegration of the U.S. petroleum industry? If divestiture and vertical disintegration raised the cost of capital and consequent required earnings necessary to remain economically viable for the severed components of previously integrated companies by a factor of proportionality equal to the relative 1951-1973 difference between the average for integrated companies and the averages for non-integrated producers and refiner-marketers, the overall weighted average rate of return on net domestic assets in the U.S. petroleum industry would have to increase by about 7.5 percent. This may not appear to be a very large number, but the U.S. petroleum industry is a large capital intensive industry.

A 7.5 increase in the required rate of return necessary to offset the loss of the net economies and operating efficiencies which would result from divestiture and vertical disintegration amounts to a *yearly cost of over half a billion dollars* on a 1974 base. This cost would ultimately have to be borne by the consuming U.S. public.

In addition, this estimate of the cost of American society of legislative amputation of the U.S. petroleum industry through divestiture and vertical disintegration is an underestimate of the *prospective cost* of such a policy. There are a number of reasons for this. Some of these reasons are:

1. the future net investment of the U.S. petroleum industry will be higher than that of 1974,

2. there is some evidence of increasing economies of vertical integration which would be foregone by an arbitrary divestiture and vertical disintegration,

3. the half a billion dollar estimate is based on 1974 dollars and unfortunately, inflation will make it larger, and

4. the trauma of divestiture and vertical disintegration will at least temporarily inhibit investment decisions with consequent real costs not included in the estimate.

On the basis of both its failure to enhance competition in an already effectively competitive industry and, most importantly, the cost burden it imposes upon U.S. consumers, divestiture and vertical disintegration of the U.S. petroleum industry is an ill-advised policy.

Conclusions

The lessons to be learned here are important. There is a dangerous tendency for us to seek costless solutions to our problems. The example at hand is the outcry with regard to "monopoly" in the energy industries. It is tempting to believe that by some miraculous process resources can be created by the stroke of a pen, a regulatory rulemaking, the passing of a law, an executive order or a court decision. Such is not the case.

It is important the Congress realize that there are no immediate miracles to be wrought by slaying imaginary dragons of monopoly, and that Congress proceed on a course that is consistent with the principles of how things get done in American society. This last, the matter of principles, is vitally important. There is a tendency, in Congress and elsewhere, to respond to the problems of policy and regulatory failures by more regulation and additional *ad hoc* policies. Such a response only prolongs and worsens the situation and makes its ultimate remedy more difficult and costly. I believe that we are, as always, in a critical era of choice. To impose a policy of divestiture and vertical disintegration upon the U.S. petroleum industry, however pure the intentions, would in my opinion be an unfortunate step down the road toward the Anglicization of our economy.

It is impossible to "make the companies pay" for an ill-advised policy such as divestiture and vertical disintegration of the U.S. petroleum industry. In a competitive economy, the companies are simply the agents of society. Society itself must pay. The initial costs of divestiture and disintegration of the U.S. petroleum industry would be at least half a billion dollars a year, and these yearly costs would grow in magnitude as the years go by.

The Chamber of Commerce argues that divestiture of vertically integrated petroleum companies will reduce competition in the petroleum industry by disallowing a form of firm organization that has proved efficient in that industry. Because of this, the net effect of the legislation will be to accentuate shortages of energy supplies, to increase the price of petroleum products to U.S. consumers, and to lead to ever more costly and desperate government efforts to mitigate the effects of the legislation.

3

THE EFFECT OF PETROLEUM DISMEMBERMENT ON PRICE & SUPPLY

STATEMENT OF BARRY A. FRIEDMAN[1] FOR THE CHAMBER OF COMMERCE OF THE UNITED STATES BEFORE THE SUBCOMMITTEE ON ANTITRUST AND MONOPOLY, COMMITTEE ON THE JUDICIARY, UNITED STATES SENATE— JANUARY 29, 1976

The Chamber of Commerce of the United States opposes legislation that seeks to dissolve the vertically-integrated petroleum companies and prevent them from diversifying into other energy-related areas. These proposals, as developed in S. 489, S. 2387 and S. 2761 among others, represent the wrong way to solve our nation's energy problems.

The National Chamber includes in its membership many petroleum companies which have a direct interest in legislative proposals relating to the economic organization of their industry. Our membership includes a much larger number of companies which relate to the petroleum industry as consumers rather than as producers. Their concern over these proposals is

---

[1]Member, New York Bar; Antitrust and Trade Regulation Staff, Chamber of Commerce of the United States.

scarcely less direct, both in terms of jobs for their employees and a reasonable return to their stockholders.

Our membership in the auto industry, for example, is absolutely dependent on the petroleum industry to provide auto users with an adequate supply of gasoline and oil at a price they can pay. Our membership in the electrical industry is at least presently dependent on the supply of fuel oil for electric utilities in adequate amounts and at reasonable prices to sustain the market for electricity-using products. Our members in the chemical industry depend heavily on the oil industry for petroleum-based raw materials. Our transportation industry members are major users of diesel fuel. The impact of high fuel prices on farmers is a source of concern to our members in the farm equipment industry.

Both commerical and domestic users of oil products are deeply interested in two principal questions about dissolution proposals:

1. Would dissolution bring lower prices?
2. Would dissolution improve the adequacy of oil supplies?

We believe that there are compelling reasons to conclude that dissolution of the integrated petroleum companies would reduce competition in the petroleum industry, foreclose a form of business organization that has been historically a significant element in the reduction of petroleum costs, and serve to increase the price of petroleum products over what the price would be in the absence of dissolution legislation.

Of primary importance to consumers is their ability to get adequate supplies of petroleum and petroleum-based products at reasonable prices. It is our belief that a program of dissolution of integrated producers would serve only to deepen and intensify, rather than dissipate, the already widespread public view that the prices of petroleum and petroleum-based products are higher than they need to be to stimulate adequate production.

Our main reasons for these conclusions are stated below in two parts:
I. Dissolution legislation would unfavorably affect prices and supply.
II. At a time when the petroleum industry faces severe cost and supply problems, dissolution would preclude the use, in this industry, of basic modern developments in management.

I

Dissolution of integrated petroleum companies has been advocated on the ground that it would decrease prices as a result, it is said, of increased competition.

As a matter of arithmetic, a decrease in prices would have to reflect a decrease in the profits component of costs, a decrease in other costs, or some combination of the two. We will examine both profits and other costs.

A. *Profits*—Profits are not now a major element in the costs of petroleum products—less than 2 cents per gallon of gasoline. In addition, all projections of future demand for petroleum indicate that this industry must earn profits sufficient to attract high levels of capital investment. In the context of continuing inflation, high interest rates, and intense government and private competition for the investor's dollar, we see no realistic prospect for reducing petroleum industry profit levels and, at the same time, attracting capital funds sufficient to meet the needs of consumers for petroleum products.

In fact, the realistic prospect is that a statutory prohibition on integration would lead investors to demand a higher level of profits to compensate for added risks of certain types of investment in the petroleum industry. We understand that Congress has already heard testimony to the effect that the construction of refineries without an assured supply of crude oil is regarded as riskier than the construction of refineries with an assured supply of crude oil. Similarly, the construction of pipelines without an assurance of traffic is also regarded as a high risk investment. Both refineries and pipelines become favorable investments when they are built in conjunction with a distribution and marketing organization capable of selling their products to consumers. The investor, taking this in mind, cannot be expected to provide capital, at favorable rates, to major capital construction projects of the petroleum industry where both the assurance of supply and the marketing operation are less secure than the present.

Consumer interests require that these capital requirements be met; because it is the use of this capital which makes it possible to produce petroleum products at reasonable costs. Dissolution legislation, leading to higher costs for capital, will thus drive consumers' prices up.

B. *Non-capital Costs*—The conjecture that non-capital costs of providing petroleum would be reduced by the dissolution of the integrated companies is also unrealistic.

1. Cost pressures in the oil industry now arise from competition between highly diverse business organizations. A comprehensive study of the energy industry has noted that concentration levels, an indicator of the existence of competition, are relatively low.[2]

---

[2]Thomas D. Duchesneau, *Competition in the U.S. Energy Industry.* Ballinger Publishing Company: Cambridge, 1975.

All that dissolution could accomplish is to *eliminate* the competitive cost pressures resulting from competition between integrated companies and the single-function companies and from competition among integrated companies. Whatever assessment anyone wishes to make of the importance of these two types of competition, it does not appear possible that their statutory elimination would decrease competitive costs in this industry.

2. Integration has itself been an important influence in reducing costs in the petroleum industry. The integrated petroleum company has been one of the major innovations in the past century in the field of economic organization.

Costs of production, storage and transportation in the petroleum industry are, over the long term, subject to inherent economies of scale. The basic production tools—refinery pressure vessels, pipelines, storage tanks, and tankers—are subject to the principle that, with increases in size, the enclosed working volume increases faster than the area and weight (and hence the cost) of the enclosing structure.[3] It is the vertically integrated company, which has fewer risks in each sector where it operates, that can make this type of investment.[4]

Reductions in costs are due to large-scale operations or to more efficient planning and coordination made possible by integration are of interest and benefit both to the investor and the consumer.

C. *Effect on Crude Prices*—Historically, sharp decreases in the price of crude oil have been caused by supply gluts due to temporary overproduction. At the present time, excess production of domestic crude is not a realistic possibility. The possibilities of excess production lie, if anywhere, in the OPEC countries.

The OPEC price increases have, predictably, resulted in decreased consumption of OPEC oil and compelled the OPEC countries to allocate production in order to maintain their desired level of prices. These reductions in output have occasioned unwanted modifications in ambitious development plans and some difficulty for financially over-committed

---

[3]A tank in the shape of a cube, one foot on a side, uses six square feet of structure (one square foot to the side) to enclose one cubic foot of space. If the cube is increased to two feet on a side, 24 square feet of structure—four times the area—encloses eight cubic feet of space, or eight times the space. As in many other fields of technology where the same general principle applies, one of the main thrusts in the development of petroleum industry technology is toward overcoming the practical engineering obstacles to larger and larger structures—a point illustrated by the rapid growth in the size of the tankers.

[4]See J. McLean and R. Haigh, *The Growth of the Integrated Oil Companies.* Harvard University Press: Cambridge, 1954.

OPEC countries; but, so far, these difficulties do not appear to have led to major departures from cartel price levels or production allocations.

The proposed dissolution of American integrated petroleum companies, far from reducing OPEC's power, would increase it.

There is historical evidence that it is actually easier to maintain cartel prices in markets where the buyers are small and numerous than in markets where the buyers are few and large. The belief that large buyers are in a favorable position to bargain for special terms is reflected, for example, in the Robinson-Patman Act; and it is a relevant item of recent oil industry history that OPEC has been particularly successful in exerting pressure on smaller companies. We have real difficulty foreseeing any outcome favorable to the American consumer from a situation in which the OPEC countries might be selling to the American market through a large number of relatively small importers, while they were selling into other industrial markets through foreign majors or government monopolies.

A further consideration is that dissolution of the American majors would involve some disposition of their overseas operations, and it seems highly probable that these dispositions would provide an opportunity to the OPEC countries to accelerate their announced plans for further integrating forward into refining and distribution. Even if it were politically desirable to prevent these facilities from being sold in the first instance to OPEC nominees, the United States would have jurisdictional problems in preventing OPEC countries from acquiring such overseas facilities from the first-round purchasers. Such a line of development would appear likely to strengthen the OPEC cartel.

In summary, the reasons advanced for believing that dissolution of the American majors might weaken the OPEC cartel appear flawed by the assumption that the OPEC countries will not take obvious measures to protect their own essential interests. The more probable prediction is that dissolution would speed up the expansion of the part played by the OPEC countries in refining, distribution, and transportation and that dissolution would, if anything, reduce the chance that OPEC oil would be imported into the United States under favorable "special deals" as compared to the chance that other industrial countries would get the benefit of such deals.

II

Explicitly, dissolution proposals distinguish between integrated and non-integrated petroleum companies, and they distinguish between petroleum companies on the basis of differences in size.

Implicitly, these proposals draw certain somewhat less obvious distinctions between companies in the petroleum industry.

For instance, some petroleum companies recognized early the severity of the energy problem and undertook to develop alternate fuel sources by diversifying their business. Others did not. Dissolution proposals distinguish between the two types of companies; many of those which sought to meet the problems posed by oil shortages would be dissolved. On its face, this legislative approach clashes with our national search for energy independence.

The dissolution proposals classify the companies into integrated and non-integrated and diversified and non-diversified. In addition, a number of the bills will exempt the smaller companies from their reach. However, size alone is just a small part of the difference between those firms that will be dissolved and those that will remain. An overlooked point is the vastly greater importance of knowledge in today's technology-rich industrial world. If one goes back far enough in history, practically all business organizations were highly specialized in terms of product and function. But in recent years progressive businessmen have come to realize more and more that the basic resource of the modern enterprise is knowledge—general knowledge of business organization, planning, controls, personnel administration, finance and more specific knowledge of how to design, how to produce, and how to market a family of products and services. The question how best to use basic organizational knowledge and competence cannot be answered, in this changing world, by old slogans to the effect that the "shoemaker should stick to his last."

On the contrary, any economic enterprise which views knowledge and competence as major resources of its management is inherently committed to seek new markets to which to apply these resources. It will look for new geographic markets and for new product markets. It will make sure that its suppliers of raw materials, components, and distribution services are doing as good a job as it could do itself. It will keep a weather eye on industries which use analogous product design, production, or marketing knowledge, with a view to taking advantage of any sign of weakness in business performance. Companies which are good at deploying their basic competence are attractive to investors for their growth in earnings, and they are attractive to ambitious management and technical personnel who see possibilities of promotion opportunities due to the expansion of the enterprise and not just due to executive turnover.

There are still many product-oriented companies which operate in a restricted field of specialization, with little effort to stretch the application of their familiar competence to new fields. There is nothing wrong with the product approach to business strategy; but, an economy composed entirely of product-limited companies would be a lackluster economy. Every advanced economy has sanctioned the development of knowledge-based enterprises, because of the contributions these enterprises make to economic expansion, the growth of international trade, increased competition, rising levels of productivity, technological innovation and ultimately, a higher and more richly varied standard of living for consumers.

Obviously, a business organization which is constantly probing its own frontiers is an uncomfortable neighbor that will make enemies among those who feel threatened by it and among those with an emotional or political bias against size, diversity, economic success, or all three. One could view these reactions more sympathetically if there were any real indication that the growth of knowledge-oriented enterprise was achieved at the price of stifling small business, reducing the number of self-employed, or precluding the development of new knowledge-based firms. But all the evidence is that during the years since World War II (the period of the most extensive development of the diversified, knowledge-based firm), the United States has seen a large increase in the formation of small business and some increase in the proportion of the self-employed.[5]

There has been some recognition among academic economists of the importance of organization to economic performance. In his 1963 Presidential Address to the Institute of Management Sciences, Kenneth Arrow, later a Nobel laureate, observed, "Truly among man's innovations, the use of organization to accomplish his ends is among both his greatest and his earliest." Thomas Cochran, a professor at the University of Pennsylvania, has suggested, in the December 1974 *American Historical Review,* that "business organization rather than technology or capital is the leading factor in bringing about economic growth." Arthur Cole, of Harvard University, has observed, in the May 1968 *American Economic Review,* that "If changes in business procedures and practices were patentable, the contributions of business change to the economic growth of the nation would be as widely recognized as the influence of mechanical inventions or the inflow of capital from abroad."

---

[5]Professor Neil H. Jacoby, a member of President Eisenhower's Council of Economic Advisers, systematically collected the evidence in Chapter 2 of his book, *Corporate Power and Social Responsibility,* (MacMillan: New York, 1973). The fear propaganda that large companies are taking over the economy uses the data focused entirely on the manufacturing sector, and even these data are highly ambiguous. See the *Anthology of Studies of Industrial Concentration by the Conference Board: 1958-1972* (The Conference Board: New York, 1973), particularly parts V and VI.

Successful forms of organization evolve by trial and error, with knowledge residing as much in practice and experience as in any easily stated set of principles which might be digested for popular understanding. The various structural proposals for disintegrating the petroleum industry amount to a prohibition of the use of the major developments in business organization of the last hundred years. The overall result would be a systematic policy of reversion to the pre-Industrial Revolution type of business organization. We do not suggest that the sponsors of this legislation intend to require a reversion to green eye shades and the quill pen. It is no doubt assumed that the surviving companies will use all the modern business gadgets, from computers to copiers. But in business organization, the gadgetry can be taken for granted. The basics begin with the views held by the members of the organization as to its purposes and goals, together with their concept of what its opportunities are, what its assets are, and what the organization ought to be doing with its assets and opportunities. These bills tell the petroleum industry to forget all it has learned about the basics of business organization and management for more than a century. Each firm in the industry would have legislatively limited business assets, objectives and goals with coordination between the parts being formalized and restricted.

Proposals to outlaw the use of modern business organization in any industry are counter-productive at best. As applied to an industry which very clearly needs all the help it can get to supply the foreseeable public demand for its highly essential products, such proposals are more than counter-productive. They border on irrationality. Over time, the effects of such legislation would be certain to show up in accentuated shortages of energy supplies, higher prices to the consumer (reflecting both production inefficiencies and supply shortages), and evermore desperate and costly government efforts to mitigate the effects of bad legislation.

In sum, the National Chamber opposes the concepts now written into S. 489, S. 2387, and S. 2761 and comparable bills. We urge this subcommittee not to approve these bills.

The Gary testimony examines the effect of petroleum industry divestiture on the industry's cost of raising capital. Gary finds that for several reasons such divestitures would increase the riskiness of investment in the industry, thus leading investors to demand a higher return from such investment. These conditions would last at least ten years and perhaps longer. In consequence, there would be a long period of underinvestment by the domestic energy industry and hence a much weakened U.S. energy position.

4

TWENTY YEARS OF CHAOS

STATEMENT OF RAYMOND B. GARY,* MORGAN STANLEY & CO., BEFORE THE SUBCOMMITTEE ON ANTITRUST AND MONOPOLY, COMMITTEE ON THE JUDICIARY, UNITED STATES SENATE—JANUARY 27, 1976

Mr. Chairman and Committee Members, I am Raymond B. Gary, a Managing Director of Morgan Stanley & Co. Incorporated, an investment banking firm headquartered in New York City. I welcome this opportunity to comment on the bill introduced by Senator Bayh, S.2387, which requires dismemberment of the major United States integrated petroleum companies. I believe that such legislation would impair the financial strength of a major portion of the U.S. petroleum industry. It would impede the industry in raising the capital necessary to satisfy the energy requirements of this nation. Instead of promoting the availability of additional energy from domestic sources, the results of such legislation would be to create an extended period of uncertainty and weakness for domestic oil companies leading to even greater dependence on foreign sources of energy.

---

*Managing Director, Morgan Stanley & Co., Inc.

Before discussing in detail why I am so concerned about the implications of the present proposals, let me provide background on the perspective from which I am speaking. Morgan Stanley is an international banking firm engaged in the underwriting and placement of securities for corporations and governments. Since 1935, when our firm was founded, we have sponsored in the form of public offerings or private placements in the world's capital markets the equivalent of over $97 billion of debt and equity securities. Morgan Stanley is also a member of the New York Stock Exchange and is involved in brokerage and market-making activities in both stocks and bonds. In addition, we provide general financial advisory services on a wide range of matters including long-range financial policy and planning. In this capacity we have been closely involved with new large construction projects many of which are related in some way to the oil and gas industry.

In the 40 years of our history, Morgan Stanley has raised approximately $16 billion for 31 companies in the petroleum industry and their subsidiaries and affiliates, including not only many of the multi-national integrated petroleum companies directly affected by S.2387 but also smaller independent companies. In 1975, we arranged financing in the amount of approximately $3.9 billion for oil companies, including the largest private placement in history, $1.75 billion of long-term debt for two of the participants in the Trans-Alaska Pipeline System.

Because we have had such extensive involvement in arranging financing for the petroleum industry, we hope that the Subcommittee will find it useful to have comments on the financial implications of the proposed legislation from an investment banker's point of view. (Attached as Exhibit I is a listing of and certain statistics for companies apparently affected by S.2387.)

Over the next decade the ability to secure funds from investors in the world's capital markets is going to be vital to the economic future of U.S. industry. For the first time in modern U.S. financial history, the supply of funds may not grow so fast as the potential demand for capital and financing considerations may act as effective constraints on the economy's capacity to finance fixed investment over the next decade.

Over the last five years, investors have become very quality conscious in choosing their investments; in the next few years, we would expect them to become increasingly selective. They will allocate their capital to the industries and companies and projects which represent the best investment opportunities. In light of this projected capital insufficiency, one element that has to be considered in evaluating the wisdom of legislation like S.2387 is the effect it would have on the ability of the affected oil companies to compete for investors' funds. We are forced to conclude that the proponents of a divestiture statute have largely ignored this element.

The petroleum industry has been and will continue to be an intensive user of capital. The era of cheap oil and cheap energy is over. Unfortunately, large discoveries of oil in the United States today are only being found in frontier areas such as the Arctic or deep offshore waters. The petroleum industry will be required to drill deeper, move farther offshore, explore in forbidding climates, transport over longer distances, and utilize more expensive recovery techniques, all of which are essential to add to our current sources of petroleum. If the credit of our U.S. based oil companies is weakened by legislation such as S.2387, they will not be able to attract the capital to do the job. Furthermore, a fragmented industry would have a seriously diminished capability of competing with foreign oil companies precisely at the time when many foreign nations are strengthening and consolidating their own national oil companies.

Prior to the Arab oil embargo of 1973, the petroleum industry enjoyed the highest degree of acceptability to investors in the capital markets of the world. Since that time, world petroleum economics have been importantly affected by the actions of the OPEC cartel. A number of factors arising largely as a result of OPEC actions,—including skyrocketing costs, unilateral nationalizations, increased taxes, and governmental controls on prices—have caused investors to become concerned about the industry's continued investment attractiveness. The confusion arising from the passage of divestiture legislation would have the most disastrous impact of all; in our view, it could prevent most of the petroleum industry from financing in any significant amounts over the next decade except at prohibitive rates.

If the supply of capital to the petroleum industry dries up, as we believe it would, there would be only one source left to look to for support in financing this most vital of our energy industries—the Federal Government. In the end, oil company divestiture could well lead to the need for a federal guarantee program, or some form of federal insurance, to provide the necessary backing for petroleum financing. We question whether this is what the Congress intends or the public wants.

My testimony is divided into two major sections. First, I will discuss the present and future needs of the petroleum industry for capital, and the circumstances which have been and will affect its ability to finance in an era of threatened and actual capital shortages. Second, I will consider the financial chaos which would ensue for the oil industry following passage of the proposed legislation.

I. THE CURRENT NEED FOR CAPITAL

Considerable study has been undertaken recently of the capital investment requirements of the U.S. economy over the next decade. Our total capital requirements in the United States between now and 1985 are awesome, and I believe no one disputes the urgent need for this capital investment. Treasury Secretary Simon has cited an estimated need for investment outlays in the decade ahead of $4 to 4 1/2 trillion. Of this amount, $1 trillion would be needed through 1985 to explore and develop additional oil and gas reserves, build refineries and pipelines, develop coal resources, construct nuclear power and electric utility plants and provide for other facilities required to meet our energy needs. These numbers are of course estimates but, whatever the exact requirement, it is clear that the needs are enormous and must be described in trillions and not billions of dollars. The critical question is whether the supply of capital will be able to satisfy these potential demands.

Availability of Capital as a Constraint

We at Morgan Stanley have been interested in the subject of the enormous need for capital and how such needs will be financed for a number of years. Our interest came about initially as a result of being involved as financial advisor to some large projects, such as the Trans-Alaska Pipeline and the Canadian Arctic Gas Pipeline. The estimated dollar requirements for such projects constantly increased in size and began to loom so large that they staggered the imagination. Most of these increases were a result of inflation and increasing emphasis on environmental requirements of the projects. As these estimated dollar totals rose, we began to question whether the funds to finance the undertakings would be available. It also became apparent that the electric utilities had enormous needs for capital to finance expansion of their generating plant capacity fired by oil, coal and gas, and also to finance new nuclear generating capacity whose capital costs are huge. Gas producing and distributing companies had similar demands and also needed capital for new sources of gas such as coal gasification plants. Other industries had additional large requirements. It seemed that none of the new projects our clients were studying had price tags of less than 1/2 billion and many were over one billion dollars. This prompted us to make an extensive study of the whole question of availability of capital.

We were particularly concerned about the next five years, since many of the specific projects on which we were working were scheduled for construction during that period. Our economic consultant, Professor Benjamin M. Friedman of Harvard University, undertook a major study of this subject, an updated version of which was subsequently published in *The Sloan Management Review* (Spring 1975) which is attached as Exhibit II. Our conclusion from this study was that whereas in the past the need for productive facilities in this country has determined the amount of capital which was raised, in the future the amount of capital which can be raised will determine the amount of productive facilities which will be built. In other words, availability of capital will act as a constraint on investment. Not all potential demands for capital will be satisfied.

Under these circumstances, only those companies or projects which represent the best investment opportunities will be able to attract sufficient capital. Lenders and equity investors are always faced with a wide selection of competitive investment alternatives vying for their attention. When capital comes into short supply, these investors derive the traditional benefits of a buyer's market, and become even more selective in the investment of their funds. They tend to demonstrate a preference for securities which appear to offer investors an attractive return with a high degree of safety. This preference for safety becomes heightened during periods of financial crisis or instability. Such selectivity was demonstrated during the difficult buyer's market in July-October of 1974, when certain lesser quality credits were altogether excluded from the public debt markets, and even the most credit-worthy electric and gas utilities experienced difficulty in raising sufficient amounts of money on acceptable terms. At that time, many utilities found that the cost of fossil fuel had risen dramatically while certain state regulatory agencies had not permitted utilities to raise their prices to the consumer. The result was declining earnings, deteriorating credit ratings, a reduction in financing alternatives and a significantly higher cost of financing. During that period no utility with credit ratings of less than Single-A was able to raise long-term funds. The only issues done by lower rated companies were done in intermediate rather than long-term maturities.

Moreover, interest rate differentials between issues of differing credit standing widened considerably. A dramatic example of the difference between strong and weaker credits came on October 1, 1974. On that day, Texas Power & Light, a Triple-A rated issuer, came to market with $50 million of 30 year bonds at 10 1/8%. The same day, Detroit Edison, a Triple-B rated issuer, also came to market. However, the maturity of its $50 million of bonds was only 5 years, not 30 years, and the interest rate on the Detroit Edison issue was 12 1/2 not 10 1/8%.

We believe that passage of S.2387, or even a continuing serious threat of its passage, may have the result of similarly diminishing access to or even excluding the petroleum industry from our market places.

Capital Requirements of the Petroleum Industry

There have been a variety of estimates with respect to the future capital requirements of the petroleum industry. A widely cited study is that done by the Chase Manhattan Bank which estimated that on a worldwide basis the industry would need $750 billion from 1970-1985 for capital and exploration expenditures. Adding $450 billion for other financial requirements and working capital additions gave a total financial need for the period of $1.2 trillion. These estimates are in 1970 dollars. Of course the factor of inflation increases considerably the actual dollar amounts of these estimates.

If we look only at the needs of the domestic petroleum industry, a reasonable estimate for capital and exploration expenditures for the decade from 1976 to 1985 would be in the range of $400 billion or more. A comparable number has been derived by the Standard Oil Company (Ohio) by using the estimates developed in the Federal Energy Administration Project Independence Blueprint and applying an annual assumed rate of inflation at 5 percent. First National City Bank in its Energy Memo of January 1976 estimates capital outlays of the oil industry in the United States at $460 billion (in 1974 dollars) for the period 1976-1985. These estimates would indicate capital and exploration outlays for the domestic petroleum industry averaging over $40 billion per year over the next 10 years, a dramatic increase above the approximately $9 billion per year spent in the prior ten years.

Historically, oil companies were able to meet their needs for capital primarily out of internally generated funds—earnings, depreciation and depletion. In fact, for The Chase Manhattan Group of Companies, in the five year period 1960 to 1964 more than 87% of cash needs came from these sources. Since that time the percentage steadily declined to 76% in the next 5 years and 72% in the 5 year period 1970 to 1974. This resulted in a corresponding increase in the need to utilize the capital markets for external financing and to raise further funds through the sales of assets and other financial transactions. Over the last 15 years the major petroleum companies covered in the Chase Manhattan Survey had to increase their reliance on external funds from an annual average of $1 billion in 1960-64, to $3.1

billion in 1965-69 and to $7.2 billion in 1970-74. Over that period, debt and other long-term credits as a percent of total capitalization increased from 17.8% at December 31, 1960 to 30.9% at December 31, 1974. (See Exhibits III and IV).

In 1974, even though it was a year of record earnings for these companies because of substantial inventory profits, they had to raise $10.8 billion from external sources of which $6.4 billion was in long-term debt and sales of capital stock.

Current Investor Concerns With Respect to the Petroleum Industry

Just as professional investors over the years have traditionally favored oil industry securities, individuals have also invested extensively in them. Millions of individuals directly or indirectly own the common stock and bonds of these companies. In the wake, however, of a number of disturbing actions by our own Government and those abroad, both debt and equity investors are beginning to express concern about the attractiveness of oil investments. At Morgan Stanley we have seen evidence of this concern displayed in the prices and yields at which oil company securities sell in relationship to other comparable quality securities.

Anyone can see what has been going on by looking into the daily newspapers; the most striking recent events, of course, have been nationalization of reserves by foreign countries, elimination of the oil depletion allowance in the United States, and increased taxes in almost all jurisdictions. The Energy Policy and Conservation Act rolling back the price of oil and continuing government oil price fixing that was recently signed into law was a continuation of policies which have impeded, and will continue to impede, the petroleum industry from forming the capital which is needed for this country to move towards our national goal of reasonable energy self-sufficiency. It is quite apparent that such actions have reduced the petroleum industry's cash flow and therefore substantially increased its need for external financing. It has been estimated that the effect of the elimination of the depletion allowance and the Energy Act could be to reduce the domestic petroleum industry's cash flow by as much as $4 billion per year, cash flow that could have been utilized in the expensive search for new oil in the United States. This amount is equivalent to almost 20% of the capital expenditures of the petroleum industry in the U.S. in 1974.

As the petroleum industry's ability to generate funds internally continues to be impaired by these policies, it becomes clearer and clearer to investors that the industry will require an unprecedented amount of external financing in the future, and that its economics will be substantially less attractive than in the past. The effects will be felt both in long-term debt and equity markets. Investors also recognize that the factors causing the decline in internal generation of funds also tend to make petroleum industry securities less attractive investments, since smaller cash flow produces a lesser ability to service existing and future debt, and indicates as well the probability that a lesser portion of earnings would be paid out to investors as dividends. From the point of view of a lender the industry may become less credit-worthy; while from that of an equity investor it appears to be turning less profitable, with the concomitant erosion in his potential for return either through dividends or through capital appreciation.

Tangible Evidence Of Investor Concern

The cost of capital to the petroleum industry has already shown signs of increasing. A differential between yields on petroleum company debt issues and non-petroleum industrial company debt issues of similar bond quality rating has developed over the past several years. We believe that this differential in interest costs has developed largely from two factors: the anticipated large amount of financing required by the petroleum industry, and the concern over the ability of these companies to maintain their bond quality ratings. For instance, while petroleum company securities used to sell at a small premium over the prices of other comparably-rated industrial securities, our more recent experience has been that they are now selling at discounts from such prices, and that these discounts have been as high as to produce a yield differential of 20 to 25 basis points from time to time. Exhibit V is a weekly yield comparison from the end of 1974 up to the present for certain Triple-A oil company and non-oil company bonds. Correspondingly, in the equity markets the common stocks of the major petroleum companies are generally trading at price levels much lower in relationship to their earnings than they have traded in the past and at a level lower than their historic relationship to the price earnings ratio of other industrial companies, as shown by the attached chart. Exhibit VI is an analysis of the price earnings ratios of 10 large oil companies and shows the decline of those multiples relative to Standard & Poor's Composite index for time periods between 1965 and 1974.

In assessing investment quality, professional investors and rating agencies are concerned not only with historic performance, as measured by various statistical financial ratios, but also long-term prospects for earnings growth, financial stability, and general economic viability. When many professional investors purchase a security they are making a judgment about investment quality which they expect will be appropriate for an extended period of time. For example, bond issues may have maturity dates as much as 30 years in the future. Professional investors, therefore, take considerable interest in such factors as supplies of raw materials, ability to transport products to the market, and availability of market outlets for the product. Our experience in selling petroleum company securities over the years has been that investors place a high value upon the fact that the larger companies are vertically integrated and are hence generally more stable and economically more efficient, exhibiting a consequent lesser risk from an investment point of view. In our view, the generally high investment quality of these larger petroleum companies is in many respects attributable to the benefits of their vertically integrated structure.

The ratings accorded to debt securities by established Bond Rating Services are important matters. Investors are becoming concerned that the petroleum companies may not be able to maintain their generally high ratings. These ratings are an evaluation of creditworthiness, and are critical factors in determining the cost and frequently the very ability to finance in today's volatile capital markets. Not only does a rating affect the terms of and the interest rate a corporation must pay on its debt securities, a rating bears directly on the breadth of market for a debt security. Quite simply, companies with the higher ratings can borrow more money. Many state and municipal pension funds, for example, can invest only in debt securities which have ratings at or above a certain level, and many small institutional investors and trust accounts rely upon rating agency appraisals because they are not adequately staffed to do their own independent analysis.

Top grade debt ratings are going to continue to be important to petroleum companies because they are going to need to borrow more than they ever have before and the largest amounts are available to the highest rated issuers. In our opinion, however, divestiture of the oil industry would result in a reduction in ratings, in many cases to a level below the minimum required for investment by a wide range of institutions. Certainly, such a reduction must inevitably bring forth a contraction in the industry's ability to borrow.

An Example: The Trans-Alaska Pipeline System

In order to illustrate what I have been saying about how important it is for the petroleum industry to maintain a strong credit position, I would like to tell you something about the financing of the Trans-Alaska Pipeline System ("TAPS" or "the System").

This is a matter with which I am personally very familiar. I was in

Anchorage in February, 1969 attending a lunch at which it was first publicly announced the System would be built, and I have worked almost continuously since that time with one or another of the participants on the financing of the System.

As you know, the Congress deemed this System to be of strategic importance to the nation when it passed the Trans-Alaska Pipeline Authorization Act in November 1973, and as you have been told many times in these hearings, the System is the largest single project ever built and financed by private enterprise. The latest estimate of the cost is in excess of $7 billion not including contingencies or interest during construction. When those factors are added, the overall cost will be in excess of $8 billion. In addition, with field development costs and the tanker fleet to bring the crude oil from Valdez to the West Coast, the grand total is over $13 billion, all of which will be spent before a cent is returned. Costs of the same order of magnitude will also be incurred to develop and deliver the gas reserves in the Prudhoe Bay field.

To set the stage, I will discuss first how oil pipelines have been financed in the past and why most of it has had to be done by oil companies.

To start off with, oil pipelines are risky investments, even for oil companies. They transport only one commodity over a fixed route in one direction. The investment therefore is inflexible and cannot be easily altered to respond to changed distribution patterns. The owners of the systems are exposed to many risks that are completely beyond their control. These include production declines, proration, government controls, imports, changes in fuel requirements, environmental complications and the development of alternate energy sources. Further, since oil pipelines do not have exclusive franchises or certificates of necessity, they compete for transportation business with other pipelines as well as other forms of transportation.

Second, they are capital intensive; it is vital, therefore, that they achieve economies of scale. The major share of pipeline costs are fixed and bear no relationship to the volumes transported. For this reason the profitability is sensitive to volume declines. In modern large-diameter pipelines a small percentage reduction in throughput can result in severe losses unless tariffs are increased.

Because of these risks—and these risks are inevitably borne by the oil industry and not by investors—most oil pipeline systems in this country have been built by the oil interests they serve. As contrasted to the practice in the gas industry, no one else has an economic incentive to build a multi-million dollar oil pipeline, nor would a third party assume these risks without some assurance of throughput to cover them.

Because lenders are acutely aware of the risks, they have almost inevitably insisted when financing pipelines that they have the credit of the appropriate shipper-owner oil company backing the credit of any pipeline borrower. The credit backing is either direct (in the case of undivided joint interest systems, such as TAPS) or indirect (in the case of pipelines financed as a project and organized in corporate form.) In the latter case the debt is secured by the pledge of completion agreements and throughput agreements undertaken by parent company shipper-owners of the pipeline. Almost uniformly, the security agreements include unconditional commitments of the shipper-owners to complete the facilities, to operate them, and if operation is interrupted for any reason, to take necessary steps to restore the facilities to operation but, most important, to pay enough to cover the outstanding indebtedness of the pipeline whether or not such completion, operation or repair ever takes place. These agreements, in fact, are firm applications of the full credit of the oil companies involved and, for the purposes of financing, are the equivalent of guaranties of the pipeline companies' indebtedness. In case of undivided joint interest systems each owner company completes its own share of the system and finances its share of the cost across the range of its entire capital structure.

Whether the credit backing is direct or indirect, the consequence for the lenders is the same—the risks of failure of the pipeline operation have been put upon the oil companies. The consequence for the oil companies is also the same—they have dedicated the parent company resources and credit to get the pipeline financed.

At this point I would like to return to TAPS, where the risks I have been talking about become prodigious in size, many times what they are for crude oil lines in the lower 48 states. The most serious risk of all (and therefore the greatest potential liability for TAPS owners) is the risk that the line may not be completed. Such a matter is worrisome for lenders for the reasons often cited—the harsh environment, escalating costs, environmental delays, weather, or any other unforeseen problem which endangers completion. A pipeline is worthless until the last mile is built.

In order to have a specific example to talk about let me tell you a little about a private placement that we completed last November. The placement was for Sohio/BP Trans Alaska Pipeline Finance Inc., a joint financing vehicle used by The Standard Oil Company (Ohio) and The British Petroleum Company to finance their share of the system. Together, these companies own just under 50% of the 1,200,000 barrel per day system and their share of the costs is presently estimated to be between $5 1/2 and $6 billion, including associated field development expenditures and tankers.

The principal amount of the private placement was $1,750,000,000, comprising two issues of guaranteed notes due 1993 and 1998, both with an interest rate of 10 5/8%. Drawdown of $1.055 billion of bonds occurred in 1975, and there are additional closings scheduled quarterly through the second quarter of 1977. The issue was placed with 76 investors including life insurance companies, fire and casualty companies, public and private pension funds, savings banks, and other institutional investors—and in almost every case these institutions made investment commitments exceeding the amounts they had previously invested in any one issuer.

It should not be surprising, therefore, for me to tell you that the economics of the project and the credit of the companies were weighed with more care than any other financing I have known. The lenders sought to ensure themselves from every conceivable angle that the project would indeed be economically viable and that the borrowers could protect themselves to the maximum extent possible against the onslaught of every risk that could be imagined. The guarantors were analyzed for their capacity to withstand massive overruns in cost or delays in time, and there were elaborate protections built into the loan documents themselves to give the lenders a right to intervene if trouble was threatened. The basic security for the financing was viewed by lenders as the oil in the ground at Prudhoe Bay; and there were elaborate provisions which had the purpose of tying the oil and the pipeline inextricably together so that the security could not be endangered. There were detailed restrictions put upon SOHIO's ability to dispose of the oil, and a prohibition against either parent selling or assigning the equity of their pipeline subsidiaries. To make sure that the strongest possible credit was involved, the lenders required both completion and throughput agreements in addition to the direct guarantees of the debt by the respective parent companies—thus, in effect, giving the lenders recourse against the project itself as well as the general credit of the parent oil companies.

Without the credit of BP and SOHIO, this financing could not have taken place. Moreover, without the credit of the other integrated oil companies participating in TAPS, there would be no pipeline and no prospect of oil reserves being produced from the Prudhoe Bay area. Yet S.2387 appears on its face to prohibit the throughput and completion agreements whereby the parent oil companies in effect guarantee the debt incurred in building this pipeline, as they generally do in other pipeline financings. What the divestiture proponents have in effect proposed is the end of all new pipeline construction and the voiding of the security behind many existing pipeline financings. Even when oil was cheap and domestic reserves adequate to supply our needs, such action by the Government would have seemed unwise; with capital scarcity upon us and a national policy designed to reduce our dependence on foreign supply, one would have to describe such a proposition as reckless.

Summary of the Current Situation

The petroleum industry is already in a position where it must surmount steep hurdles in order to provide for a major portion of this country's energy needs. At a time when projected demand for capital is enormous in all industries, the petroleum industry is going to require capital in unprecedented amounts. At the same time a variety of governmental actions are beginning to impair the industry's credit standing and significantly reduce its cash flow. In addition, there is a prospective capital insufficiency emerging in which lack of availability of capital will act as a constraint on the amount of productive facilities that can be built.

Now the petroleum industry must face the even gloomier prospect that it must meet these challenges while at the same time dismembering itself under legislative fiat. Let me describe the serious financial consequences that would result from the passage of a divestiture bill such as S.2387.

II. INTERIM PERIOD FOLLOWING PASSAGE OF THE PROPOSED LEGISLATION

In our opinion, enactment of the legislation would result in substantial confusion and uncertainty as to the financial, legal and operating outlook for the petroleum industry. In this environment we believe it will be extremely difficult or, in some cases, impossible for the affected companies and other segments of the industry to finance. This conclusion will obviously have important effects on operating and planning decisions of the industry.

Future Capital Expenditures

What will happen to capital expenditure programs? They will undoubtedly have to be curtailed. Some programs, of course, will be continued if at all possible, such as partially completed pipeline projects and undeveloped oil fields which require further expenditures to place them into production. But other capital expenditure programs would be reduced while management reviews which sectors are to be divested and studies the potential economic viability of individual sectors standing alone. We must assume that such legislation and its implications would occupy virtually all the time of top management until some solution has been reached. For instance, it would not be surprising for a company electing to stay in the producing sector to place its refining, marketing and transportation operations on a care and maintenance basis only. This is because there would be doubts as to whether any additional investments in such facilities would be recovered on divestiture. Moreover, it might not be possible to secure the external funds needed for such additional projects, or for that matter, the funds necessary to complete existing projects.

How Would Divestiture Be Accomplished

It would seem most unlikely that any significant part of the assets to be divested could be sold for cash. For one thing, the market would be flooded with a glut of oil industry facilities being offered for sale. For another, in a capital restricted environment, there would hardly be a large series of buyers for tens of billions of dollars of assets unless it might be foreign entities which could be at variance with our national interests. Potential buyers such as other oil companies not affected by the legislation would certainly have difficulty securing such funds if they can be buyers at all. As pointed out in the testimony of Peter A. Bator this morning, the definition of "control" in the bill would impede any such sales from being made in exchange for securities of the buyer, since ownership of such securities would imply continuing control of the prohibited assets.

We doubt that companies outside the petroleum industry would want to make major investments in any aspect of the industry during this period because of the uncertainties faced by the new oil company segments. We also assume that antitrust principles would prevent accomplishment of the required reorganization through the swapping by the companies among themselves of the various segments of their existing business.

It appears, therefore, that the distribution will have to be accomplished in very large part by "spin-offs" to existing shareholders. However, there are serious problems even with this approach. The assets of the surviving company would be materially reduced, yet its obligations might remain undiminished. Such a wholesale distribution of assets to shareholders would not be permitted under the existing debt instruments of many companies, and would raise serious questions under the debt instruments of the others. As we heard this morning from Mr. Bator, even potential violations of covenants that could lead to defaults would in all probability require court determination at the insistence of holders of debt and persons representing these holders, such as indenture trustees. And whether the resolution is voluntary, under court decree or under order from the Federal Trade Commission, it will be necessary in all likelihood to allocate the outstanding debt of each divesting oil company among the segments to be divested. The debt might be allocated according to the book value of assets, earnings, or cash flow of each segment if such financial statistics could be constructed. However, there is no way to predict with certainty how much debt the individual segments would be able to support.

What effect would allocation of debt have on the opportunities for segmented oil companies to raise capital? We believe lenders will be distressed about such a result. After all, allocation changes the nature of the original investment; holding debt of several segments of a fragmented company is substantially different from holding debt of the integrated whole. Each segment is inherently weaker, riskier, and more vulnerable to swings in earnings than the original company. Lenders provide funds to an integrated petroleum company in the belief that they are protected by its asset and earnings strength as well as the provisions of and covenants contained in the relevant financing documents. There are good and valid reasons why indentures and loan agreements include such covenants as negative pledge clauses, sale and leaseback restrictions, dividend and debt limitations, sale merger and conveyance of assets provisions—they are written to protect investors, many of which are fiduciaries and have a duty to protect their beneficiaries from an undermining of the security of their investments.

One solution to the removal of the protection of these covenants will undoubtedly be proposed: let all the outstanding debt become joint and several obligations of the existing company and the new spin-off companies. This cross guarantee arrangement might not create as good a credit for the existing debtholders as the credit of the existing integrated company, but it would at least provide the security backing of the same assets. Apparently, however, this arrangement would not be allowed under the provisions of the legislation since it implies continuing mutual interest and possible "control" under the statutory definition. The investors are not even given Hobson's Choice, but no choice at all—they will be forced to accept lesser credits and the risk that such a result entails. Bond holders and trustees on their behalf can be expected to take every action open to them—including litigation,—to protect the security of their investments, but the court remedy is expensive and time consuming and not necessarily very productive.

Impracticality of Rapidly Working Out a Fair and Equitable Plan

Anyone who recognizes the complexities inherent in slicing up a major industry must reasonably come to the conclusion that it is going to take an extended period of time to accomplish. As you have heard this morning, every party who has an interest in the proceeding (creditors, equity investors, joint venture partners, labor unions, and anyone else with contractual relationships) will want to be represented before the FTC and the courts to protect those interests in any proposed or revised plan. This means a multitude of litigants and years of uncertainty and confusion as plans are made, revised, opposed and changed again. I believe, therefore, that an extended period of time (far longer than the short three year period provided by S.2387) will be required for a company and the FTC to devise (and the courts in various appeals to approve) a plan which complies with the legislation, establishes new businesses, and is as fair and equitable to all parties as the legislation permits. In any event, while plans are being studied, debated and litigated, the industry is not going to be making much progress and no one is going to be anxious to put up new capital.

Effect on Foreign Investments of the Affected Companies

S.2387 purports to act extraterritorially—that is, it could force a company which is deemed to be, for example, a major producer in the United States to get rid of all its domestic and foreign downstream assets. It is clear that in many circumstances foreign tenders would be able to challenge a purported allocation of contractual obligations resulting from an FTC divestiture order in a foreign court, and have a good chance of enforcing their grievances by seizing foreign assets of the oil company.

The complexity of domestic divestiture is difficult enough; I won't try to evaluate the possible consequences on the oil companies' foreign operations themselves. Some of the foreign refineries and other assets could be sold to foreign oil companies, especially those rich in capital. But under the postulated circumstances, divestiture would have all of the attributes of a bankruptcy sale with foreign buyers in a dominant position to acquire a multitude of U.S. investor-owned foreign assets at substantial discounts from their true value. In summary, S.2387 would seriously damage the credit of U.S. oil companies overseas, might disadvantageously affect that of other U.S. companies in foreign markets, and could also lead to a massive windfall for foreign oil companies.

Financing During the Interim Period

I have stated above that we believe that it will be extremely difficult or impossible for a large sector of the petroleum industry to finance once the proposed legislation is passed. In order to amplify on that statement let me pose a series of questions:

—What would be the reaction of investors in petroleum company stocks and bonds?

—What would happen to the market prices of outstanding debt and equity securities?

—Will it be possible to do any financing at all after passage of a divestiture statute?

Investors have no liking for uncertainty; the passage of the proposed legislation would immediately create long lasting uncertainty for the industry. Our firm believes that investors, large and small, will attempt to dispose of their oil company securities, almost certainly at lower prices under confused market conditions. We fear that billions of dollars of security values are going to be wiped out, to the detriment not only of large institutional investors, but also of their direct and indirect beneficiaries, such as life insurance policy holders, pension fund beneficiaries, and individual investors. (Exhibit VII sets forth the composition of share ownership of the six largest oil companies and Exhibit VIII illustrates the type of investors purchasing recent bond issues).

The sell-off would extend even to sophisticated lenders, who would be dismayed at the legal tangles you have heard about this morning. Realizing that legal positions bargained for to bring the maximum amount of security are susceptible to unilateral revision, such lenders would obviously reassess their securities holdings and their investment policy toward the industry.

What would happen to a company trying to sell debt after legislation had been passed requiring split up, but before the method of effecting it and the legal questions had been fully resolved? Both the rating agencies and potential investors would want to know what assets would be available to support the obligation. They would want to be able to evaluate the economic viability of the company behind the security. But the investor would be unable to analyze several critical financial yardsticks.

First, it would not be possible to calculate the asset backing or debt equity ratio for a new debt issue. The professional investor would know that at some point during the life of the issue the company was to be divested of a large, perhaps a major, part of its assets and that a certain amount of debt might, or might not, be passed along to the segments. As far as making calculations, however, the investor would be in the dark.

Second, it would also be virtually impossible to predict the future earnings of the company. This is, after all, the principal measure of a company's ability to service its debt, and the most important element in assessing the market prospects for its common stock. While it may be possible to make some estimates of future earnings from the production segment, economic projections for the refining and marketing divisions would be pure conjecture due to uncertainties regarding prices and volumes for purchases and sales of crude and product.

Third, the investor would have no way of gauging the future marketability and price of the new debt security. He would be aware of the fact that the credit ratings of oil company securities would most likely decline—perhaps even to levels below that permitted for investment. He would also be aware that there were many billions of dollars of already outstanding oil company debt (approximately $21 billion at December 31, 1974 for the twenty companies listed on Exhibit I) that might have had their investment ratings lowered because of this uncertainty and a large part of which might be potentially for sale. There would virtually be no way to evaluate with any degree of accuracy the credit of companies in such a situation. In addition, there would remain the serious question of whether the rating agencies would be able to assign any ratings whatsoever to the debt of such companies.

Fourth, under the possible solution of joint and several liability, each company would be contingently liable for obligations far in excess of their ability to service, and would be subject to the risk of failure by another company over which it had no control or influence.

Finally, and in the last analysis, who would the investors for new issues of oil companies be? Most traditional lenders, having already purchased oil company securities prior to the advent of divestiture legislation, would be suing to protect the security of their outstanding loans to the affected companies. As investors, or more importantly as fiduciaries, they would be unlikely to lend one penny more, on whatever terms.

What of the market for equity securities during this period? This market is part institutional and part individual. The concerns that investors would have in connection with debt securities witl be equally reflected in the equity market. Professional security analysis during the critical period will be speculative at best, and institutions could be expected to be large sellers on balance of oil company stocks, as they look to reinvest the funds in industries susceptible of being appraised.

The individual investor in stocks looks either to dividends or to potential capital gains. The significant reduction of the flow of debt funds to oil companies will result, as I indicated, in a serious cash shortage for them. It should be noted that in 1974 the net long-term debt increase of the 29 oil companies in the Chase Survey—which totaled $2.15 billion—was equivalent to 47% of the total cash dividends paid to shareholders. Under conditions of cash shortage the reduction of dividends would be one of the most tempting areas in which to reduce cash outflow. Upon such a reduction, of course, millions of investors would suffer from diminshed incomes after already having suffered a probable decline in the market value of their savings. As most of the companies in the oil industry would be going through a long period of confusion, restructuring and restraint, there would be little prospect for capital gains. The market for oil company equity securities would be one of depressed disarray.

How long tould these conditions of uncertainty continue? In my view, at least ten years, and perhaps longer. The process of untangling the initial state of confusion will take a certain amount of time. Thereafter, there will follow a period of many more years while the new entities are being tested for their economic viability after the divorce from the inherent economic strength of vertical integration. Undoubtedly, a number of the segments will encounter serious problems and some may well fail. The stronger ones will eventually survive. However, until they can demonstrate a pattern of successful earnings for a sustained period and until the strong and the weak have been separated, neither can expect significant institutional investor support in the provision of additional funds. Hence, many portions of the industry will go through a lengthy period of stagnation, involving growing obsolescence of plant and inability to finance new projects.

Long Range Consequences

What will the oil industry look like after the completion of a divestiture program, ten to twenty years after the passage of a statute like S.2387? I regret that I do not have a crystal ball, and it would be hard to be confident about any predictions even if I did. Moreover, hypotheses in many areas go far outside the confines of traditional investment banking. For example, I believe that costs will be higher generally—duplication of management functions in the separated segments will guarantee that—but I have no idea what magnitude the increases might run. And while I have an opinion that divestiture would reverse a positive trend toward economies of scale, I could not document or quantify the assertions made during these hearings on this point—such as, (i) that fragmented research and the attendant reduction in research budgets will mean fewer new ideas, (ii) that smaller companies will be unwilling and unable to undertake any but the smallest projects, or (iii) that the segmented producing industry will be in a far weaker position than our current integrated companies to negotiate with foreign governments over the crude supplies we will undoubtedly continue to require.

I do believe, however, that the host of smaller companies which will be in business after the completion of divestiture will find it more costly and more difficult to get the financing they will need. Each new sector will lack the greater stability of an integrated operation and consequently will be more subject to risks and earnings fluctuations. As such, its cost of capital must be higher to compensate for these risks, and indeed there may well be a number of new companies which will not be able to raise the funds they require at any reasonable price. The overall effect of these changes upon a highly capital intensive industry has to be higher financing costs and hence higher revenue needs. These revenues can come only from higher selling prices, ultimately reflected in heating bills and at the pump.

III. CONCLUSION

If S.2387 is enacted, it is our view that a major portion of the oil industry may be effectively closed off from the capital markets for an indefinite period. As I have noted, the market for capital is becoming more and more selective, and with the legal and financial uncertainties that will undoubtedly accompany a divestiture program, and the long delays for final resolution, investors will place their funds in companies in industries that they can appraise more readily and from which they can expect a surer and safer return.

The consequences of this to oil company financing cannot be overstated. To the extent the exploration dollar cannot be raised, it will not be spent and the new oil will not be found. This could not come at a more critical time for national energy policy. Our dependence upon foreign petroleum sources will have to increase even further, with all the consequences that dependence may cause in areas of defense and foreign policy.

Divestiture is not an experiment which can be tried without serious consequences. The price for enacting such legislation will have to be paid by someone—if not by the consumer in the price of the products then certainly by the taxpayer: either prices will have to be raised to provide a sustained earning power for the industry, or the Federal Government will have to step in, with programs of guarantees, insurance, or even direct subsidies.

It is important to realize that credit strength and the ability to finance important capital expenditures due to credit strength is not something which can be restored for a company or an industry at will. It takes a long time to build. The Congress must realize that if America's oil industry is torn asunder under this bill, if the contractual rights of petroleum company debt holders are abrogated, if the basic credit strength of the industry is dissipated, the decision will be irreversible. The strength of our vertically integrated oil industry is not something that Congress or anyone else will be able to restore.

LIST OF EXHIBITS

EXHIBIT I

Certain Statistics for Companies Apparently Affected by Provisions of U.S. Senate Bill S.2387

EXHIBIT II

"Financing the Next Five Years of Fixed Investments" by Professor Benjamin M. Friedman, *Sloan Management Review,* Massachusetts Institute of Technology, Spring 1975, Vol. 16, No. 3. (Not included.)

EXHIBIT III

Sources of Funds of the Chase Manhattan Group of Petroleum Companies 1960-1974

EXHIBIT IV

Capital Expenditures and Sources of Capital of the Chase Manhattan Group of Petroleum Companies 1960-1974

EXHIBIT V

Weekly Yield to Maturity Comparison for Selected Aaa/AAA Oil Company and Non-Oil Company Long-Term Bonds

EXHIBIT VI

An Analysis of the Price Earnings Ratios of Selected Oil Companies for the Ten Years Ending 1974 Relative to the Standard & Poor's Composite Index

EXHIBIT VII

Composition of Ownership of the Six Largest U.S. Oil Companies

EXHIBIT VIII

Summary of Sales by Type of Institution of High Grade, Long-Term Petroleum Company Debenture Issues

EXHIBIT I
Page 1

Certain Statistics for Companies Apparently Affected by Provisions of U.S. Senate Bill S.2387

Company	Areas Affected by Proposed Legislation				Total (3) Assets ($MM) (3)	Total Long Term Debt (3)	Number of Common Shareholders ($MM) (3)	Total Stockholders' Equity (Book Value) ($MM) (4)	Market Value of Common Stock as of 1/16/76 of Employees	Number
	Annual Domestic Production (2) 36.5MM Barrels or 200 BCF	Annual Domestic Refining (2) 75 MM Barrels	Annual Worldwide Marketing (2) 110MM Barrels	Transportation (2)						
Amerada Hess Corporation	No	Yes	Yes	Yes	$ 2,255	$ 641	19,196	$ 945	$ 461	5,779
Ashland Oil, Inc.	No	Yes	Yes	Yes	1,716	331	59,368	662	545	27,000
Atlantic Richfield Company	Yes	Yes	Yes	Yes	6,152	1,219	132,863	3,455	4,188	28,800
Cities Service Company	Yes	Yes	Yes	Yes	2,898	569	122,944	1,674	1,123	17,400
Continental Oil Company	Yes	Yes	Yes	Yes	4,673	893	69,192	2,054	3,498	41,174
Exxon Corporation	Yes	Yes	Yes	Yes	31,322	3,052	707,000	15,724	20,243	133,000
Getty Oil Company	Yes	Yes	No	Yes	3,004	158	16,632	1,835	3,185	11,364
Gulf Oil Corporation	Yes	Yes	Yes	Yes	12,503	1,471	372,415	6,329	4,576	52,700
Marathon Oil Company	Yes	Yes	No	Yes	1,800	208	42,891	997	1,332	9,465
Mobil Oil Corporation	Yes	Yes	Yes	Yes	14,074	1,729	226,100	6,436	5,169	73,100
Pennzoil Company	Yes	No	No	Yes	1,798	797	46,303	515	651	9,487
Phillips Petroleum Company	Yes	Yes	Yes	Yes	4,028	658	131,621	2,274	4,342	30,802
Shell Oil Company	Yes	Yes	Yes	Yes	6,129	977	31,917	3,560	3,454	32,287
Standard Oil Company of California	Yes	Yes	Yes	Yes	11,640	1,015	274,000	6,450	5,074	39,540
Standard Oil Company (Indiana)	Yes	Yes	Yes	Yes	8,915	1,427	163,556	5,125	6,139	47,217
The Standard Oil Company (an Ohio Corporation)	No	Yes	Yes	Yes	2,621	805	39,536	1,244	1,925	20,300
Sun Oil Company	Yes	Yes	Yes	Yes	4,063	679	48,211	2,247	1,152	27,707
Tenneco Inc.	Yes	No	No	No	6,402	2,054	238,275	2,142	2,201	81,000
Texaco Inc.	Yes	Yes	Yes	Yes	17,176	1,897	340,520	9,003	6,854	76,420
Union Oil Company of California	Yes	Yes	Yes	Yes	3,459	648	76,400	1,923	1,442	15,364
					$146,628	$21,228		$74,594	$77,554	779,906

EXHIBIT [1]
Page 2

Notes:

(1) U.S. Senate Bill S.2387 states that it shall be unlawful for companies to control businesses which qualify under more than one of the following criteria:

    (a) *Annual Domestic Production* greater than 36.5 million barrels (100,000 BBL/D) of crude oil, condensate, and natural gas liquids or 200 billion cubic feet (547,945 MCF/D) of natural gas.

    (b) *Annual Domestic Refining* greater than 75 million barrels (205,479 BBL/D) of refined products.

    (c) *Annual Worldwide Distribution or Marketing* greater than 110 million barrels (301,370 BBL/D) of refined products.

    (d) *Domestic or International Transportation* of crude oil or refined products in pipelines.

(2) Based on 1974 data as available from public sources.

(3) As of 12/31/74, reported in the Annual Report or 10-K of the company.

(4) Calculated as: (Common Shares Outstanding on 9/30/75 times Closing Common Stock Price on 1/16/76.)

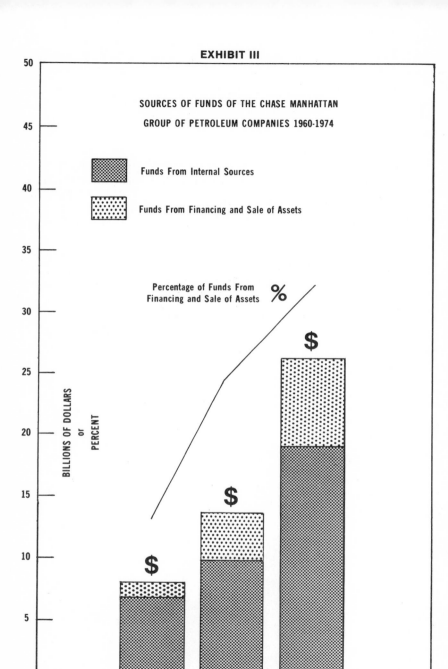

EXHIBIT III

SOURCES OF FUNDS OF THE CHASE MANHATTAN
GROUP OF PETROLEUM COMPANIES 1960-1974

Funds From Internal Sources

Funds From Financing and Sale of Assets

Percentage of Funds From
Financing and Sale of Assets %

BILLIONS OF DOLLARS
or
PERCENT

1960-1964   1965-1969   1970-1974

5 Year Averages

EXHIBIT IV

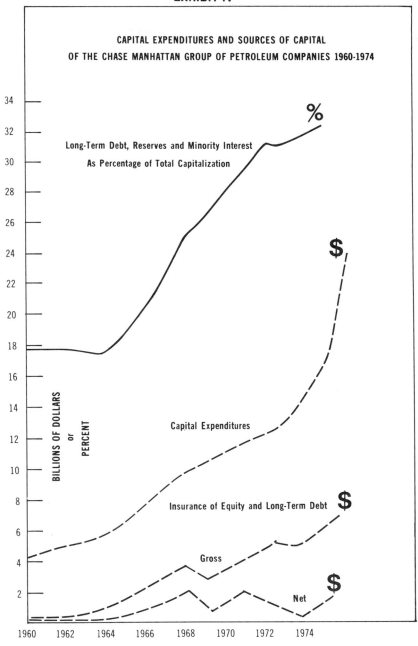

CAPITAL EXPENDITURES AND SOURCES OF CAPITAL
OF THE CHASE MANHATTAN GROUP OF PETROLEUM COMPANIES 1960-1974

EXHIBIT V
Page 1

Weekly Yield to Maturity Comparison for Selected Aaa/AAA Oil Company Long-Term Bonds

Week Ended	Exxon Pipeline Co. 9% Debs. due 2004	Exxon Pipeline Co. 8 7/8% Debs. due 2000	Mobil Oil Co. 7 3/8% Debs. due 2001	Mobil Alaska Pipeline Co. 8.45% Debs. due 2005	Standard Oil Co. (Indiana) 9.20% Debs. due 2004	Standard Oil Co. 8 3/8% Debs. due 2005	Texaco Inc. 7 3/8% Debs. due 2001	Texaco Inc. 8 7/8% Debs. due 2001	Average Yield
1974									
November 1	8.82		8.54				8.62		8.66
8	8.79		8.49				8.51		8.60
15	8.76		8.43				8.51		8.57
22	8.89		8.54				8.62		8.68
29	8.87		8.60				8.67		8.71
December 6	8.88		8.60				8.67		8.72
13	8.90		8.54				8.62		8.69
20	8.95		8.60				8.67		8.74
27	9.03		8.71				8.67		8.80
1975									
January 3	9.03		8.71		9.05		8.67		8.87
10	8.69		8.31		8.77		8.36		8.53
17	8.83		8.49		8.86		8.46		8.66
24	8.83		8.45		8.84		8.46		8.65
31	8.71		8.29		8.75		8.35		8.53
February 7	8.63		8.21		8.70		8.31		8.46
14	8.69		8.25		8.75		8.31		8.50
21	8.58		8.14	8.42	8.63		8.22		8.40
28	8.60		8.25	8.50	8.72		8.31		8.48
March 7	8.66		8.26	8.48	8.72		8.34		8.49
14	8.81		8.37	8.58	8.89		8.45		8.62
21	8.98		8.69	8.81	9.06		8.65		8.84
27	9.02		8.60	8.88	9.03		8.75		8.86
April 4	9.02		8.66	8.96	9.12		8.85		8.92
11	9.05		8.71	8.93	9.20		8.85		8.95
18	9.00		—	8.91	9.05		8.77		8.93
25	9.02		—	8.93	9.08		8.88		8.98
May 2	8.95		—	8.83	8.99		8.75	—	8.88
9	8.93		—	8.86	8.98		8.70	8.90	8.87
16	8.90		—	8.78	8.94		8.65	8.83	8.82
23	8.94		—	8.83	8.98		8.73	8.875	8.87
30	8.97		—	8.84	9.00		—	8.93	8.94
June 5	8.88		—	8.71	8.93	—	—	8.81	8.83
13	8.76		—	8.56	8.72	Syndicate	—	8.69	8.68
20	8.71		—	8.54	8.70	8.50	—	8.67	8.62
27	8.85		—	8.68	—	8.61	—	8.80	8.74
July 3	8.88	—	—	8.73	—	8.61	—	8.80	8.76
11	8.88	—	—	8.73	—	8.63	—	8.81	8.76
18	8.88	—	—	8.72	—	8.61	—	8.80	8.75
25	8.93	—	—	8.78	—	8.69	—	8.84	8.81
August 1	8.97	—	—	8.88	—	8.80	—	8.92	8.89
8	9.12	—	—	9.02	—	8.93	—	9.08	9.04
15	9.17	—	—	9.09	—	8.99	—	9.17	9.11
22	9.17	—	—	9.09	—	9.02	—	9.17	9.11
29	9.05	—	—	9.01	—	8.86	—	9.04	8.99
September 5	9.10	—	—	9.05	—	8.90	—	9.07	9.03
12	9.20	—	—	9.14	—	9.04	—	9.16	9.14
19	9.11	—	—	9.06	—	8.98	—	9.08	9.06
26	9.10	—	—	9.09	—	9.00	—	9.13	9.08
October 3	9.15	—	—	9.14	—	9.04	—	9.20	9.13
10	8.98	—	—	8.93	—	8.89	—	8.97	8.94
17	8.88	8.86	—	8.81	—	8.75	—	8.85	8.83
24	8.86	8.875	—	8.78	—	8.68	—	8.83	8.81
31	—	8.78	—	8.73	—	8.66	—	8.78	8.74
November 7	—	8.80	—	8.73	—	8.66	—	8.82	8.75
14	—	8.85	—	8.78	—	8.71	—	8.85	8.80
21	—	8.97	—	8.78	—	8.84	—	8.97	8.89
28	—	8.95	—	8.81	—	8.82	—	8.95	8.88
December 5	—	8.96	—	8.88	—	8.86	—	8.97	8.92
12	—	8.96	—	8.92	—	8.83	—	8.97	8.92
19	—	8.68	—	8.64	—	8.56	—	8.68	8.64
26	—	8.59	—	8.55	—	8.47	—	8.60	8.55
1976									
January 2	—	8.62	—	8.57	—	8.48	—	8.64	8.58
9	—	8.59	—	8.52	—	8.43	—	8.61	8.54
16	—	8.62	—	8.52	—	8.42	—	—	8.52

Source: Internal records of Morgan Stanley & Co. Incorporated

EXHIBIT V
Page 2

Weekly Yield to Maturity Comparison for Selected Aaa/AAA Non-Oil Company Industrial Long-Term Bonds

Week Ended		E. I. duPont de Nemours and Company 8.45% Debs due 2004	General Electric Co. 8-1/%2 Debs due 2004	General Motors Corp. 8-5/8% Debs due 2005	The Procter & Gamble Co. 8-1/4% Debs due 2005	Warner-Lambert Co. 8-7/8% Debs due 2000	Average Yield
1974							
November	1	—	8.57	—	—	—	8.57
	8	—	8.51	—	—	—	8.51
	15	—	8.44	—	—	—	8.44
	22	—	8.57	—	—	—	8.57
	29	—	8.52	—	—	—	8.52
December	6	—	8.55	—	—	—	8.55
	13	—	8.44	—	—	—	8.44
	20	—	8.46	—	—	—	8.46
	27	—	8.55	—	—	—	8.55
1975							
January	3	8.57	8.59	—	—	—	8.58
	10	8.31	8.29	—	—	—	8.30
	17	8.43	8.38	—	—	—	8.41
	24	8.43	8.40	—	—	—	8.42
	31	8.31	8.34	—	—	—	8.33
February	7	8.29	8.26	—	—	—	8.28
	14	8.36	8.33	—	—	—	8.35
	21	8.24	8.20	—	—	—	8.22
	28	8.36	8.27	—	—	—	8.32
March	7	8.36	8.35	—	Syndicate	—	8.36
	14	8.47	8.44	—	8.40	—	8.44
	21	8.71	8.69	Syndicate	8.59	—	8.66
	27	8.73	8.69	Syndicate	8.62	—	8.68
April	4	8.71	8.68	8.78	8.62	—	8.70
	11	8.75	8.68	8.82	8.67	8.88	8.76
	18	8.75	8.68	8.82	8.67	8.82	8.75
	25	8.80	8.74	8.85	8.72	8.875	8.80
May	2	8.71	8.64	8.77	8.62	8.82	8.71
	9	8.70	8.64	8.75	8.62	8.79	8.70
	16	8.63	8.59	8.71	8.58	8.71	8.64
	23	8.66	8.65	8.75	8.62	8.75	8.69
	30	8.70	8.69	8.78	8.62	8.75	8.71
June	5	8.57	8.57	8.66	8.53	8.70	8.61
	13	8.45	8.44	8.55	8.35	8.56	8.47
	20	8.43	8.42	8.53	8.33	8.53	8.45
	27	8.54	8.52	8.625	8.47	8.68	8.57
July	3	8.57	8.53	8.625	8.46	8.68	8.57
	11	8.53	8.52	8.61	8.48	8.68	8.56
	18	8.04	8.52	8.65	8.46	8.65	8.56
	25	8.61	8.59	8.68	8.55	8.68	8.62
August	1	8.71	8.72	8.81	8.66	8.85	8.75
	8	8.77	8.84	8.94	8.80	8.94	8.86
	15	8.96	8.91	9.01	8.80	8.98	8.93
	22	8.95	8.90	9.01	8.90	8.98	8.95
	29	8.82	8.77	8.90	8.80	8.88	8.83
September	5	8.86	8.81	8.93	8.82	8.90	8.86
	12	9.01	8.96	9.06	8.90	8.98	8.98
	19	8.93	8.89	9.03	8.85	8.93	8.93
	26	8.91	8.87	9.00	8.82	8.93	8.91
October	3	8.93	8.89	9.01	8.82	8.98	8.93
	10	8.69	8.64	8.78	8.60	8.82	8.71
	17	8.58	8.54	8.66	8.49	8.70	8.59
	24	8.58	8.54	8.67	8.46	8.70	8.59
	31	8.54	8.50	8.625	8.43	8.65	8.55
November	7	8.54	8.52	8.65	8.46	8.68	8.57
	14	8.63	8.57	8.69	8.53	8.70	8.62
	21	8.74	8.69	8.81	8.64	8.85	8.75
	28	8.74	8.67	8.78	8.64	8.85	8.74
December	5	8.74	8.68	8.79	8.64	8.82	8.73
	12	8.74	8.68	8.79	8.64	8.82	8.73
	19	8.45	8.41	8.51	8.34	8.53	8.45
	26	8.39	8.33	8.36	8.27	8.48	8.37
1976							
January	2	8.39	8.33	8.45	8.28	8.48	8.39
	9	8.37	8.31	8.44	8.27	8.48	8.37
	16	8.36	8.31	8.44	8.25	8.48	8.37

Source: Internal records of Morgan Stanley & Co. Incorporated.

EXHIBIT VI

An Analysis of the Price Earnings Ratios of Selected Oil Companies for the Ten Years Ending 1974 Relative to the Standard & Poor's Composite Index

Ranking Fortune 500		1965	1966	1967	1968	1969	1970	1971	1972	1973	1974	Average 10 Years 1965-1974	Average 5 Years 1965-1969	Average 5 Years 1970-1974
		Absolute Price Earnings Multiple (1)												
18	Atlantic Richfield Company	12.8	12.2	13.5	24.0	25.4	18.6	18.2	18.6	18.9	11.2	17.3	17.6	17.1
16	Continental Oil Company	17.4	13.1	13.9	12.8	11.7	8.5	11.6	9.7	8.5	6.4	11.3	13.8	8.9
1	Exxon Corporation	17.1	14.2	11.7	12.8	12.6	10.4	11.0	11.5	8.6	5.5	11.6	13.7	9.4
7	Gulf Oil Corporation	13.7	11.2	12.6	13.5	13.0	10.3	10.8	12.1	6.0	3.8	10.7	12.8	8.6
5	Mobil Oil Corporation	14.1	12.1	11.7	12.6	12.6	9.9	9.9	11.1	7.1	4.2	10.5	12.6	8.4
25	Phillips Petroleum Company	14.4	12.5	12.3	18.6	17.7	16.2	17.1	17.9	18.2	9.1	15.4	15.1	15.7
14	Shell Oil Company	16.2	14.8	14.7	14.3	13.3	12.2	13.2	13.2	11.5	5.6	12.9	14.7	11.1
6	Standard Oil Company of California	14.4	12.9	12.0	12.1	11.5	8.7	9.4	10.5	7.3	4.0	10.3	12.6	8.0
13	Standard Oil Company (Indiana)	14.7	13.2	14.1	13.5	12.7	9.8	13.9	13.9	12.2	6.6	12.5	13.6	11.3
4	Texaco, Inc.	17.0	14.1	13.7	13.2	12.7	9.6	10.4	10.5	7.2	4.5	11.3	14.1	8.4
												12.38	14.06	10.69
		Multiples Relative to the S&P Composite Index (2)												
	Atlantic Richfield Company	76	81	81	141	150	116	106	108	145	123	113	106	120
	Continental Oil Company	104	87	83	75	69	53	67	56	66	70	73	84	62
	Exxon Corporation	102	94	70	75	75	65	64	67	66	60	74	83	64
	Gulf Oil Corporation	81	74	75	79	77	64	63	70	46	42	67	77	57
	Mobil Oil Corporation	84	80	70	74	75	62	58	65	55	46	67	77	57
	Phillips Petroleum Company	86	83	74	109	105	101	99	104	140	100	100	109	91
	Shell Oil Company	96	98	88	84	79	76	77	77	88	61	82	89	76
	Standard Oil Company of California	86	85	72	71	68	54	55	61	56	44	65	76	54
	Standard Oil Company (Indiana)	87	87	84	79	75	61	81	81	94	72	80	82	78
	Texaco, Inc.	101	93	85	78	75	60	61	61	55	49	72	86	57
												79.3	86.9	71.6

NOTES: (1) Annual Ratios are based on average price for the year and the full years earnings.

EXHIBIT VII

Composition of Ownership of the Six Largest U.S. Oil Companies (1)

	Number of Shares Held	Percentage of Total
	(millions)	
Individuals	595	57.0%
Estates, Individual Trusts and Common Trusts	162	15.5
Retirement Plans and Profit Sharing Funds	93	9.0
Foundations and Charitable and Educational Institutions	76	7.0
Investment Companies, Brokers and Securities Dealers	42	4.0
Insurance Companies	35	3.5
Other	42	4.0
Total	**1,045**	**100.0%**

(1) Information provided by the American Petroleum Institute. Companies included: Exxon Corporation, Gulf Oil Corporation, Mobil Oil Corporation, Standard Oil Company of California, Standard Oil Company (Indiana) and Texaco Inc.

EXHIBIT VIII

Summary of Sales by Type of Institution of
High Grade, Long-Term Petroleum Company Debenture Issues

Institutions	Exxon Pipeline 9% Due 2004 (000)	Mobil Alaska Pipeline 8.45% Due 2005 (000)	Texaco Inc. 8 7/8% Due 2005 (000)	Shell Oil Company 8 3/4% Due 2005 (000)	Standard Oil Company (Indiana) 8 3/8% Due 2005 (000)	(000)	%
Insurance Companies							
Life	$ 21,795	$ 12,480	$ 15,035	$ 21,727	$ 19,870	$ 90,907	6.5%
Other	5,610	9,430	1,750	1,580	23,020	41,390	3.0
Non-Profit Organizations	9,725	8,922	8,345	8,430	8,605	44,027	3.1
Savings Banks	6,937	19,286	21,495	21,020	31,025	99,763	7.1
Commercial Banks (1)	90,652	103,265	97,465	68,104	91,725	451,121	32.3
State and Municipal							
Pension Funds	65,560	74,260	95,002	72,086	46,675	353,583	25.4
Corporations	6,755	12,060	11,600	12,590	8,010	51,015	3.6
Investment Trusts	17,253	28,115	32,320	32,640	42,890	153,218	11.0
Individuals	16,135	15,266	9,696	10,597	13,136	64,830	4.6
Dealers & Others	9,668	16,651	6,822	1,092	14,766	47,852	3.4
	$250,000	$300,000	$300,000	$250,000	$300,000	$1,400,000	100.0%
Offering Date	11/17/74	2/19/75	5/6/75	5/15/75	6/12/75		

NOTE: (1) Primarily corporate pension funds and individual trust funds managed by banks.

Jacoby examines evidence on international petroleum markets over the past twenty years or so and finds that the industry has been characterized by large-scale entry, normal profit rates and falling real crude oil prices until 1970, when OPEC began to exert economic power. In Jacoby's view, forced vertical disintegration would cripple industry exploration and R&D and thus would strengthen OPEC and increase U.S. dependence upon that body. He also argues that divestiture would reduce the ability of U.S. firms to bargain effectively with OPEC producers and would lead to foreign integrated firms becoming a large force in international petroleum markets.

5

INTERNATIONAL ASPECTS OF DISMEMBERMENT

STATEMENT OF NEIL H. JACOBY*, UNIVERSITY OF CALIFORNIA, LOS ANGELES, BEFORE THE SUBCOMMITTEE ON ANTITRUST AND MONOPOLY, COMMITTEE ON THE JUDICIARY, UNITED STATES SENATE—FEBRUARY 18, 1976

1. Introduction

Mr. Chairman and Members of the Subcommittee:

My name is Neil H. Jacoby, and I am Professor of Business Economics and Policy in the Graduate School of Management of the University of California, Los Angeles. For many years I have studied the petroleum industry in the United States and abroad as a university scholar and also as a director of a multinational oil company. From these practical as well as theoretical perspectives I welcome this opportunity to discuss with you basic economic issues raised by S.2387, introduced by Senator Birch Bayh.

---

*Professor and Dean Emeritus, Graduate School of Management, University of California, Los Angeles.

If enacted, the Bayh Bill would require the vertical disintegration of all large American petroleum companies within three years. Such radical surgery on the corpus of the U.S. economy, whose petroleum industry produces around 7 percent of the GNP, would have incalculable consequences. In an endeavor to contribute to an understanding of the structure and behavior of the petroleum industry, of the role played by vertical integration, and of the probable consequences of forced vertical integration, I shall present economic data and analysis that complement rather than repeat previous testimony to this Subcommittee. I shall not enter into the enormous financial, legal, international and other problems created by a vertical dismemberment of the large oil companies, because they have been pointed out by previous witnesses.

May I state my major conclusions at the outset: Forced vertical disintegration of large U.S. oil companies would lead to higher-priced petroleum products, would increase dependence upon foreign energy, would strengthen and prolong the effectiveness of the OPEC cartel, and, paradoxically, would probably make for a less competitive structure of the industry. It is therefore contrary to the public interest, and should be defeated.

2. Anomalies in the Theory Underlying the Bayh Bill

Let us first observe some anomalies in the premises underlying S.2387. In introducing the Bill Senator Bayh stated the theory that inspired this proposal for vertical disintegration of large oil companies. He said: "The lack of competition in the oil industry is the result of the *unique convergence* (italics added) of two factors: intense concentration and vertical integration. Neither of these economic phenomena is automatically anti-competitive; however, in concert they provide a small number of companies with extensive control over an essential commodity."[1]

Senator Philip A. Hart, a co-sponsor of the Bill, offered a different reason why it is needed. He correctly noted that vertical integration per se is neither good nor bad, and that each vertically integrated industry should be judged on its own merits. But in the petroleum industry, he asserted, vertical integration is anticompetitive for two reasons: First, the industry is "unlike all others in the degree of open cooperation—and cooperation between the participants in joint production, joint transportation and joint bidding." Secondly, ownership and control of gathering lines, product lines and crude lines by the major oil companies effectively foreclose transportation to new entrants and make smaller companies "stay in line."[2]

---

[1] Congressional Record, Senate, September 22, 1975.
[2] Ibid.

Neither of these statements satisfactorily explains why *all-out vertical disintegration* of large oil companies is needed to restore competition, assuming for the sake of argument that it is lacking. Economic theory clearly attaches a greater probability of noncompetitive behavior to a high order of *horizontal* integration (i.e., concentration of market shares) than to a high degree of vertical integration in an industry. Indeed, the ultimate degree of horizontal integration is monopoly in the literal sense; whereas the perfect vertical integration of a firm is quite consistent with effective competition, if there is an adequate number of such firms competing in the market. If, indeed, it is a combination of these two conditions that creates the problem, as Senator Bayh asserts, then it would be more logical and effective to propose *horizontal* divestiture as a remedy. Why has he opted for vertical dismemberment?

If Senator Hart is correct in his theory that it is a combination of vertical integration with joint arrangements and pipeline control that creates a non-competitive U.S. petroleum industry, the obvious solution would be to limit or preclude joint bidding and production and control of pipelines by large oil companies. I believe that a thorough inquiry will show that such joint ventures do not "interlock" the participating oil companies in a common management. They are really a means of spreading the high risks of such investments, which benefits the public. Even if it be assumed that such practices are objectionable, they could be cured by specific reforms. Complete vertical disintegration of the large companies would be unnecessary. Yet, Senator Hart also proposes to "throw out the baby with the bathwater" in supporting the Bayh Bill.

These anomalies in the premises underlying the Bayh Bill suggest that it was hastily drafted without thorough analysis of all of the relevant facts regarding the structure and behavior of the American petroleum industry.

The preponderant weight of the evidence shows:

First: that the industry is comparatively unintegrated.

Second: that the industry is comparatively unconcentrated.

Third: that the industry is effectively competitive.

Fourth: that *forced vertical disintegration would damage the public interest* by destroying efficiencies, increasing risks, raising petroleum product prices, retarding the movement toward energy independence, and probably leading to horizontal integration and a less competitive structure of the industry.

3. The U.S. Petroleum Industry is Relatively Unintegrated Vertically

Vertical integration is a pervasive phenomenon in all advanced industrial economies. Many steel companies integrate backward through ownership of coal mines and ore mines, or forward into fabrication of finished products. Most chemical companies integrate backward through ownership of phosphate, sulfur, potash and other deposits, and forward into specialized products and pharmaceuticals. Motor vehicle manufacturers may own steel and glass-making plants, manufacture their own parts, and even sell and service their vehicles. Food manufacturers often own farms, process and pack food products, and retail them. Even farmers integrate vertically, as in the case of the hog farmer who grows his own feed, or the grower who markets fruits and vegetables through a roadside stand.

Manifestly, there must be weighty advantages to be derived from vertical integration in order to make it so universal a phenomenon in both market and centrally planned economics and in both government-owned and privately-owned enterprises. It is a reasonable inference that vertical integration in the U.S. petroleum industry—as in other industries—came about as a result of a quest for economics of production and limitation of risks, that is, from normal competitive motives.

The potential gains from vertical integration have been well formulated by Professor Oliver Williamson, and also by Professor Edward J. Mitchell in testimony to this Subcommittee.[3] They include the following:

1. There is stronger assurance of technical complementarity of successive industrial processes. Thus, a refinery can be designed so as to maximize efficiency for a particular type of crude oil input.

2. There is greater certainty of execution of business plans, because all stages of the production process are under the control of the firm. Thus, a chain of retail service stations can be assured a source of supply of refined products, and consumers benefit from a more dependable flow of petroleum products and services of uniform, high quality.

3. There are economies of time, transport costs, and investment in inventory because the integrated firm can better coordinate successive operations. For example, a better coordination of crude oil production with tanker loading schedules can reduce time and speed up transportation.

---

[3] See Oliver Williamson, *Corporate Control and Business Behavior* (New York: Prentice Hall, 1970), Chapt. 2. See also *Congressional Record*, Senate, January 22, 2976. In theory, vertical integration will occur whenever the costs to the firm of transacting in markets (including premiums for bearing risk) exceed the costs of vertical unification.

4. There are reductions in costs of bargaining and contracting, because transfers of products within the firm can be made more quickly and inexpensively than by negotiating with independent firms in markets.

5. There are lesser costs of information needed for decisions, because the pertinent data are available within the firm and can quickly be communicated among its members, and need not be procured from external sources. The fact that crude oil and its major products are fluids which are relatively costly to store above ground has made continuity of control from well to pump a causal factor of special importance in the vertical integration of the petroleum industry.

The gains from vertical integration are substantial. In their penetrating and massive study of *Integration and Competition in the Petroleum Industry* (Yale University Press, 1959), Professors Melvin de Chazeau and Alfred E. Kahn came to the conclusion that vertical integration had fostered the growth of the industry by reducing risks and costs of capital, providing coordinated use of specialized talents, and permitting a better synchronization of the flow of crude oil and products. "They are advantages not lightly to be dismissed in the unforeseeable contingencies of the future," they concluded.[4]

The advantages of vertical integration—reduced costs of production, reduced risks, and reduced costs of capital are, of course, reflected in lower prices, improved products and more ample services to consumers of petroleum products, given effective competition.

Despite strong technical and economic reasons for vertical integration, *no petroleum enterprise is perfectly integrated.* All either buy or sell products or services in carrying on their operations from exploration to marketing. Even the largest firms contract for seismological, drilling and other services. Even the largest do not attain, except by accident, a perfect balance between their crude production, transport facilities, refinery runs and product sales. All participate in the intermediate petroleum markets, as buyers, as sellers, or as both.

There is also a substantial number of thriving unintegrated firms accounting for a substantial share of the business at every stage of the industry[5]. For obvious reasons, unintegrated firms normally operate at a higher

---

[4] *Op. cit.,* p. 566.

[5] The fact that *un*integrated refiners and marketers, as a group, expanded their market shares at the expense of the integrated companies during the past twenty years vitiates the argument that the latter generally "squeezed" the profit margins of the unintegrated firms.

level of risks than do the integrated companies. Being at the mercy of fluctuating market conditions for both their inputs (raw materials) and outputs (sales), their annual profits fluctuate more widely and are less predictable. However, there is evidence that unintegrated firms are compensated for these higher risks by a somewhat higher rate of return on investment. At each stage of the industry there is competition among integrated companies, between integrated and unintegrated firms, and among unintegrated firms. The Bayh Bill would go far to eliminate two of these three types of competition.

The U.S. petroleum industry is pluralistic in structure. It contains thousands of individual enterprises of a wide range of sizes, degrees of integration, areas of operation, and business strategies and policies. It is neither monolithic nor oligopolistic at any stage.

Of primary importance is the fact that the *U.S. petroleum industry has relatively little vertical integration* compared with U.S. manufacturing industries in general. As Professor Edward T. Mitchell has noted in his testimony to this Subcommittee, citing studies of Adelman and Gort, petroleum is among the least—and possibly the least—vertically integrated among all thirteen U.S. manufacturing groups.[6] Although several different measures of vertical integration may be applied, this conclusion holds for all measures.

The implication of relatively low vertical integration in the petroleum industry is that, if vertical integration really is an evil to be routed out of the U.S. economy, Congress should first require vertical divestment in a dozen other manufacturing groups before attacking the oil industry! If, indeed, it is the "unique convergence" of "intense" concentration and vertical integration that makes the petroleum industry non-competitive, as Senator Bayh has asserted, certainly one cannot find the cause in its relatively low *vertical* integration. One is therefore obliged to turn to the degree of *horizontal* integration, that is, of concentration in the industry.

4. The U.S. Petroleum Industry is Relatively Unconcentrated

It is a fact that *the U.S. petroleum industry is also relatively unconcentrated* in comparison with U.S. manufacturing industry as a whole. This is true irrespective of whether concentration is measured with respect to

---

[6] Testimony of Edward T. Mitchell, *Congressional Record*, Senate, January 22, 1976. See M. Adelman, "Concept and Statistical Measurement of Vertical Integration," *Business Concentration and Public Policy* (Princeton: National Bureau of Economic Research, 1955). See also M. Gort, *Diversification and Integration in American Industry* (Princeton: National Bureau of Economic Research, 1962).

crude oil production, ownership of crude oil reserves, ownership of refining capacity, or product marketing. The conventional wisdom that the industry is dominated by a few giants is refuted by the facts, most of which were analyzed in two recent studies by the staff of the Federal Trade Commission.[7]

The standard by which the degree of concentration in American manufacturing industries is normally measured is the share of the market accounted for by the top four firms, weighted by value added. Table 1 shows the distribution of value added by American manufacturing industries in 1970 by successive classes of four-firm concentration ratios. The weighted average concentration ratio was 40.1 percent.

Table 1

Distribution of Bureau of the Census Four-Firm Concentration Ratios for Manufacturing Industries, 1970

4-Firm Concentration Ratio	Share of Value Added
0-9	4.94
10-19	14.71
20-29	21.58
30-39	14.64
40-49	14.46
50-59	9.48
60-69	5.68
70-79	7.06
80-89	1.67
90-100	5.78
Weighted average concentration ratio	40.1

Source: U.S. Department of Commerce, Bureau of Census, *Annual Survey of Manufactures, 1970, Value of Shipment* Concentration Ratios, M70 (AS) - 9, (Washington: U.S. Government Printing Office, 1972).

Four-Firm Percent of Market	Eight-Firm Percent of Market	Degree of Concentration
75% or more	90% or more	Very High
65-75%	85-90%	High
50-65%	70-85%	Moderately High
35-50%	45-70%	Moderately Low
Under 35%	Under 45%	Low

[7] See *Concentration Levels and Trends in the Energy Sector of the U.S. Economy* by Joseph P. Mulholland and Douglas V. Webbink. Staff Report to the Federal Trade Commission, Washington, D. C. (March 1974), p. 244. See also Preliminary Federal Trade Commission Staff Report on its *Investigation of the Petroleum* Industry, Washington, D. C. (1973).

Table 2 summarizes concentration in the U.S. petroleum industry during the same year 1970. It shows that four-firm concentration was 27.1 percent in crude production, 35.5 percent in ownership of crude reserves, 34.0 percent in refining capacity, and 30.0 percent in product marketing. These figures are all substantially *under* the weighted average for manufacturing industries as a whole.

Concentration in the U.S. petroleum industry may also be judged by reference to the following standards for manufacturing industries suggested by Professor J.S. Bain, a respected specialist in industrial organization:[8] By these standards, concentration in the U.S. petroleum industry should be rated "low" at the four-firm level and "moderately low" at the eight-firm level. The evidence thus emphatically contradicts Senator Bayh's characterization of concentration of the U.S. petroleum industry as "intense."

Moreover, the data show that no one firm towers over the industry in the sense in which General Motors outshadows other motor vehicle manufacturers or International Business Machines Corporation overshadows other suppliers of electronic data processing services and equipment. The largest firm, Exxon, accounted for only 8.5 percent of U.S. crude oil production in 1970, owned 11.6 percent of domestic crude oil reserves, and owned 9.2 percent of refining capacity. It was not even the

Table 2

Concentration in the U.S. Petroleum Industry

Dimension	Percent of U.S. Industry Output Accounted For By			Total Number of Firms (Estimated)
	Top Firm	Top Four Firms	Top Eight Firms	
Crude Oil Production (1970)	8.5	27.1	49.1	9,000-10,000
Crude Oil Reserves (1970)	11.6	35.5	58.5	9,000-10,000
Refining Capacity— Gasoline (1970)	9.2	34.0	59.8	131
Product Sales (1973) (Gasoline)	8.0	30.0	52.4	15,000 wholesalers 200,000 retailers

Sources: Crude Oil production and reserves from *Concentration Levels and Trends in the Energy Sector of the U.S. Economy* by Joseph P. Mulholland and Douglas W. Webbink, Staff Report to the Federal Trade Commission, Washington, D.C., March 1974, pp. 63-65. Gasoline Refining Capacity from U.S. Federal Trade Commission, *Preliminary Federal Trade Commission Staff Report on its Investigation of the Petroleum Industry* (Washington, 1973). Table II-3. Gasoline Sales from Harold Wilson, "Exxon and Shell Score Gasoline Gains," *Oil and Gas Journal*, June 3, 1974.

---

[8] J.S. Bain, *Industrial Organization* (New York: John Wiley and Sons, 1959), pp. 124-33.

largest vendor of motor fuel, the Number 1 position being occupied by Texaco with 8.0 percent of the national market. Being a huge industry, petroleum involves numerous giant firms as well as a host of medium and small enterprises at all levels of operation. Although concentration of domestic crude oil production and ownership of reserves has risen moderately over the past twenty years, it is still significantly lower than in the foreign oil industry, which, as will be shown, is effectively competitive. Judged by purely *structural* tests, the U.S. petroleum industry has been and is competitive. The next question is whether it has met the tests of competitive *behavior*.

5. Available Evidence Indicates Competitive Behavior by the U.S. Petroleum Industry

In determining whether the behavior of an industry is effectively competitive, economists usually apply a number of tests: Is it possible for new firms to enter the industry and have they, in fact, done so? Do prices of products sensitively reflect changes in costs and in demand? Do the pressures of competition cause firms to make product improvements, to introduce new products, and to amplify the services they offer consumers? Does the rate of return on investment tend toward a normal level?

A complete and up-to-date analysis of all of the behavioral parameters of the U.S. petroleum industry has not been made to my knowledge. However, there is a good deal of evidence on the profitability of petroleum investment in the United States, much of which as been cited by Professors Mitchell, Erickson and Mancke in testimony to this Subcommittee. All of that evidence points to the conclusion that returns to investment in the petroleum industry have not exceeded the average return to investment in American manufacturing industries as a whole. As Professor Erickson noted, the average rate of return on equity investment in the 125 companies in *Moody's Industrials* during the period 1951-1971 was 12.6 percent per annum. For the eight largest petroleum companies it was 11.9 percent.[9]

Because standard accounting measures of profit can depart in a number of ways from the economic definition, Professor Edward J. Mitchell measured the profitability of oil investment in a different way. In effect, he calculated the annual rate of return to the investor represented by the aggregate gain in the market value of common stocks over considerable periods of time. His conclusion was the investments in stocks of American

---

[9] *Congressional Record*, Senate, January 29, 1976. Testimony of Professor Edward W. Erickson.

petroleum companies were significantly *less* profitable than investments in the 500 stocks in the *Standard and Poor's Index* over the period 1953 to 1972. He also found that stock investments in the eight largest U.S. oil companies charged by the FTC with monopolizing the industry earned an average return of 12.1 percent a year, more than 20 percent *less* than the yield of investments in stocks in the Standard and Poor's Index.[10] One must look hard, indeed, to discover monopoly profits in this record.[11]

6. Effective Competition in the Foreign Oil Industry Supports the Thesis of Effective Competition in the U.S. Industry.

In determining whether there is effective competition in the U.S. petroleum industry, it is pertinent to examine the structure and behavior of the foreign oil industry in the non-Communist world outside of North America. The analogy of the foreign to the domestic petroleum industry is close because the leading firms in the U.S. industry are the same multinational companies that predominate in the non-Communist world of oil. Of the 29 large private oil companies of the world included in the annual *Financial Analysis* published by the Chase Manhattan Bank, all but four are based in the United States, and two of those (British Petroleum and Royal Dutch Shell) have important U.S. investments.[12] The total assets of these 29 companies at the end of 1974 amounted to $132.8 billion, of which $68.5 billion or 51.6 percent was invested in the United States and $64.3 billion or 48.4 percent was invested in other countries. The technology of producing, transporting, refining and marketing crude oil and its products is generally the same abroad as it is in the United States. The business policies and practices of oil companies abroad generally conform to those at home.

---

[10] See *Congressional Record*, Senate, Testimony of Professor Mitchell, January 22, 1975. Also Edward J. Mitchell, *U.S. Energy Policy: A Primer* (Washington: American Enterprise Institute, 1974), Table B-1.

[11] The following studies conclude that the behavior of the industry has been consistent with effective competition: Edward A. Erickson and Robert W. Spann, "The U.S. Petroleum Industry," *The Energy Question: An International Failure of Policy*, eds., Edward W. Erickson and L. Waverman (Toronto: University of Toronto Press, 1974); Thomas D. Duchesneau, *Competition in the U.S. Energy Industry*. A Report to the Energy Policy Project of the Ford Foundation (Cambridge: Ballinger Publishing Co., 1975); Edward A. Mitchell, *U.S. Energy Policy: A Primer* (Washington, D. C.: American Enterprise Institute, 1974).

[12] The other two foreign-based companies included in the survey are Compagnie Francaise de Petroles of France and Petrofina Societe Anonyme of Belgium. This survey excludes numerous smaller U.S.-based and foreign-based companies and all government-owned companies. See Chase Manhattan Bank, *Financial Analysis of a Group of Petroleum Companies* 1974, pp. 2, 31.

Hence, it is a reasonable inference that that degree of competition which prevails in the foreign oil industry will prevail within the United States.

I have conducted an intensive study of the evolution of the structure and behavior of the foreign oil industry since World War II, with the objective of measuring the effectiveness of competition. The results were published at the end of 1974 by the Macmillan Company in *Multinational Oil: A Study in Industrial Dynamics*, and I shall try to summarize them here.

Ever since the publication in 1952 of a Federal Trade Commission Staff Study entitled *The International Petroleum Cartel*, which was followed in 1953 by the filing of a lawsuit by the Department of Justice against seven large U.S. and foreign oil companies—the so-called "seven sisters"—there has been a widespread belief that the foreign oil industry has been in the hands of a corporate cartel.[13] Less widely known is the fact that this lawsuit was subsequently ended by consent decrees entered into with three of the five U.S. companies and that it was subsequently dismissed as against the remaining two companies for lack of evidence. Hence, it is illuminating to ask whether or not the structure and behavior of the international oil industry, as it evolved after World War II, met the conditions of a cartel.

Economic theory teaches that the identifying features of an effective cartel are these:

1. It is able to preclude new firms from entering the market, thus preserving the market shares of its members.

2. It restricts the supply of products.

3. It maintains or raises prices of products.

4. It divides markets among its members.

5. It realizes persistently high monopoly profits.

What does the evidence show with respect to each of these tests of effective cartelization?

Technical and political conditions caused the foreign oil industry to emerge from World War II in a highly concentrated condition. In 1948 a handful of very large firms together owned most of the crude oil reserves, and refined and distributed most of the petroleum products. But the explosive growth in petroleum demand and easier conditions of entry led a

---

[13] *The International Petroleum Cartel*, Staff Report to the Federal Trade Commission. Submitted to the Subcommittee on Monopoly of the Select Committee on Small Business, U.S. Senate, August 22, 1952.

horde of entrants into the industry. Between 1953 and 1972 at least 300 private and 50 government firms entered. And in 1972 there were at least 50 vertically integrated international oil companies in operation.[14] The entrants carved out for themselves large segments of the market. The massive *deconcentration* in the structure of the industry is shown in Table 3. Judged by Professor Bain's standards, concentration in all four divisions of the industry was either "high" or "very high" in 1953. Twenty years later, by 1972, concentration had fallen to a "moderately low" level. (However, a comparison of Tables 2 and 3 shows that the foreign industry remained *more* concentrated than the domestic industry.)

Because of the special interest in the "seven largest" firms that dominated the industry at the end of World War II, changes in concentration over the period 1953-1972 are measured in terms of the "seven largest" versus "all other" firms in Table 4. It shows that the share of the "seven largest" in concession areas dropped from 64 to 24 percent; their share of crude reserves fell from 92 percent to 67 percent; their share of crude oil production declined from 87 percent to 71 percent; their role in refining capacity shrank from 73 percent to 49 percent; their owned tanker capacity dropped from 29 percent to 19 percent; and their product marketing sales declined from 72 percent to 54 percent. Market shares of the newcomers rose commensurately.

Manifestly, the foreign oil industry totally failed to pass the first test of an effective cartel—ability to preclude new entrants.

Table 3
Concentration of the Foreign Oil Industry, 1953 and 1972
(Percentages of the total market)

Division of the Industry	1953			1972		
	Top Firm	Top Four Firms	Top Eight Firms	Top Firm	Top Four Firms	Top Eight Firms
Proven Crude Oil Reserves	35.7	73.5	95.8	14.3	46.7	74.6
Crude Oil Production	24.9	69.0	91.0	14.9	49.2	75.1
Refining Capacity	22.3	63.5	78.5	13.1	38.3	50.8
Sales of Petroleum Products	26.2	61.5	75.0	14.0	42.9	59.4

Source: Neil H. Jacoby, *Multinational Oil* (New York: The Macmillan Company, 1974) pp. 187, 193, 199 and 207

---

[14] Neil H. Jacoby, *Multinational Oil* (New York: The Macmillan Company, 1974), p. 120.

Table 4.
**Market Shares of the "Seven Largest" Firms Combined and of "All Other" Firms
Combined in the Foreign Oil Industry, 1953 and 1972**
(Percent of Total)

Division of the Industry	1953		1972	
	"Seven Largest" Firms	"All Other" Firms	"Seven Largest" Firms	"All Other" Firms
Concession Areas Held	64	36	24	76
Proven Crude Oil Reserves	92	8	67	33
Crude Oil Production	87	13	71	29
Refining Capacity	73	27	49	51
Tanker Capacity Owned	29	71	19	81
Product Sales	72	28	54	46

Source: Neil H. Jacoby, *Multinational Oil* (New York: Macmillan, 1974) p. 211.

Supply

A second test of an effective cartel is ability to restrict the supply of the cartelized product. The fact is that crude oil production in the foreign non-Communist world rose from 3.1 million barrels per day in 1948 to 31 million barrels per day in 1972. This tenfold increase over a period of 24 years represented an average compound growth of 10 percent per year.[15] (If one adds the approximately 1 million barrels per day exported by the Communist Bloc to the West, the growth rate rises to 11 percent per annum.) One cannot infer the existence of any effective mechanism for long-term output restriction from this record.

Price

Prices of crude oil and its products generally rose during the post-war era up to 1957, as a consequence of powerfully expanding demand combined with the special Korean War requirements of 1950-53, the cessation of Iranian output during the Mossadecq period of 1951-54 and the closure of the Suez Canal in 1956-1957 during the Franco-British war with Egypt. After the reopening of the Suez Canal in 1957, burgeoning crude oil supplies and the advent of U.S. import quotas gave rise to a buyer's market. *Posted* prices f.o.b. ports of origin were cut in 1959 and 1960, and deepening discounts from these posted prices made *delivered* prices fall even more steeply during the thirteen years from 1957 to 1970. To cite a dramatic example, the average price of Saudi Arabian Oil delivered into Japan fell from $3.42 per barrel in 1958 to $1.84 in 1970.[16] The record shows that actual

[15] *Op. cit.,* pp. 71-2.
[16] *Op. cit.,* p. 228.

transaction prices sensitively reflected changes in supply-demand relationships. There was no evidence of the high and rigid pricing associated with an effective cartel. Beginning in 1970, OPEC began to exercise its growing power and prices rose thereafter.

Market Shares

How successfully did the large international oil companies divide markets and stabilize their market shares? The facts show that substantial, nonsystematic shifts took place in the market shares of individual companies in crude oil production among the "seven largest," both from year to year and over longer periods of time. As shown in Table 5, there were radical changes in the relative market shares over the 10-year period 1953 to 1972. Exxon's share fell from 24.9 percent to 13.7 percent of the foreign world market; BP's share dropped from 20.6 percent to 14.9 percent. Gulf's share diminished from 11.2 percent to 8.1 percent. Shell's share nearly stayed constant, while the shares of Texaco and Socal rose. These changes were inconsistent with any overt or tacit market-sharing agreement among them.[17]

The common sense of the matter is that they were the unplanned result of a vigorous competition for markets, old and new.

Table 5.

Shares of Crude Oil Production by the "Seven Largest" Companies in the Foreign Oil Industry, 1953 and 1972

(Percent of the Industry)

Company	1953	1972
Exxon	24.9	13.7
British Petroleum	20.6	14.9
Shell	12.3	11.3
Gulf	11.2	8.1
Texaco	6.7	9.3
Socal	6.1	8.6
Mobil	5.3	5.0
Total—"Seven Largest"	87.1	70.9
Total—"All Others"	12.9	29.1
TOTAL INDUSTRY	**100.0**	**100.0**

Source: Jacoby, *Multinational Oil.* p. 177

---

[17] *Op. cit.*, pp. 204, 210 and Figure 9.2 on p. 176.

Profits

Finally, have firms in the foreign oil industry persistently earned above-normal incomes, as would be expected if they constituted an effective cartel? As is shown in Table 6, rates of earnings on U.S. direct investment in the foreign petroleum industry were abnormally high (25-30 percent per annum) in the early post-World War II period up to about 1957. Thereafter, with declining prices, profits fell off rapidly and fluctuated within a range of 11 to 14 percent on net worth per annum consistently up to 1972, which was about equal to rates of earnings on U.S. investment in foreign manufacturing and other industries.[18] The foreign oil industry thus constitutes an almost classic case of competitive adjustment to changes in supply demand relationships. There was an absence of monopoly profits because there was no monopoly power.

To Sum Up: During the 1950s and the 1960s, the foreign oil industry gained an increasingly competitive structure, and its behavior constitutes a classic case of competitive adjustment to changing circumstances. While

Table 6.

**Rates of Earnings on U.S. Direct Investment in Foreign Industries, Annually
1955-1972**

(Percentage of Net Income to Net Assets)

Year	Petroleum	Mining and Smelting	Manufacturing	Other Industries
1955	30.2	13.1	13.0	10.2
1956	28.8	14.6	12.1	9.7
1957	23.8	10.7	10.8	10.0
1958	16.2	7.7	10.3	9.2
1959	13.8	11.0	11.6	9.3
1960	13.6	13.1	10.5	9.1
1961	13.9	11.7	9.9	9.4
1962	14.6	12.0	10.9	11.6
1963	14.7	12.0	11.6	10.4
1964	13.7	15.0	12.4	10.3
1965	12.5	15.6	11.9	10.9
1966	11.7	16.8	10.9	9.8
1967	11.8	17.1	9.3	9.2
1968	12.3	16.3	10.4	9.7
1969	11.1	14.4	12.4	11.3
1970	11.0	11.9	11.6	11.1
1971	12.5	8.1	11.9	11.7
1972	9.9	6.2	14.1	12.2

Source: Neil H. Jacoby, *Multinational Oil* p. 248. Petroleum data from Chase Manhattan Bank. Other data from
U.S. Department of Commerce, *Survey of Current Business,* various issues.

[18] *Op. cit.*, pp. 247-48.

competition was unlike the classical textbook model, it was indubitably effective. There was no monopolistic behavior to cause similar responses in the domestic industry. If effective competition prevailed in the foreign oil industry, it may safely be inferred that it was also effective within the much less concentrated domestic industry.

The proponents of the Bayh Bill have not only failed to sustain the burden of proof that the U.S. petroleum industry is *not* competitive; they have failed to refute the substantial evidence that it is effectively competitive. Thus their contention that vertical disintegration is needed to restore competition falls to the ground.

7. Vertical Disintegration Would Damage Consumers, Impair National Security and Probably Lead to Higher Concentration

Substantial benefits have been derived by oil companies from vertical integration—reduced costs of production and lower risks and costs of capital. Given the effective competition that has prevailed in the industry, these benefits have been passed on to consumers of petroleum products in lower prices, improved products and more ample services. Such socially desirable effects are the proper objectives of Congressional policy. If vertically integrated firms were forced to disintegrate, these benefits would vanish. Other things remaining the same, prices of petroleum products would rise, product improvements would diminish, and services would shrink. Consumers would suffer, and the social consequences would be adverse as well.

Forced vertical disintegration would severely damage the national interest in achieving a larger measure of independence from foreign countries with respect to supplies of energy. The breakup of large American oil companies would inevitably cripple the ability of a fractionated industry to finance high-risk exploration in the outer continental shelves, in the Arctic, and in other remote and inhospitable regions where large reserves of crude oil may remain to be discovered. It would equally diminish the financial capacity of the industry to finance research and development aimed at producing synthetic fuels from shale, coal and tar sands, as well as from geothermal, solar and other exotic sources. Unless the Federal government undertook these tasks, in a first step toward nationalization of the petroleum industry, vertical disintegration would deliver a lethal blow to the concept of Energy Independence.

A little noted but no less important potential consequence of *vertical disintegration* of the U.S. petroleum industry would be a significant rise in its *horizontal integration* (concentration). A primary motive for vertical integration has been the desire to limit risks. Refiners enter crude oil production to assure a supply of crude, or they acquire service stations to assure marketing outlets for products. Forced vertical disintegration would restore to the smaller single-stage surviving companies the higher level of risk that was reduced by vertical integration. Many of these companies would be unable to survive periods of business adversity. They would suffer bankruptcy or seek mergers to become larger and stronger companies, better able to carry high risks. Horizontal integration is also a device for reducing risk by geographical diversification of markets and extending product lines. With foreclosure of vertical integration as a risk-limiting strategy, strong market forces would be created to produce larger and financially stronger firms. After a decade or so, the oil industry might well end up with a *higher level of concentration at each stage* than obtains today. The ironic result of legislation intended to produce smaller firms in the petroleum industry might be to enlarge their average size.

8. Vertical Disintegration Would Weaken—Not Strengthen—the Power of the OPEC Cartel

Some argue that vertical disintegration of the big U.S. oil companies would hasten the break-up of the OPEC cartel by making it more difficult for the oil-producing countries to allocate supplies of crude oil among markets and countries. The big oil companies, it is said, assist the OPEC in maintaining its monopoly power because they profit by it.[19]

This argument is erroneous. It is untrue that the OPEC could not function without the "cooperation" of seven big oil companies. These companies do *not* decide the total amount of crude oil to be produced by the OPEC members, or "prorate" the total allowable output among the producing countries. Those decisions are made by the OPEC. Indeed, it is precisely *OPEC's* ability to restrict aggregate oil production and to prorate the total among its members that enables it to maintain its high price of crude oil. The oil companies are helpless bystanders in these decisions. They merely buy oil from OPEC's members at OPEC's prices and sell what the market will take at a price which will, hopefully, cover their costs and yield a profit.

Multiplying the number of buyers of crude oil from such countries as Saudi Arabia, Kuwait or Iran would actually make it *easier* for the OPEC to maintain a high price and a low output of crude oil. OPEC would then be

---

[19] Testimony of Anthony Sampson, *Congressional Record*, Senate, February 3, 1976.

dealing with many economically weak buyers instead of a small number of economically strong buyers. It would be able to play off the many small buyers against each other more readily than it can under present circumstances. These buyers, if U.S. oil companies operating in the *post-divestiture* period, would have even less bargaining power with the OPEC than the little they have today, because they would lack control over the transportation, refining and marketing facilities the OPEC needs. While world oil markets would probably operate less smoothly than today, because of poorer coordination of flows of crude oil and petroleum products, supplies would continue to be allocated in accordance with changes in supply-demand relationships in the various countries. This allocation process can occur with many buyers of crude oil as well as with few. OPEC does not need to maintain the present structure of the industry in order to maintain its monopoly power.

Moreover, OPEC monopoly power has been exercised against the oil companies as well as against consumers of petroleum products. The evidence shows that their profits per barrel of OPEC crude oil during 1974 and 1975 have averaged *less* than they did before 1973.

Another flaw in the argument is that *horizontal* rather than vertical disintegration of the big oil companies would be the appropriate remedy, *if* the public interest would be served by multiplying the number of buyers of Middle East oil. The *vertical* disintegration proposed by the Bayh Bill would leave the number of buyers of OPEC oil undisturbed. But it would, as noted previously, weaken the bargaining position of those buyers with the OPEC members, by depriving them of their downstream facilities. The four stockholders of ARAMCO, for example—Exxon, Mobil, Socal and Texaco—would be forced to divest their transportation, refining and marketing assets if they elected to remain in the business of producing and selling crude oil. From OPEC's point of view, they would be less reliable offtakers of oil than the integrated oil companies of foreign nations with which the U.S. firms compete. However, horizontal disintegration of U.S. oil companies would also strengthen rather than weaken the OPEC for reasons already stated.

The only effective way for the United States to weaken the OPEC cartel is first, to conserve energy, second, to develop alternative energy sources of comparable magnitude, and third, to take leadership in forming a coalition of the important oil-importing nations which can join with the OPEC nations in writing a world petroleum agreement. Passage of the Bayh Bill would weaken the bargaining position of U.S. oil companies and would hurt U.S. consumers. It would thereby operate to extend the effective life of the

OPEC cartel, and delay the day when normal economic forces destroy its power.

9. Conclusion

The case against enactment of the Bayh Bill is overwhelming. The theses on which it is based are false. The U.S. petroleum industry is relatively unconcentrated, both vertically and horizontally. Available evidence shows that its behavior is as effectively competitive as is its structure. This conclusion is buttressed by the competitive behavior of the *foreign* oil industry, despite a somewhat more concentrated structure than that of the domestic industry. Vertical disintegration would damage consumers of petroleum products and impair the national security interest in lessened dependence upon foreign supplies of energy. It probably would lead to bankruptcies or mergers to achieve financially stronger firms better able to survive the inherent risks of the oil industry—risks that would be increased as a consequence of the Bayh Bill. And it would serve to strengthen the OPEC cartel and prolong its effectiveness.

Mancke examines whether conditions in the U.S. oil industry
suggest the existence of monopoly power there. He finds that in
all stages of the industry there are many firms, entry is relatively
easy, and profit rates are normal. Further, the notion that major
integrated firms "squeeze" independent oil firms is implausible
because such tactics would have cost billions of dollars annually
to implement. Mancke concluded that the industry is competitive,
that divestiture would raise fuel prices, and that legislation to
achieve divestiture diverts attention from more fundamental U.S.
energy problems.

6

COMPETITION IN THE PETROLEUM INDUSTRY

STATEMENT OF RICHARD B. MANCKE,* THE FLETCHER SCHOOL OF LAW AND DIPLOMACY, TUFTS UNIVERSITY, BEFORE THE SUBCOMMITTEE ON ANTITRUST AND MONOPOLY, COMMITTEE ON THE JUDICIARY, UNITED STATES SENATE — JANUARY 1976

**The cost of a barrel of average quality foreign crude oil delivered to
the U.S. East Coast was about $2.30 in 1969; by year end 1975 these costs
had soared to about $13 (not including a $2 per barrel tariff). Because presently developed domestic energy supplies are inadequate to fully supply the
United States' needs, sharply higher prices for all crude oil products and

---

* Associate Professor of International Economic Relations at Fletcher School of Law and
Diplomacy, Tufts University.

**This paper expands the discussion that appears in Chapter 7 of Richard B. Mancke,
Squeaking By: U.S. Energy Policy Since the Embargo (New York: Columbia University Press,
1976).

their substitutes—chiefly coal, natural gas, and uranium—have been an inevitable consequence of this nearly six-fold increase in foreign oil's delivered costs.[1] Reacting to these soaring energy costs and to the public's growing sense of helplessness and unease, a variety of widely quoted opinion makers—including both elected and appointed public officials, consumerists, editorialists, and even some Persian Gulf potentates—have been quick to resurrect the charge that the United States' energy problems have been caused in large part by the monopolistic abuses of the giant, politically powerful, integrated oil companies.

Competition vs. Monopoly

Whenever a product's price exeeds the cost of producing an additional unit, producers will find it profitable to produce and sell that unit. Unfortunately for them, if each producer follows what he perceives to be his self-interest and produces all units for which price exceeds cost, industry output will expand, causing prices to fall and profits to dwindle. The price fall will stop only when the profit incentive to expand output ceases. This level of output will be reached only when price equals the total costs of producing additional units.

Business: They produce and sell crude oil from domestic and, frequently, foreign sources; they transport crude oil from the wellhead to refineries and ship finished oil products to retailers; and they produce and sell a great variety of refined products and petrochemicals. In addition, they are also substantial suppliers of other kinds of energy. Are the "opinion-makers" correct? Have the large integrated oil companies succeeded in monopolizing one or more of these markets? To answer this question economists customarily examine three types of empirical evidence:

1.   Whether the market structure is more conducive to competition or monopoly. Generally the most competitive markets have many strong companies and/or can be easily entered by new firms or by firms presently doing business in other, often-related, industries.

2.   Whether the firms doing business in the relevant market engage in

---

[1]When the price of a product rises, cost-conscious consumers turn to cheaper substitutes. If supplies of these substitutes cannot be expanded to fully satisfy the new demands, their prices will be bid higher. At any specified time the United States can expand its domestic energy production above previously planned levels only if there are substantial new investments. These will take many years to begin production. (E.g., even if the goals of Project Independence are met, the U.S. will remain a substantial oil importer in 1985.) Hence, absent price controls, higher prices for imported oil will lead to similar hikes in the prices of oil substitutes.

conduct, either explicit or implicit, that facilitates collusive behavior. Common examples of explicit anti-competitive conduct include agreements to fix prices or divide markets and legal or marketing tactics aimèd at harassing present or potential competitors. Implicit collusive conduct is most likely in markets with relatively few firms that face similar and well-known costs and demands. Implicit collusion is almost never found in industries with many firms facing dissimilar and uncertain costs and demands.

3. Whether most of the firms in the relevant industry earn persistent and otherwise unexplainable high profit rates.

Judged by these three criteria, there can be no doubt that those oil-exporting countries which are members of the Organization of Petroleum Exporting Countries (OPEC) presently possess and exercise enormous monopoly power. These nations account for over 95 percent of the non-Communist international crude oil trade.[2] They meet regularly to fix international oil prices. Moreover, because most of the world's known low-cost oil supplies are located within their borders, and it will take until the 1980's before large new non-OPEC sources can be found and developed, at present OPEC members have little to fear from entry threats. Finally the $11-plus price charged for nearly all of the crude oil sold by the OPEC countries in early 1976 is ten to one hundred times greater than its total resource cost.[3] Because, relative to current and projected levels of demand, the OPEC countries presently have huge quantities of low-cost oil reserves, the persistence of price-cost differentials of this magnitude offers conclusive proof that the OPEC countries are monopolistic sellers of crude oil in international markets.

Even the crudest empirical evidence establishes overwhelmingly that the major oil-exporting countries are enormously successful monopolists. Therefore, the remainder of this paper addresses a more interesting and, in terms of its likely effect on shaping the direction of future domestic energy policy, more important question: do the major oil companies also exercise significant monopoly power in any of the important markets in which they presently do business? After assessing the evidence—most of which is collected from published government or oil company sources—I conclude that the oil companies no longer possess measurable monopoly power in any important energy market. Moreover, the economic structures in all stages

---

[2]For elaboration see Mancke, *Squeaking By,* Chapters 3 and 6.

[3]The price was in excess of $11 per barrel for each barrel of oil sold. The total resource costs ranged between 10 cents and $1 per barrel. In most cases oil companies paid all production costs; in addition, they paid the exporting countries royalties and taxes in excess of $11 per barrel.

SHERMAN ACT SECTION 2 PRECEDENTS COMPARED

I. Major Cases Finding Defendant to Violate Section 2

Case	Entry	Number/Strength of Competitors	Reasons for Success	Defendant's Market Share
Alcoa (1945)	None	No domestic competition	Patent monopoly, cartels and pre-emption of raw materials	80-90% of industry for 25 years.
United Shoe (1953)	Only one significant entrant	No significant competitors	Merger, acquisition, discriminatory 10 year leases	85% of market for 40 years
American Tobacco (1946)	None in 8 years	Several small competitors	Conspiracy to fix prices and exclude competitors	75% of cigarette market for 40 years, declining slowly
Grinnell (1966)	None effective	No significant competitors	Mergers and agreements not to compete	87-91% of market

II. Major Cases Finding Defendant Not to Violate Section 2

Case	Entry	Number/Strength of Competitors	Reasons for Success	Defendant's Market Share
du Pont (1956)	Substantial	Many in flexible wrappings; only 2 in cellophane	Competitive achievement and willingness to take risks	75% of cellophane, 20% of flexible wrappings.
Hughes Tool (1954)	Some successful entrants	Four significant competitors	Best product and excellent service	75% of roller bit industry and stable for 20 years

Source: Cravath, Swaine & Moore, *Pretrial Brief for International Business Machines* (submitted to the U.S. District Court Southern District of New York, January 15, 1975), pp. 4-5.

Table 2

Company Shares of Domestic Net Crude Oil Production and Proved Domestic Crude Oil Reserves

Company	Share of Domestic Production (in 1969)	Share of Domestic Proved Reserves (in 1970)
Exxon, U.S.	9.76%	9.92%
Texaco	8.47%	9.31%
Gulf	6.78%	8.97%
Shell	6.08%	5.98%
Socal	5.31%	8.97%
ARCO	5.11%	7.48%
Standard of Indiana	5.09%	8.46%
Mobil	3.94%	4.87%
Getty	3.38%	3.85%
Union	2.88%	3.18%
Sun	2.47%	2.67%
Continental	2.21%	2.77%
Marathon	1.64%	2.37%
Phillips	1.55%	3.55%
Cities Service	1.28%	2.49%
Amerada Hess	1.04%	2.49%
Tenneco	0.99%	0.90%
Skelly	0.88%	1.09%
Superior	0.74%	1.03%
Top 4	31.09%	37.17%
Top 8	50.54%	63.88%

Source: U.S. Federal Trade Commission, *Preliminary Federal Trade Commission Staff Report on Its Investigation of the Petroleum Industry,* (June, 1973), Tables II-1 and II-2.

Table 3

Concentration in U.S. Net Crude Oil Production

	As a Percent of Total U.S. Production		
	1965	1970	1974
Four largest firms	24.6	26.5	25.9
Eight largest firms	39.0	42.3	42.1

Source: Presentation by Ted Eck, Standard Oil of Indiana. Reprinted in Bureau of National Affairs, *Energy Users' Report (November 13, 1975), p. A-19.*

of the oil business are such that the successful exercise of monopoly power is virtually impossible unless the oil companies receive direct governmental assistance.

The Evidence: Market Structure and Conduct in the Major Facets of The Domestic Petroleum Industry

Domestic Crude Oil. The oil industry is built upon a foundation of crude oil. There are three steps in crude oil production: exploration, development, and operating. Exploration refers to the search for new oil reserves in places where its presence is suspected but unsure; development is the installation of the production facilities that are necessary before previously discovered oil reserves can be extracted; operating takes place when crude oil from previously developed reserves is actually produced. Compared with either other natural resource based heavy industries—such as steel, aluminum, or copper—or large manufacturing industries—such as automobiles, computers, or electrical equipment—American crude oil production is not highly concentrated in the hands of just a few giant firms. Instead, there are more than 20 large companies (annual petroleum sales greater than $1 billion) that are significant participants in the crude oil industry. Tables 2 and 3 summarize, respectively, the Federal Trade Commission's (FTC) and Standard Oil of Indiana's assessments of the American crude oil industry's present large firm concentration. According to the FTC, the largest producer of crude oil in the United States, Exxon, accounted for less than 10 percent of all production in 1969; the FTC credits the eight largest crude oil producers with barely more than 50 percent of all U.S. production. Indiana Standard's data suggest that the FTC's estimates of the leading firms crude oil production shares may be too high. Instead, they show that the eight largest crude oil producers' share of total U.S. production peaked at only 42.3 percent in 1970 and fell slightly over the next few years. Because of both data limitations and legitimate disagreements as to what are the "correct" definitions to use when calculating production shares, all such estimates are necessarily imprecise. Because the FTC is currently trying to prove that the eight largest integrated U.S. oil companies (Indiana Standard is number seven in crude production) do exercise substantial monopoly power in most phases of the oil business, it seems reasonable to infer that the crude oil production share estimates presented in Tables 2 and 3 offer plausible upper and lower bounds. However, regardless of whether the reader judges the low or high production share estimates more plausible, the key fact deserving emphasis is that this industry is far less concentrated than most other American manufacturing or mining industries that contain one or more giant firms.

Besides the presence of many large firms, there are literally tens of thousands of small companies that presently compete in the American crude oil industry. The role played by small companies is especially crucial in the vital exploration phase. In 1974 small companies (defined as not in the largest 30) drilled 86.2 percent of all exploratory wells.[4] The chief reason for the large number and vitality of small companies is the absence of significant scale economies in producing crude oil from onshore Lower 48 sources. Hence, new entry into this part of the oil business is easy. Dean James McKie has described the most common ways that firms enter the oil industry:

> Many oil-producing companies originated as successful wildcat enterprises. While a few firms may begin with a large supply of capital and immediately undertake an extensive drilling program, the typical firm got its start through a series of fortunate single ventures, often involving exploratory deals with established major or independent firms. New corporations and partnerships are frequently budded from the existing ones.
>
>   . . . A geologist or petroleum engineer may gain enough experience on his own, making good use of the associations he has built up in the industry . . . An employee of a drilling contractor may work up from platform hand to superintendent. Once known to purchasers of drilling services and sellers of equipment, he finds it relatively easy to set up his own firm . . . After operating as a contract driller for some time, he may be willing to put one of his rigs into a wildcat venture on a speculative basis . . . In this way drilling contractors frequently become independent producers. . .
>
>   Another way to enter oil and gas exploration is via brokerage. Exploration enterprise swarms with middlemen anxious to arrange producing deals . . . A speculative broker may arrange a prospecting deal among other parties . . . and usually retains for himself a small interest in the venture. Since the technical training and apprenticeship are not strictly necessary, this route is crowded with hopeful shoestring promoters along with the experienced entrepreneurs.[5]

The twin facts that the domestic crude oil industry embraces tens of thousands of viable firms and that new entry continues to be easy offer strong support for the inference that the economic structure of this market is effectively competitive. However, one caveat is necessary. To acquire rights to produce crude oil from either the Alaskan North Slope or the U.S. Outer Continental Shelf presently requires an initial investment totaling millions of dollars. The importance of oil supplies from these two frontier areas will grow rapidly over the next several years. While the growing importance of crude oil from frontier sources will make it more difficult for

4"Independents Claim Big Exploration Role," *Oil and Gas Journal* (April 21, 1975), p. 58.
    5James McKie, "Market Structure and Uncertainty in Oil and Gas Exploration," *Quarterly Journal of Economics,* LXXXIV (1960), p. 569.

small, one-man companies to enter the business, it seems unlikely to seriously diminish effective competition. Presently, the nineteen large oil companies listed in Table 2 are all active participants in one or both of the United States' promising frontier oil regions. Many smaller oil companies are also active in these areas. In addition, many large industrial companies and public utilities (e.g., Bethlehem Steel, Peoples Gas, Reynolds Industries, and Union Pacific Railroad) have also invested large sums in the search for frontier oil. I suspect that no other large American industry enjoys the participation of so many large and wealthy firms.

When an industry has many firms and entry is easy, collusive behavior becomes nearly impossible unless all of the industry's major firms are tied together by explicit price-fixing and market-sharing agreements. Such agreements would violate Section 1 of the Sherman Act. There is no evidence that they exist in the American crude oil industry.

Another instance in which crude oil producers would find collusion highly profitable would be if they could agree to limit the amounts they must bid to acquire production rights to potentially commercial Outer Continental Shelf (OCS) and Alaskan North Slope oil lands. Rights to individual 5-6,000 acre tracts are auctioned to the firm or individual submitting the highest sealed bid. Since 1970, more than $12 billion has been paid to the U.S. government by firms acquiring OCS tracts. If they colluded, the oil companies would agree among themselves, prior to bidding, which firm would make the high bid on each tract thought likely to contain commercial quantities of petroleum. In addition to the fact that no direct evidence of such collusion has ever been offered, there are two reasons for inferring that it has never taken place. First, oil companies take elaborate and expensive precautions to insure that their competitors don't learn their bidding intentions. To illustrate, in the week just prior to Alaska's 1969 sale of petroleum rights to state-owned lands located near the giant Prudhoe Bay field, one oil company required all of its concerned employees to remain together in a private rail car that was shuttled back and forth across western Canada. Second, the winning bid is often several times higher than that offered by the closest competitor.[6] In sum, all available market structure and industry conduct evidence supports the inference that the market for American-produced crude oil is effectively competitive in the mid-1970's.

---

[6]It is interesting to contrast the bidding for oil land rights with the bidding during the 1950's by manufacturers of electrical equipment on multi-million dollar orders for electric turbines. The electrical equipment manufacturers did collude prior to the "secret" bidding. Thus, the winning bid (in this case the low bid) was always only slightly less than the bid offered by competition.

Transportation. Crude oil products are the most versatile and readily transportable major type of energy. Hence, they tend to be consumed far away from the wellhead and therefore transportation is a key stage in the oil business. All of the United States' imports of crude oil and refined products, with the exception of those from Canada, are shipped via tanker. Within the U.S. approximately 75 percent of crude and 27 percent of products is carried by pipeline; the remainder is carried by tankers, barges, and trucks.[7]

Oil companies own as much as one-third of non-U.S. private tanker capacity. The remaining capacity is chartered, either under short-term (spot) contracts or long-term contracts averaging five years duration. Economists who have studied the tanker market agree that it is one of the most competitive in the world.[8] Thus, Professor M.A. Adleman has written:

> *Each individual ship available for spot charter is, in effect, like a separate firm and the worldwide market allows no protected enclaves . . . In any given month, several dozen ships are offered for oil company use all over the world by several hundred owners, none with over 5 percent of total tonnage. Tacit collusion would be impossible, and no attempt at open collusion has been made since World War II . . . [The] "spot" charter market therefore seems purely competitive.*

> *The time-charter market is linked to the spot market at one end, and at the other to the cost of creating new capacity. Here entry is open and cheap . . . Moreover, there are no strong economies of scale in ship operations. Many owners have only one ship . . . But to say that many competent firms cluster on the boundaries of the industry, and that minimum capital requirements are low, is to say that entry is easy and market control impossible.*

> *With many ships availabe in the short-run, and easy entry for the long-run what possibility is left for control in the meantime? Little if any in theory, and none can be observed in practice. Tankship owners, oil companies and independents cannot control the long-term supply even in concert, for anyone contemplating a production or refining investment and needing the transport services has time to charter a ship or buy a new one.[9]*

Since the 1973-74 oil embargo, there has been a new trend in the world tanker market: many OAPEC countries have begun to acquire tanker

---

[7]U.S. Federal Trade Commission, "Preliminary Federal Trade Commission Staff Report on Its Investigation of the Petroleum Industry" in U.S. Senate Permanent Subcommittee on Investigations of the Committee on Government Operations, *Investigation of the Petroleum Industry* (Washington: G.P.O., July 12, 1973), p. 23.

[8]See M.A. Adelman, *The World Petroleum Market,* chapter 4 and Zenon Zannetos, *The Theory of Oil Tankship Rates* (Cambridge, Mass.: M.I.T. Press, 1966). R. Mancke, *The Failure of U.S. Energy Policy,* pp. 122-125 discusses the Jones Act—a law that raises shipping costs between two or more U.S. ports.

[9]M.A. Adelman, *The World Petroleum Market,* pp. 105-106.

fleets. Already the charge is being made that OAPEC tankers pose a new threat to the security of oil importers because they may refuse to deliver oil. Since the trnd to increased OAPEC tanker ownership seems likely to continue, this charge will be heard with increasing frequency. It should be ignored. The oil exporting countries will have monopoly power as long as they can act together to limit crude oil sales. Their control over access to crude oil production already gives them this power. Hence, even if they could monopolize the tanker market (and for the reasons discussed above this is unlikely) it would not enhance their total monopoly power.

The United States is traversed by an extensive network of crude oil and refined petroleum products pipelines. Gathering lines collect crude oil from wells and transport it to larger diameter main trunklines that go to one or more refineries. Product pipelines carry gasoline and other products from the refinery to local or regional storage facilities. Because large pipelines are expensive to build, most are owned directly by individual major oil companies or by several majors participating in joint ventures.[10] Because of the physical fact that a cylinder's volume (hence crude oil throughput) increases proportionately faster than its circumference (hence capital costs), pipelines enjoy extensive scale economies; i.e., larger pipelines have lower unit transportation costs. The twin facts that in any specified geographic area the pipeline business is relatively concentrated and that pipelines enjoy extensive scale economies suggest that established pipeline companies may face little competition.[11] In part for these reasons, interstate pipelines come under the "common carrier" regulatory jurisdiction of the Interstate Commerce Commission.

The Interstate Commerce Commission (ICC) has the responsibility for insuring that the interstate pipelines do not discriminate against non-owners. It attempts to do this by regulating rates and assuring that all shippers are granted access. Nevertheless, many non-pipeline owners have charged that the ICC has been derelict in performing this duty. They maintain that a variety of business practices have been used to deny them access to common carrier lines. These alleged practices include requiring unnecessarily large minimum-size shipments, granting non-owners irregular shipping dates, limiting available storage at the pipeline terminal, and imposing unreasonable product standards upon pipeline customers.[12] Scheduling pipeline shipments is not a trivial task—to minimize unit costs

---

[10]U.S. Federal Trade Commission, "Preliminary Staff Report," p. 23.

[11]Pipelines may face significant competition from alternative modes of transportation, especially tankers and barges.

[12]U.S. Federal Trade Commission," Preliminary Staff Report," p. 26.

the line must be operated continuously near full capacity but, to prevent product contamination it is necessary to separate shipments of different products. For these and similar reasons, the unit costs of providing pipeline services to a large customer are less than if the same service is provided to a small customer. Since any interstate pipeline is forced by the ICC to charge all customers the same rates for the same services, it would be surprising not to find instances when a pipeline's owners—who tend to be relatively small shippers—might disagree over the necessity for different business practices. In order to get redress for the alleged inequities, the customers would complain to the ICC. Absent contrary empirical evidence, the fact that the ICC—which has a tradition of issuing regulations that effectively subsidize high-cost shippers—has found few of these complaints to be justified, supports the inference that the large oil companies are not presently exercising substantial monopoly power in the pipeline industry.

Refining. The oil refining industry transforms crude oil into more useful petroleum products. Table 4 lists the principal products of U.S. refineries—gasoline accounts for nearly 50 percent of the total. As of 1 January 1974 the United States had 132 oil refining companies; 17 had a daily capacity in excess of 200,000 barrels.[13] Table 5 lists the FTC's estimates of the share of domestic gasoline refining capacity of the 20 largest companies in 1970. The largest, Exxon, accounted for less than 10 percent of the total. Table 6 shows that between 1965 and 1975 the eight largest refiners accounted for roughly 55 percent of the industry's total capacity. When compared with other major American heavy industries, oil refining is not highly concentrated.

Depending on their complexity and size, new oil refineries cost from $50 to $500-plus million. Many, including the Federal Trade Commission, infer that such high capital requirements constitute a significant barrier to new entry. The evidence summarized in Table 7 suggests that the significance of entry barriers has been exaggerated. Sixty firms have chosen to become oil refiners since 1950. Events immediately following the elimination of oil import quotas in May 1973 also fail to support the inference that high capital requirements make it nearly impossible for firms to enter the oil refining business. As Professor Leonard Weiss has testified in his role as an expert witness for the Antitrust Division of the Justice Department in U.S. vs. I.B.M.:

I mentioned . . . the number of firms, including some independents I have never heard of, who set out to build refineries between May and July of 1973,

---

[13]Leo Aalund, "Refining Capacity Registers Largest Nickel and Dime Jump in History," *Oil and Gas Journal* (April 1, 1974), p. 76.

Table 4
Principal Products of U.S. Refineries in 1969

Product	Percent
Gasoline	45.5
Distillate Fuel Oil	21.6
Jet Fuel	8.2
Residual Fuel Oil	6.8
Kerosene	2.6
Lubricants	1.7

Source: U.S. Federal Trade Commission, *Preliminary Federal Trade Commission Staff Report on Its Investigation of the Petroleum Industry* (1973), p. 18.

Table 5
Top Twenty Companies Share of U.S. Gasoline Refining Capacity, 1970

Company	Share (percent)	Cumulative Shares
Exxon, U.S.A.	9.22	9.22
Texaco	9.19	18.41
Indiana Standard	7.94	26.35
Shell	7.69	34.04
SOCAL	6.72	40.76
Gulf	6.47	47.23
Mobil	6.30	53.53
ARCO	6.25	59.78
Sun	4.54	64.32
Phillips	4.24	68.56
Union	3.24	71.80
SOHIO	3.09	74.89
Cities Service	2.26	77.15
Ashland	2.11	79.26
Continental	2.03	81.29
Marathon	1.92	83.21
Getty	1.76	84.97
Tenneco	1.35	86.32
Clark	1.21	87.53
American Petrofina	0.85	88.38

Source: U.S. Federal Trade Commission, *Preliminary Federal Trade Commission Staff Report on Its Investigation of the Petroleum Industry*, (1973), Table II-3.

Table 6
Concentration in U.S. Refining Operating Capacity
(1965-1974)

	As a Percentage of Total U.S. Operating Capacity		
	1965	1970	1974
Four largest firms	30.4	31.8	29.8
Eight Largest firms	53.5	56.7	53.0

Source: Presentation by Ted Eck, Standard Oil of Indiana. Reprinted in Bureau of National Affairs, *Energy Users' Report* (November 13, 1975), p. A-19.

Table 7
New Entrants Into U.S. Refining
(1950-1975)

	Number of New Entrants
1950-1972	47
1972-1975	13
Total	60

Backgrounds of 23 largest entrants during
1950-1972 prior to becoming refiners:

Crude oil producers	8
Refined products marketers	6
Acquisition of integrated operation	1
Antecedents not readily available	8
Total	23

Source: Presentation by Ted Eck, Standard Oil of Indiana. Reprinted in Bureau of National Affairs, *Energy Users' Report* (November 13, 1975), p. A-20.

> *and it is just astounding—and these were one hundred million dollars and many one hundred million dollar investments—that shook my belief in capital require-ment as a high barrier to entry quite a bit.[14]*

Because of the OAPEC embargo and the resulting sharp fall in projections of future U.S. petroleum demands, many of these plans to build new refineries were subsequently canceled. Nevertheless, as of year-end 1974 eleven companies were still planning to complete new U.S. refineries in the mid-1970's. They are listed in Table 8. The diversity of these firms does not support the contention that large firms in the American refining industry enjoy the protection of high entry barriers.[15]

Marketing. Marketing is done by jobbers who purchase refined oil products and supply retail dealers. Many jobbers are completely independent from refiners and dealers; others own their own retail outlets, and others are simply marketing extensions of the oil refiners. Also jobbers may carry branded or unbranded products. Table 9 presents the FTC's estimates of the national gasoline market shares of the leading 25 marketers in 1973. The largest, Texaco, had less than 8 percent of the market. Table 10 shows that the share of the eight largest refined product marketers has fallen by more than 9 percentage points since 1964. A rising market share for independents accounts for most of this fall. After examining evidence of this type the Federal Trade Commission concluded: Gasoline marketing is the most competitive area of the petroleum industry and has the largest number of independent companies."[16] Absent evidence of collusive conduct in regional or local markets, I concur.

The Evidence: Market Structure, Conduct and Performance in International Oil Markets

Available evidence on both the structure of the world crude oil market and the conduct of the international oil companies supports the judgments that, in the years prior to the formation of the Organization of Petroleum Exporting Countries in 1960, the major international oil companies en-

---

[14]Leonard Weiss, *Deposition for U.S. vs. I.B.M.,* United States District Court Southern District of New York (June 11, 1974), pp. 354-55.

[15]Further evidence on the viability of small refiners can be inferred from the fact that in 1973 refiners with less than 75,000 barrels daily capacity accounted for 39.2 percent of total expansion. See Leo Aalund, "A Close Look at Added New Refining Capacity in U.S.," *Oil and Gas Journal* (April 18, 1974), p. 33.

[16]U.S. Federal Trade Commission, "Preliminary Staff Report," p. 21.

joyed significant but eroding monopoly power.[17] However, by the early 1970's their monopoly power had disappeared.

Prior to the mid-1950's virtually all of the oil traded internationally was produced by the subsidiaries of eight companies: British Petroleum (BP), Compagnie Francaise des Petroles (CFP), Exxon, Gulf, Mobil, Royal Dutch Shell, Standard Oil of California (Socal), and Texaco. In the Middle East these companies were joint participants in a variety of crude oil producing and marketing consortia. Moreover, encouraged by the American, British, and French governments, the charters of these consortia included clauses severely restricting competition between the eight. Two examples will suffice to illustrate this point.

1. American oil companies first entered the Middle East by acquiring a share in the Iraq Petroleum Company from BP, CFP, and Shell. "The price of establishing the first American presence in the Middle East was the 1928 Red Line Agreement which obligated the consortium members not to compete against each other within the area of the old Ottoman Empire."[18] Exxon and Mobil—who acquired the entire American interest in the Iraq Petroleum Company in the early 1930's—were subject to the anti-competitive strictures of the Red Line Agreement until 1947.

2. In 1933 Socal obtained an exclusive 60-year oil concession in Saudi Arabia. Desiring both additional financing and marketing facilities, Socal took in Texaco as an equal partner and formed a new subsidiary named Caltex. Caltex's Aramco subsidiary discovered and began to develop enormous low cost crude oil reserves in Saudi Arabia. The appearance of this oil on the world market following the conclusion of World War II threatened the market power of the other six established international majors. The prospects for Exxon and Mobil, whose only Middle East oil came from their jointly held minority interest in the Iraq Petroleum Company, were especially bleak. Both firms needed more oil to supply their Western European affiliates but they were prevented from acquiring new Middle East sources by the Red Line Agreement. Hence, they feared that "Caltex . . .would be able to use Aramco to build up a marketing organization no other firm could compete against. Exxon and Mobil therefore decided to offer their markets and their capital to Caltex in return for a piece

---

[17]See M.A. Adelman, *The World Petroleum Market,* chapters 5-7; and Subcommittee on Multinational Corporations, United States Senate Committee on Foreign Relations, *Multinational Oil Corporations and U.S. Foreign Policy* (Washington: G.P.O., January 2, 1975).

[18]Subcommittee on Multinational Corporations, *Multinational Oil Corporations and U.S. Foreign Policy,* p. 36.

Table 8

New U.S. Refining Capacity Set for 1975-77

Company	Date Set	Location	Added Capacity (barrels/day)
Exxon U.S.A.	1976	Baytown, Texas	250,000
	1975	Baton Rouge, La.	14,000
	1975	Bayway, N.J.	30,000
ECOL Ltd.	1976	Garyville, La.	200,000
SOCAL	1975	Perth Amboy, N.J.	80,000
	1975	Pascagoula, Miss.	40,000
	1976	Richmond, Calif.	175,000
	1976	El Segundo, Calif.	175,000
Dow	1977	Freeport, Texas	100,000
ARCO	1976	Houston, Texas	95,000
Champlin	1976	Corpus Christi, Texas	60,000
Clark	1975	Hartford, Ill.	45,000
Vickers	1975	Ardmore, Okla.	30,000
Texaco	1977	Lockport, Ill.	25,000
Douglas Oil	1975	Paramount, Calif.	15,000
Energy Co. of Alaska	1977	Fairbanks, Alaska	15,000

Source: Leo R. Aalund, "Inflation and Uncertainty Cut U.S. Refining Buildup," *Oil and Gas Journal* (November 25, 1974), p. 37.

of Aramco."[19] After considerable negotiation, Caltex accepted the Exxon-Mobil offer.

Broadening Aramco's ownership to include two companies that had access to other sources of crude oil, both within and outside the Middle East, seriously reduced the competitive impact of Saudi oil. Aramco, when solely owned by Caltex, had sold its oil at cost (which was far below the prevailing world price) to Socal and Texaco. Both companies then reaped high profits when refined products made from it were sold in Western European markets. Having access to lower cost crude oil, the Caltex partners threatened to offer severe price competition in refined products markets that had traditionally been dominated by the other international majors. Shortly after Exxon and Mobil assumed partial ownership of Aramco, they persuaded Caltex to agree that Aramco should be transformed into a profit-maximizing entity that would sell oil to its owners at the world price. The net result of this change was to eliminate the special incentive for Socal and Texaco to expand refined products sales and thus competition in world oil markets was reduced.

Beginning in the mid-1950's several companies (both American and foreign) joined the eight majors in producing Middle Eastern crude oil. Because the most promising Persian Gulf oil concessions were under the

---

[19]*Ibid.*, p.

Table 9
Share of U.S. Gasoline Market—1973

Company	Percent of U.S. Market	Cumulative Shares
Texaco	7.97	7.97
Exxon	7.64	15.61
Shell	7.47	23.08
Indiana Standard	6.90	29.98
Gulf	6.75	36.73
Mobil	6.49	43.22
SOCAL	4.78	48.00
ARCO	4.37	52.37
Phillips	3.92	56.29
Sun	3.67	59.96
Union	3.05	63.01
Continental	2.30	65.31
Cities Service	1.66	66.97
Marathon	1.52	68.49
Ashland	1.48	69.97
Clark	1.25	71.22
SOHIO	1.23	72.45
Hess	1.00	73.45
BP	0.81	74.26
Tenneco	0.78	75.04
Murphy	0.66	75.70
Getty	0.65	76.35
American Petrofina	0.63	76.98
Skelly	0.60	77.58
Triangle	0.57	78.15

Source: Harold Wilson, "Exxon and Shell Score Gasoline Gains," *Oil and Gas Journal* (June 3, 1974), p. 78 cites results of the Lundberg Survey.

Table 10

Concentration in Petroleum Product Markets

Refined Product Sales			
		As a Percentage of Total U.S. Refined Product Sales	
	1964	1970	1974
Four largest firms	34.8	33.8	31.2
Eight largest firms	61.7	57.0	52.3

Gasoline Sales		
	As a Percentage of Total U.S. Gasoline Sales	
	1970	1974
Four largest firms	30.8	29.9
Eight largest firms	35.0	51.9

Market Share of Independents		
	1968	1974
Marketing	19.8	29
Refining	26.8	29.8

Source: Presentation by Ted Eck, Standard Oil of Indiana. Reprinted in Bureau of National Affairs, *Energy Users' Report* (November 13, 1975), p. A-19.

nearly exclusive ownership of the eight majors, the new competition was, initially, on a very small scale. This was not the case in Libya. Not wanting to be controlled by any single economic entity, that country's 1955 Petroleum Law established a fragmented pattern of oil concessions. Many American companies that had previously had no significant oil reserves acquired Libyan concessions. Several of these companies had discovered and developed large oil reserves by the late 1950's. Libyan developments, coupled with rising European sales of Soviet crude oil and natural gas, resulted in a rapid increase in the level of competition between firms that produced and sold crude oil on world markets.

World oil markets were glutted by 1959—the international oil companies responded by cutting their posted prices. Supplies were too great; the glut continued; posted prices were cut a second time in 1960. In return for permission to produce and sell a nation's oil, the oil companies pay royalties and taxes to the host country. These payments were a fraction of the posted price. Hence, the decision by the international majors to meet competition by cutting their posted prices meant that the oil-exporting countries would receive lower per barrel revenues. Naturally, these countries were incensed by the oil companies' "arbitrary" price cuts. Meeting in 1960, representatives of five countries (Iran, Iraq, Kuwait, Saudi Arabia and Venezuela), which together supplied 80 percent of all oil entering world trade, established OPEC. Throughout the 1960's OPEC was able to prevent further cuts in the posted price of crude oil. Nevertheless, because world oil markets continued to be glutted, the price at which oil actually sold fell throughout the 1960's. Thus, oil that would have sold for about $1.50 per barrel at Persian Gulf ports in 1960 could be bought for about $1.10 per barrel in 1969.[20] Roughly 90 cents of this total price was paid as royalties or taxes to the oil exporting nation; the oil company had to pay for all production costs out of the remaining 20 cents. Hence, by the late 1960's the international oil companies could not have been earning sizeable monopoly profits.

By the early 1970's several hundred producing companies were participating in the world petroleum market (see Table 11). Also, as the OPEC members gained power and successfully demanded that they be given partial ownership over their oil, the number of effective restrictive agreements between the majors dwindled rapidly. In sum, because of sharp changes in both the structure of the world petroleum market and in the conduct of the industry's firms, the available evidence no longer supports the inference that the large international oil companies continue to exercise significant monopoly power in the world crude oil market. The fact that they lack monopoly power explains why after paying royalties and taxes most Persian Gulf producers presently retain only 25 cents on each barrel of crude oil sold.[21] This covers their exploration, development, and operating costs but does not permit monopoly profits. Hence, it is fatuous to blame present and near-future international energy problems on the monopolistic practices of the international oil companies.

The Evidence: Structure and Conduct in the Markets for Other Energy Products

Most large oil companies are also significant suppliers of natural gas; in addition, many are substantial participants in the coal industry and some are making preparations to enter the business of enriching uranium. Are these products sold in monopolistic markets? Does the fact of substantial oil company participation have deleterious implications for competition?

Natural Gas. Crude oil and natural gas are found in similar, frequently the same, geological structures and tend to be produced by methods utilizing roughly the same technology. Thus, crude oil and natural gas are often

---

[20]M.A. Adelman, *The World Petroleum Market,* pp. 160-91.

[21]"Divestiture Heat Still on in the Senate," *Oil and Gas Journal* (November 17, 1975), p. 43. Citing Exxon senior vice-president William Slick who stated that Exxon made 35 cents/bbl on light Arabian crude early in 1973, when crude was selling for $2/bbl, compared to profits of 25 cents/bbl today from $11.50 market prices.

Table 11

Independent Oil Companies Overseas

(Other than largest seven)

	Number	Percent of Concession Area
1953	28	35
1972	330	69

Source: Presentation by Ted Eck, Standard Oil of Indiana. Reprinted in Bureau of National Affairs, *Energy User's Report* (November 13, 1975), p. A-20.

produced as joint products and, even when they are produced separately, there are real economies that are only available to firms having the capability of producing both products. Hence, it was inevitable that large crude oil producers also became large producers of natural gas.

Most natural gas is sold at the wellhead to large natural gas pipeline companies. These companies, in turn, ship natural gas to customers (usually local natural gas distribution companies or large firms) in either intrastate or interstate markets. Because the Federal Power Commission (FPC) enforces strict price ceilings on all gas sold in interstate markets, the arbitrary distinction between intrastate and interstate natural gas is, nonetheless, important. Since the early 1960s the FPC has held the price of interstate natural gas far below the price of all competitive fuels. Thus, in 1975 when the delivered cost of imported crude oil (including a $2 per barrel tariff) was more than $14 per barrel, the FPC allowed new reserves of natural gas to be sold to interstate customers at 50 cents per thousand cubic feet (Mcf). At this price natural gas would be competitive with crude oil priced at only $2.80 per barrel. Such a low price, coupled with natural gas's low-polluting properties, encourages soaring demands. But, the low price also discourages firms from making the investments necessary to discover and develop new natural gas reserves sufficient to prevent the depletion of already developed reserves. As a result of FPC-mandated below-market clearing prices, most areas of the United States have suffered severe and worsening natural gas shortages since the late 1960s. Only customers located in states blessed with substantial natural gas that could be sold at higher unregulated intrastate prices have not suffered these costly shortages.[22]

One of the principal justifications for natural gas wellhead price controls was that absent price regulation its producers would be able to exercise substantial monopoly power. Market share data of the type summarized in Table 12 casts doubt on this justification—the natural gas industry is not highly concentrated. Even more persuasive are the numerous detailed

---

[22]In 1975, new reserves of natural gas sold at about $2.00 per Mcf in intrastate markets.

Table 12

Company Shares of Natural Gas
Sold to Interstate Pipelines, 1970

Producer	Volume (mcf)	Percent of Total	Cumulative Percentage
Exxon	1,300,642,683	9.0	9.0
Gulf Oil	813,738,549	5.6	14.6
Shell Oil	785,667,041	5.4	20.0
Pan American Petroleum (Stand. Ind.)	767,439,589	5.3	25.3
Phillips	707,235,036	4.9	30.2
Mobil Oil	650,890,489	4.5	34.7
Texaco	607,433,789	4.2	38.9
Atlantic Richfield	561,540,880	3.9	42.8
Union Oil of California	548,896,648	3.8	46.6
Continental Oil	461,297,727	3.2	49.8
California Co. Division of Chevron	367,213,888	2.5	52.3
Sun Oil	361,622,934	2.5	54.8
Alberta & Southern Gas (Canadian)	304,529,422	2.1	56.9
Tenneco	252,971,722	1.8	58.7
Cities Service	243,511,899	1.7	60.4
Superior Oil	240,211,285	1.7	62.1
Westcoast Transmission (Canadian)	223,257,230	1.5	63.6
Trans-Canada P.L.Ltd.	199,655,647	1.4	65.0
Pennzoil Producing	184,440,676	1.3	66.3
Getty Oil	173,480,911	1.2	67.5
Total: Top 20	9,502,706,323		
Total: Other	4,938,030,621		
Grand Total	14,440,736,944		

Source: FPC, Sales by Producers of Natural Gas to Interstate Pipeline Companies, 1970.

studies by Professor Paul MacAvoy and colleagues.[23] All of these studies buttress MacAvoy's 1962 conclusion that:

> Studies of most field and supply markets in Texas, Louisiana, Oklahoma, etc. indicate the presence of systematic competition or monopsony throughout the period in which regulation was proposed. The problem to be solved by regulation seems not to have existed.[24]

Economists are a notoriously disputatious lot. Nevertheless, I know of no reputable academic economist who presently argues that natural gas producers possess substantial monopoly power. In sum, because they have been used to justify the FPC's unfortunate regulation of natural gas wellhead prices, the totally unsupported assertions that the business of producing this product is monopolized must be judged a costly myth.

Coal. More than 3,500 companies presently produce coal in the United States. Table 13 lists the 20 largest coal producers in 1972. Together these 20 firms accounted for only 55 percent of total domestic production. The 20 largest coal producers have diverse backgrounds. Besides "coal companies" their ranks include companies that are chiefly known for their interests in other industries. For example, Peabody Coal, the industry's largest producer, is presently owned by Kennecott Copper. Most steel companies, which are among the nation's largest coal consumers, are substantial coal producers—U.S. Steel and Bethlehem Steel were the nation's sixth and seventh largest producers in 1972. Some electric utilities (most notably, the industry's giant, American Electric Power) produce a significant fraction of their coal needs. And, several oil companies are also substantial coal producers.

In addition to the fact that coal production is not concentrated, there are two reasons for concluding that present producers possess little or no monopoly power. First, most coal is consumed by either electric utilities or steel companies. These companies are large and sophisticated consumers. Because they burn huge quantities of coal, they find it profitable to search for the best buy. They actively solicit competitive bids rather than meekly accepting prices quoted by coal companies. Moreover, because many electric utilities and steel companies are themselves substantial coal producers, they would respond to monopoly coal prices by expanding their

---

[23]Paul MacAvoy and Robert Pyndyck, *Price Controls and the Natural Gas Shortage* (Washington: American Enterprise Institute, 1975); Stephen Breyer and Paul MacAvoy, *Energy Regulation by the Federal Power Commission* (Washington: Brookings Institution, 1974).

[24]Paul MacAvoy, *Price Formation in Natural Gas Fields* (New Haven: Yale University Press, 1962), pp. 252-53.

Table 13
Top Twenty Companies Share of U.S. Coal Production in 1972

Rank	Group	Tonnage (bituminous and lignite) (tons)	Percent of Total	Cumulative Percentage
1	Peabody Coal Co.	71,595,310	12.1%	12.1
2	Consolidated Coal (0)	64,942,000	11.0	23.1
3	Island Creek Coal (0)	22,605,114	3.8	26.9
4	Pittston Coal	20,639,020	3.5	30.4
5	Amax	16,380,303	2.8	33.2
6	U.S. Steel (S)	16,254,400	2.8	36.0
7	Bethlehem Mines (S)	13,335,245	2.3	38.3
8	Eastern Associated Coal Corp.	12,528,429	2.1	40.4
9	North American Coal Co.	11,991,004	2.0	42.4
10	Old Ben Coal Corp. (0)	11,235,910	1.9	44.3
11	General Dynamics	9,951,263	1.7	46.0
12	Westmoreland Coal Co.	9,063,919	1.5	47.5
13	Pittsburgh & Midway Coal Co. (0)	7,458,791	1.3	48.8
14	Utah International	6,898,262	1.2	50.0
15	American Electric Power	6,329,389	1.1	51.1
16	Western Energy Co.	5,500,700	0.9	52.0
17	Rochester & Pittsburgh	5,137,438	0.9	52.9
18	Valley Camp Coal	4,777,674	0.8	53.7
19	Zeigler Coal Co.	4,201,164	0.7	54.4
20	Midland Coal	3,899,478	0.7	55.1
	Total: Top 20	320,428,813	55.1	
	Total: Others	269,571,187	44.9	
	Total U.S. Production	590,000,000		

Source: Thomas Duchesneau, *Competition in the U.S. Energy Industry* (Cambridge, Mass.: Ballinger Publishing, 1975), p. 75.

Note: O denotes owned by an oil company.
S denotes owned by a steel company.

own production. Second, the U.S. has enormous presently undeveloped but economic coal reserves. Most of these are owned by federal and state governments. But huge quantities are also owned by existing coal producers, several Indian tribes, and the large western land grant railroads. Most of these undeveloped reserves have not been leased. Existing coal companies can expect substantial new entry when they are.

Available structure and conduct evidence supports the conclusion that the coal industry is highly competitive and that oil company participation has not resulted in reduced competition. Nevertheless, one caveat is necessary. There are two ways that a firm can enter an industry—either by starting a grass roots coal-mining operation or by acquiring an existing firm. Because grass roots entry raises the number of firms in the industry, many economists prefer it to entry by acquisition. Oil companies have used both methods to enter the coal business. However, those oil companies that are presently the largest coal producers—Continental, Occidental, Sohio, and Gulf—all took the less desirable acquisition route.

Because petroleum products are close substitutes for coal in many uses, the oil companies' coal acquisitions might also be opposed on the grounds that they are really horizontal mergers and therefore violate Section 7 of the Clayton Act. The Justice Department's Antitrust Division—subscribing to the rather narrow view that coal and petroleum are sold in different markets—has not felt that Section 7 is not applicable. Hence, these acquisitions have not been opposed. Because of the rather high degree of inter-fuel substitutability, I feel that the Antitrust Division was remiss in failing to challenge these acquisitions. However, if one agrees with my position, logical consistency also compels him to admit that the crude and refined oil market share data summarized earlier overstates the importance of the large oil companies in the combined coal-oil market. This, in turn, reduces even further the already low probability that the large oil companies possess the power to set monopoly prices.

Enriched Uranium. Enriched uranium 235 fuels all of the United States' commercial nuclear reactors. Three federally owned gaseous diffusion plants presently produce all enriched uranium. These huge plants—the largest would cost over $6 billion to replicate—were initially used to provide the uranium necessary for nuclear weapons. Present enriching capacity will be inadequate to supply anticipated 1980s nuclear fuel needs. President Ford has proposed allowing privately-owned firms to build the necessary new enriching capacity. To enable them to raise financing for the enormous expenditure, he has proposed federal guarantees of up to $8 billion.

Four groups of companies have proposed building uranium enrichment plants. Uranium Enrichment Associates (UEA)—a joint venture of Bechtel, Goodyear Tire, and the Williams Companies—has proposed an enormous $6 billion gaseous diffusion plant. The other companies—Centar (a partnership of Atlantic-Richfield and Electro Nucleonics), Garrett (a Signal Oil subsidiary), and Exxon Nuclear (an Exxon subsidiary)—propose building plants that would use the commercially untested centrifuge enrichment process. Each of these plants would cost about $1 billion and have roughly one-third the capacity of UEA's proposed diffusion plant.

The present cost of enriched uranium is only a small fraction of the cost of coal or residual fuel oil on an energy content basis. This fact, coupled with the fact that the enormous size of uranium enrichment plants entails that this industry must be highly concentrated at least through the 1980s, raises the spectre that the enrichment companies may enjoy considerable monopoly power. The danger is real but exaggerated. Compared to coal or oil-fired electricity generating plants, nuclear plants take much longer to build and are far more expensive to construct. Thus, an electric utility would choose to build new nuclear generating capacity only if lower costs for enriched uranium (compared with costs for comparable quantities of coal or fuel oil) more than offset the sharply higher capital costs. Presently electric utilities in most areas of the country appear to prefer new coal-fired generating capacity to new nuclear-fired capacity. This suggests that enriched uranium producers will not be able to raise prices substantially above present real levels. In sum, because of the higher costs of new nuclear electricity generating capacity, the difference between the cost of enriched uranium on the one hand and the cost of coal or fuel oil on the other hand does not offer a valid measure of the price hikes potentially available to enriched uranium producers.

The Evidence: Oil Company Profitability

Available market structure and conduct evidence supports the unpopular inference that the American oil industry is more competitive than most other comparable large American manufacturing or mineral industries. Available evidence, summarized below, on the oil industry's profitability also supports this inference.

Total Profitability. The best test of the successful exercise of monopoly power is the persistence of abnormally high *industry* profits over a long period of time.[25] Judged by the most common measure—the after-tax rate of return on equity investments—profits of most American oil companies were below the average for all U.S. industrial firms for the ten years prior to 1973.[26] Largely as a result of embargo-caused higher crude oil prices, oil company profits rose sharply in 1973 and 1974. Nevertheless, even then they were only slightly higher than the average earned by all U.S. manufacturing companies. Moreover, they began to fall off in the last quarter of 1974, and this trend accelerated in 1975. The fact that unusually high profits were earned for a period of less than two years that coincided with a period of unanticipated supply shortages is not evidence of monopoly.

Accounting profitability measures are only loosely related to the economist's profit definition and thus the evidence just cited should be regarded as suggestive but not conclusive. Professor Edward Mitchell has described several problems plaguing the accounting profit data.:

> *Expenditures that should be capitalized, such as advertising and research and development, frequently are not. Depreciation charges usually reflect simple arithmetic rules rather than actual changes in the value of assets. Future income not yet confirmed by sales contracts is ignored. Even without these problems, the procedure of estimating the rate of return on capital by the ratio of income to stockholders' equity . . .can give widely disparate answers for a given true rate of return depending upon the particular time pattern of cash flows.*[27]

In an attempt to circumvent the problems of interpreting accounting profit data, Mitchell calculated the profits that would have been realized by owners of oil company common stocks. Specifically, he calculated oil company's stockholders' profits over a specified period by subtracting the sum of the common stock's purchase price at the start of the period and all dividends (assumed to be reinvested in the company's common stocks) paid during the period from the value of the initial and acquired stock at the

---

[25]Because of successful innovations, etc. individual firms can earn "above-normal" profits for long periods of time even though they possess no monopoly power. However, it is unlikely that most firms in an industry would enjoy persistent "above-normal" profits unless the industry were characterized by unusual risks or the member firms enjoyed monopoly power. For elaboration see Richard B. Mancke, "Interfirm Profitability Differences: A Reinterpretation of the Evidence," *Quarterly Journal of Economics* (May 1974), pp. 181-93.

[26]See *Oil and Gas Journal* (February 18, 1974) p. 38. For more elaboration see Edward Erickson and Robert Spann, "The U.S. Petroleum Industry," in Edward Erickson and Leonard Waverman, *The Energy Question,* vol. 2 (Toronto: University of Toronto Press, 1974), pp. 6-12.

[27]Edward Mitchell, *U.S. Energy Policy: A Primer* (Washington: American Enterprise Institute, 1974), p. 91.

period's close.[28] Table 14 reprints Mitchell's calculations of the average annual rates of return realized by oil company stockholders over two periods, 1953-72 and 1960-72. Based on this data Mitchell concludes:

1. *"American petroleum companies were significantly less profitable than the S & P (Standard & Poor's) 500's over the 1953 to 1972 period. Indeed, not one of the twenty-one American petroleum companies equalled the S & P 500's rate of return!"*

2. *"The eight companies charged by the Federal Trade Commission with monopolizing the industry earned an average rate of return of 12.1 percent, more than 20 percent below the S & P norm for the 1953 to 1972 period."*

3. *"From 1960 to 1972 domestic producers realized less than half the rate of return of the S & P 500."*[29]

The rather poor profit performances realized by these major oil companies is inconsistent with the charge that they have been exercising substantial monopoly power.

Profitability of Offshore Oil Investments. Because of the relatively much higher costs of lease acqusition and production, fewer firms are actively involved in producing offshore oil. Moreover, offshore oil is frequently produced by joint ventures of several oil companies. For these reasons, monopoly returns seem especially likely to be realized in this sub-business. Nevertheless, a rather large number of economic studies have failed to find any evidence of monopoly.[30] For example, a U.S. Bureau of Mines study concluded that the typical successful offshore tract in the Gulf of Mexico yielded a return on total assets of between 14 and 17 percent—

[28]Mitchell comments: "One criticism of this approach is that initial period stock prices may already capitalize expected future monopoly profits. Therefore, rates of return calculated on initial stock prices would only reflect normal rates of return, even though monopoly profits were being earned . . . As a practical matter this probably has little effect on our calculated rates of return. Any monopoly profits earned in the petroleum industry would . . . .require lax antitrust and regulatory policy and a passive Congress and executive. The uncertainty of future public policy would mean that these monopoly profits would be discounted at a very high rate and that monopoly profits that might accrue four or five years in the future would be accorded a very small value in present stock prices . . . Monopoly profits earned continuously for a couple of decades should definitely show up in our figures." E. Mitchell, *U.S. Energy Policy: A Primer,* pp. 92-93.

[29]E. Mitchell, *U.S. Energy Policy: A Primer,* pp. 93-95.

[30]See Jesse Markham, "The Competitive Effects of Joint Bidding by Oil Companies for Offshore Lease Sales," in Jesse Markham and Gustov Papanek, eds., *Industrial Organization and Economic Development* (Boston: Houghton Mifflin, 1970), pp. 116-35. Edward Erickson and Robert Spann, "The U.S. Petroleum Industry" in E. Erickson and L. Waverman, *The Energy Question,* Vol. 2, and C.J. Jirik, *Composition of the Offshore U.S. Petroleum Industry and Estimated Cost of Producing Petroleum in the Gulf of Mexico,* U.S.D.I. Information Circular 8557 (Washington: G.P.O., 1972).

many tracts are unsuccessful.[31] After examining the process of leasing offshore lands, Professors Erickson and Spann concluded that "oil and gas companies earn no more than a competitive rate of return on offshore drilling."[32]

The Evidence: Special Monopoly Arguments

When judged by the conventional market structure, industry conduct, and industry performance criteria, the conclusion that the American oil industry is relatively competitive is unavoidable. Hence, proponents of the thesis that the American oil industry is monopolized have had to develop a special monopoly argument.[33] As outlined by the Federal Trade Commission: "the major oil companies in general and the eight largest majors in particular have engaged in conduct . . .squeez[ing] independents at both the refining and marketing levels."[34] This ability to squeeze "has its origin in the structural peculiarities of the petroleum industry" which allow the majors to "limit effectively the supply of crude oil to a point which reduces refinery profits to zero. Clearly, such a system creates a hazardous existence for independent refiners who have little or no crude production."[35]

Squeezing could be both profitable and successful only if the integrated majors enjoyed special advantages over their independent competitors. The Federal Trade Commission mistakenly argued that they enjoyed two: import quotas—which were abolished in 1973—and the oil depletion allowance—abolished for large oil companies in 1975:[36]

1. *"The import quota clearly contributed to profits earned in producing crude oil by elevating prices, but the quota increased profits to the major in another way. The right to import went only to existing refineries. Thus the major companies . . . were able to purchase oil at the world price as an*

---

[31]L.K. Weaver, *et. al., Composition of Offshore U.S. Petroleum Industry.*

[32]E. Erickson and R. Spann, "The U.S. Petroleum Industry," p. 17.

[33]This argument is by no means original with the FTC. It was developed initially by de Chazeau and Kahn. Recent adherents include the Federal Trade Commission. See Melvin de Chazeau and Alfred Kahn, *Integration and Competition in the Petroleum Industry* (New Haven: Yale University Press, 1959), pp. 221-29.

[34]U.S. Federal Trade Commission, "Preliminary Staff Report," p. 43.

[35]*Ibid.,* pp. 17, 43.

[36]Based on arguments similar to those outlined in the text, the FTC has issued a complaint charging the eight largest American oil companies with antitrust violations. In an unprecedented move, the FTC judge hearing the case issued a brief (October, 1975) arguing that, because of changed circumstances since the charge was brought (especially OPEC's success at raising world oil prices and the abolition of both oil import quotas and the oil depletion allowance), the charge should be withdrawn. The full Commission ruled against this suggestion. I suspect that political considerations rather than economic analysis lay behind the Commission's ruling.

input for their refineries, which produced final products at elevated domestic prices."[37]

2. *"Oil depletion allowances[allowed]* . . . a crude oil producing firm . . . to subtract from its gross income before taxes an amount equal to 22 percent of its total revenues from crude production . . . Under this system the major integrated firms have an incentive to seek high crude prices. The high crude prices are, however, a cost to the major firms' refineries. Thus, an increase in crude prices implies an increase in crude profits but a decrease in refinery profits. The integrated oil companies gain because the depletion allowance reduces the tax on crude profits, while refinery profits are not subject to the same advantageous depletion allowance."[38]

The arguments just summarized are fallacious.

Under the Mandatory Oil Import Quota Program the general rule for allocating the valuable oil import rights was that they be given to domestic refiners as a percentage of their total crude oil imports. However, the allocation formula was a sliding scale that granted small refiners a far larger proportion of imports. Table 15 calculates the value in 1969 of the per barrel subsidy which the sliding scale would have awarded three refiners of very different size. The small refiner received a per barrel subsidy more than five times higher than the largest. This result was not atypical. But, this means that the FTC was wrong when it stated that the allocation of oil import rights provided the large integrated majors with a tool for squeezing their smaller independent competitors.

The FTC's second charge was that, because the oil depletion allowance reduced the effective tax rate on crude oil profits, the large integrated majors have incentives to raise the price of crude oil and thereby diverted taxable profits from refining operations to crude oil operations. As a result, the FTC continued, independent refiners would be squeezed. Although sounding plausible, this charge was flawed since, using the FTC's own data, 16 of the 17 largest integrated majors would have found profit-shifting unprofitable.

The FTC's analysis was wrong because it failed to take proper account of the fact that most of the integrated majors were not self-sufficient in crude oil. To operate their U.S. refineries at desired levels they had to buy crude oil from independent producers. Assuming that the oil depletion allowance was 22 percent, profit-shifting would only yield profits for those companies able to produce at least 93 percent of their crude oil needs.[39] Table 16 reproduces the FTC's estimates of crude oil self-sufficiency for the

---

[37]*Ibid.,* p. 15.

[38]*Ibid.,* p. 17.

[39]The proof can be found in Richard Mancke, *The Failure of U.S. Energy Policy,* Footnote 33 to chapter 7.

Table 15
Per Barrel Subsidies Awarded to Three
Oil Refiners in 1969[a]

Firm	1 Daily Total Crude Oil Input[b]	2 Daily Total Crude Oil Imports Allowed by Sliding Scale	3 Gross Value of Daily Import Rights[c]	4 Per Barrel Subsidy to Refiner[d]
Standard Oil of New Jersey	992,000 barrels	35,810 barrels	$53,715	5.41¢
Clark Oil	97,651 barrels	8,886 barrels	$13,329	13.65¢
Husky Oil	11,000 barrels	2,060 barrels	$ 3,090	28.09¢

[a]These calculations are intended to be illustrative only. They are premised on two simplifying assumptions: 1) The refineries of all three firms are located in Districts I-IV. 2) None of these firms was claiming "historical" import rights.
[b]Estimates of daily crude oil inputs are obtained from Moody's. These are approximations.
[c]The right to import one barrel of oil into Districts I-IV was worth about $1.50 in 1969 (see *The Oil Import Question*). Thus the product of $1.50 times the daily crude oil imports allowed yields the gross value of import rights.
[d]Obtained by dividing column three by column one.
Source: Richard Mancke, *The Failure of U.S. Energy Policy* (New York: Columbia University Press, 1974), Table 7-4.

17 largest integrated American refiners in 1969. Except for Getty Oil, only the sixteenth largest, none of these integrated giants produced more than 93 percent of its total domestic needs. Hence, none owned enough crude oil self for profit-shifting to be profitable. The after-tax losses assuming any of these firms had adopted this strategy would have ranged from a low of 3 cents on each dollar of profits shifted by relatively oil-rich Marathon to a high of 48.3 cents on each dollar of profits shifted by relatively oil-poor Standard Oil of Ohio.[40] None of these 16 integrated majors would choose to bear these high costs. This implies that, even if it were possible, profit-shifting would never be practiced and thus that independent refiners would never be "squeezed."

The Evidence: A Concluding Comment

Five significant factual conclusions were established in the preceding discussions:

1. Many firms (both large and small) participate in each stage of the oil business and entry appears to be relatively easy.

2. Many firms (both large and small) produce natural gas and/or coal and entry is relatively easy.

3. There is no evidence that oil companies are presently engaged in wide-ranging collusive practices.

[40]*Ibid.*, Footnote 36 to chapter 7.

4. The large oil companies have not enjoyed abnormally high profits that have persisted over a long period of time.

5. The special "squeezing" arguments are implausible because adoption of the hypothesized tactics would have cost the large oil companies (i.e., the alleged squeezers) billions of dollars annually to implement.

To summarize, after examining a great variety of empirical evidence this paper concludes that the oil companies no longer possess observable monopoly power in any important energy market. Moreover, the economic structures of the key stages of the oil business are such that the successful exercise of monopoly power is virtually impossible unless the oil companies receive direct governmental assistance. Though these conclusions may surprise the lay reader and certainly are inconsistent with present popular perceptions, they will be neither surprising nor new to most academic economists who have more than a passing acquaintance with both the oil industry and the field of industrial organization. These "experts" are nearly unanimous in agreeing that the oil companies possess little or no independent monopoly power. Before concluding with a discussion of the high costs because a large portion of energy policymakers' efforts are aimed at remedying a non-existent oil company monopoly problem, it should prove helpful to discuss four factors which might explain the sharply different assessments of the public and of the, presumably unbiased, academic experts.

First, economic theory suggests that relative size, not absolute size, is an important determinant of whether the firms in an industry are likely to possess monopoly power. Review of U.S. antitrust case law reveals that the courts have also stressed the importance of relative (to the market) firm size while downplaying the role of absolute firm size. Nevertheless, precisely because the actions of large firms are so visible, the American public has always equated absolute size with monopoly power. The major oil companies are among the very largest and most visible companies doing business in the United States. Huge accounting profits (but not high profit rates) are an inevitable corollary of large absolute firm size. This makes these companies obvious targets for public criticism.

Second, nearly 80 percent of all domestically produced crude oil comes from just four states—Texas, Louisiana, California, and Oklahoma. Just two states—Louisiana and Texas—presently produce nearly 75 percent of all domestic natural gas. Because of their close proximity to the petroleum sources, citizens of these states pay lower petroleum costs; they also pay significantly lower state taxes because the oil companies pay large rents to the oil states.[41] Because citizens from other regions—especially the Northeast—pay higher petroleum prices and receive none of the rents, they are often angry. The large oil companies are obvious, though inappropriate, targets for this anger. The fact that some "Texans" have earned huge fortunes in the oil business also offends popular sensibilities. Anyone who has seen the cliche depiction of oil barons in recent movies such as *Oklahoma Crude* or *The Drowning Pool* or in a film classic like *Spindletop,* cannot doubt that many Americans believe that oil men are innately evil.

Third, in the not too distant past two government policies—state-enforced market demand prorationing and federally-enforced oil import quotas—did allow the producers of American oil to charge above competitive prices. Specifically, beginning in the early 1930s most of the large oil-producing states began to enforce so-called market demand prorationing regulations which limited, often severely, the maximum rate of crude oil production from each well.[42] State prorationing laws were passed in order to remedy the economic distress due to the sharp Depression-caused drop in crude oil demands and a concurrent sharp rise in crude oil supplies (because of the "fortuitous" discovery of the giant East Texas oil field) which had caused oil prices to tumble. Prorationing did reverse the price fall. Moreover, because there were only a few important oil-producing states and these (assisted by the Federal government's enforcement of the Connally Hot Oil Act) were able to coordinate their respective prorationing policies, these regulations offered a tool by which monopolistic crude oil prices were maintained long after the Depression.[43]

Prior to the late 1940s the United States was self-sufficient in crude oil; the Gulf-coast states actually exported large quantities to Western Europe. But toward the end of the decade their share of the West European market was quickly eroded by expanding sales from lower-cost Persian Gulf sources. By 1950, Persian Gulf oil was supplying most of Western Europe's petroleum needs. Having nearly total control of this market, some Persian Gulf producers began exporting to the United States. This had the effect of undermining the oil states' ability to use prorationing to fix a high price for U.S. crude. Specifically, in the fact of swelling imports, American crude oil's high price could be maintained only if the oil states continually tightened their prorationing policies. But, even if this succeeded, domestic producers knew that their profits would decline with a fall in the domestic

[41]For a discussion of the nature of petroleum rents see Richard B. Mancke, *The Failure of U.S. Energy Policy,* chapter 4.

[42]Actually the prorationing laws exempted low-productivity stripper wells. This exemption made only a minor difference.

[43]For elaboration see R. Mancke, *The Failure of U.S. Energy Policy,* pp. 72-76.

share of the oil market. Thus, the U.S. oil industry sought to end the erosion of their product's market share by persuading the government to restrict oil imports severely. The industry's pleas were rewarded when President Eisenhower issued an Executive Order establishing mandatory oil import quotas in 1959.[44] A prestigious Presidential Cabinet Level Task Force issued a report in 1970 which maintained that American consumers were spending roughly $5 billion per year more for oil as a result of the enforcement of oil import quotas.[45]

Prorationing and (somewhat later) oil import quotas did result in above competitive crude oil prices throughout the 1950s and 1960s. I was one of their harshest critics at that time.[46] However, the situation changed dramatically in the early 1970s because the United States' oil supplies were no longer sufficient to meet most domestic demands and the price of foreign oil began its seemingly inexorable sharp rise. Prorationing has had almost no restrictive effects on output since 1972 and oil import quotas were abolished by a Presidential Executive Order in May 1973. In sum, the domestic oil industry no longer benefits from any government-sponsored monopolistic restrictions. Those who continue to blast the industry for enjoying the fruits from such restrictions are either ignorant or deliberately deceitful.

Fourth, as a direct result of the OAPEC embargo, the United States has suffered enormously higher energy costs, a sharp deterioration of its oil security, and worldwide political humiliation. The American public has quite naturally sought a villain upon which blame for our present energy problems can be placed. The large oil companies offer an inviting target. The fact that there is no evidence that these companies presently possess any monopoly power is of little importance to the oil companies' demagogic accusers. Professor M.A. Adelman alluded to this problem when he told a Senate Committee in January 1975:

> Sheik Yamani and his colleagues knew that the oil companies are in the public doghouse, and that millions of people will call a price hike a reduction if

---

[44]The publicly proclaimed rationale for these quotas was that they were necessary to prevent rising dependence on "insecure" foreign oil and thus protect vital security interests. Throughout the 1960s most academic economists felt that the real reason for oil import quotas was to prevent lower oil prices.

[45]U.S. Cabinet Task Force on Oil Import Controls, *The Oil Import Question* (Washington: U.S. Government Printing Office, 1970), p. 22.

[46]As a staff economist for the President's Cabinet Task Force on Oil Import Controls and in several articles including "The Longer Supply Curve of Crude Oil Produced in the United States," *Antitrust Bulletin* XV (1970) and "The Cost of Oil Import Controls" in *Oil Prices and Phase II*, Hearings before the Subcommittee on Priorities and Economy in Government of the Joint Economic Committee, 92nd Congress, First Session (Washington: G.P.O., 1972), pp. 56-61.

Table 16

**The FTC's Estimates of the
Domestic Self-sufficiency of 17 Leading
Refiners in 1969***

Company	Self-sufficiency (Percent of runs to stills)
Standard (New Jersey)	87.4
Standard (Indiana)	50.5[a]
Texaco	81.0[b]
Shell	62.1
Standard (California)	68.8[a]
Mobil	42.2[c]
Gulf	87.6[a,d]
ARCO	64.9
Sun	46.7[e]
Union	64.3[a]
Standard (Ohio)	6.7[a]
Phillips	51.8[a]
Ashland[f]	12.6
Continental	64.0
Cities Service	49.9
Getty[g]	137.2[d]
Marathon	88.1

Source: *Preliminary Federal Trade Commission Staff
Report on Its Investigation of the Petroleum Industry* (July 1973), p. 20.
[a]Other liquids included in crude production.
[b]Estimated.
[c]Other liquids included in refinery runs.
[d]Excludes crude processed for company's account.
[e]Crude production includes Canada.
[f]12 months to September 30, 1969.
[g]Includes subsidiaries.

you can only make the companies out as villains. The public attitude toward the
multinational oil companies brings me back to the bad old days of Joe McCarthy.
Then, many of our people, frustrated, angry, and a bit fearful of the unreachable
leaders of the "monolithic Communist bloc," went out determined to find and
bash an enemy at home. Today, unable to do anything about high oil prices,
many of our citizens are inclined to take it out on the multinational oil companies.[47]

Conclusion

There is no evidence that the large vertically integrated oil companies
are presently exercising monopoly power in any of the four major stages of
the oil business: the production of crude oil, the transportation of crude oil

[47]M.A. Adelman, *Statement to the Senate Foreign Relations Committee, Subcommittee
on Multinational Corporations* (January 29, 1975).

and refined products, the refining of crude oil, and the marketing of refined oil products. Indeed, all available evidence supports the opposite inference. Hence, there is neither economic nor legal justification for forcing the integrated oil companies to divest one or more of their major operations. Nevertheless, this has not stopped numerous Congressmen—including several prominent Presidential aspirants—from backing legislation designed to force oil company divestiture on the grounds that this will help to alleviate our present energy problems by eliminating their alleged major cause—the oil companies' monopoly power. Absent Congressional naivete, the real aim of this intellectually dishonest legislation seems dubious: it is politically popular to attack the "monopolistic" oil companies. There are at least three reasons for opposing political pandering of this kind.

The first objection is a practical one. If adopted, divestiture is likely to result in higher (rather than lower) fuel prices since oil companies will have higher costs because divestiture eliminates some real integration economies. (Other papers in this volume discuss integration economies in considerable detail.) Moreover, merely raising the threat of divestiture discourages oil companies from making investments of the magnitude necessary if the United States is to reduce its oil import dependence.

Second, the United States presently faces several very real energy policy questions requiring serious and sustained public attention: How can we reduce our still-growing dependence on insecure and expensive oil imports? How can we reduce the environmental and health risks attributable to the necessarily higher production and consumption of domestic fuels like coal, oil shale, and nuclear power? And, how can the United States guarantee American consumers that they will have access to adequate energy supplies without paying unnecessarily high prices? Finding answers to these questions is of vital importance to all Americans. Both Congress and the President ought to be examining and, at some point, legislating and adopting policies designed to achieve such valuable goals as reducing the monopoly power presently exercised by the OPEC countries, reducing U.S. petroleum demands, and increasing U.S. petroleum supplies.[48] Congress has been especially remiss about tackling this task. Instead, many members have found that it is far easier to rant and rave about the non-existent oil company monopoly problem. Thus, as of year-end 1975, more than two years since the start of the OAPEC oil embargo, the U.S. Congress had avoided passing a single measure that held promise of substantially alleviating any of our energy problems. Americans can only hope that the

---

[48]For elaboration see Richard Mancke, *Squeaking By: U.S. Energy Policy Since the Embargo* (New York: Columbia University Press, 1976).

Congressional practice of benign neglect of our real energy problems does not prove fatal.

The third objection to the oil company divestiture legislation is that, though it will have a short run political payoff, in the long run it will make no contribution to solving our real energy problems and thus the public will eventually realize that it has once again been duped and, as a result, there will be further deterioration in public trust in our political institutions. Obviously, this objection is not restricted to politically attractive attempts to force oil company divestiture—it also applies to the many simplistic and intellectually indefensible decisions that ultimately culminated in the debilitating disasters of Vietnam and Watergate and in the well mentioned but too ambitious social legislation that was passed under the rubric of the Great Society. Today most politicians proudly claim to be statesmen-practitioners of a new, more realistic, and much more honest politics. Their advocacy of intellectually dishonest, but politically popular, legislation aimed at punishing oil companies raises serious doubts as to the truth of their claims.

7

Mitchell poses three criteria for divestiture to be a desirable social policy: (1) the domestic oil industry must be monopolistic; (2) that monopoly must rest on vertical integration; and (3) the benefits of divestiture must outweigh the costs. Mitchell finds that the domestic oil industry is competitive, that vertical divestiture would not make the industry more competitive, and that vertical integration is a widespread business practice that reduces costs. Thus, divestiture fails to meet any of the three posed criteria and would be a mistaken policy.

THE CASE FOR VERTICAL INTEGRATION

STATEMENT OF EDWARD J. MITCHELL*, UNIVERSITY OF MICHIGAN, BEFORE THE SUBCOMMITTEE ON ANTITRUST AND MONOPOLY, COMMITTEE ON THE JUDICIARY, UNITED STATES SENATE—JANUARY 22, 1976

Mr. Chairman and members of the Committee. I am Edward J. Mitchell, Professor of Business Economics at the Graduate School of Business Administration of the University of Michigan and Director of the National Energy Project of the American Enterprise Institute.

I appear today to discuss the wisdom and consequences of forcing vertically integrated petroleum companies to divest themselves of billions of dollars of assets and of reorganizing the U.S. petroleum industry into separate producing, refining, transportation, and marketing companies, each operating at only one stage in the industrial chain.

The ostensible purpose of this coerced reorganization is to make the petroleum industry more competitive and, thereby, lower the price consumers pay for oil products. For this divestiture to have the desired consequences three conditions must be met:

* Director of the National Energy Project at the American Enterprise Institute; Professor of Business Economics at University of Michigan, Graduate School of Business.

(1) the industry must be monopolistic or less than competitive as it stands, with artifically high prices for oil products;

(2) the monopolistic elements in the industry must be contingent upon vertical integration (otherwise vertical divestiture would not destroy the monopoly); and

(3) the benefits of increased competition induced by divestiture must more than offset the loss of the economies of vertical integration.

For vertical divestiture to be sound public policy *each* of these three premises must be valid. If any one is invalid the argument for divestiture fails.

If he is to be taken seriously, an advocate of divestiture must develop strong arguments based on economic logic and objective facts that each of these premises is valid. I believe it is impossible based on the current state of knowledge to establish *any* of the three premises with respectable economic research.

A number of questions or issues bear directly on the divestiture issue and the validity of the three premises. I have dealt with many of them in my research and my conclusions are as follows:

(1) Vertical integration is not presumptively anti-competitive.

(2) Senator Bayh's statement,[1] that "no other industry is so completely vertically integrated" is incorrect; the petroleum industry has a relatively low degree of vertical integration.

(3) The petroleum industry is competitive.

(4) Vertical divestiture would not make the petroleum industry more competitive.

(5) There is no evidence of monopoly profits in the petroleum industry.

(6) There are substantial cost savings from vertical integration including lower operating costs and lower capital costs.

(7) Small non-integrated firms are not squeezed out of the industry and entry by new firms is not difficult.

(8) Vertical integration is not confined to large privately-owned American oil companies; it is common among both small and large, government-owned and privately-owned companies throughout the world.

---

[1]Senator Birch Bayh, "Opening Statement for Anti-trust Monopoly Subcommittee Hearings on Vertical Integration in the Oil Industry," September 23, 1975 (mimeo.), p.3.

Is Vertical Integration Presumptively Anti-Competitive?

A look at the economic literature on vertical integration shows that there is no presumption that vertical integration weakens competition. The majority of writers believe that vertical integration has no weakening effect on competition and indeed that it reduces the harmful effects of monopoly where monopoly does exist. These writers include Bork, Liebler, Peltzman, Spengler, Schmalensee, and Warren-Boulton.[2] A smaller number, notably Edwards and Mueller,[3] believe there are some circumstances where vertical integration permits anti-competitive actions, such as market "squeezes." But even these writers do not find vertical integration presumptively anti-competitive. As Corwin Edwards puts it, vertical integration "tells nothing either about power or abuse of power. Hence it implies neither monopoly nor absence or monopoly. In so far as the monopoly problem is concerned, it is a neutral term."[4]

The prevailing view of economists is that monopoly is a horizontal phenomenon, and that monopoly prices are feasible when a firm or a cartel has a very large share of the market at one particular stage of the production process and has the means to keep other firms from entering and existing firms from expanding. Whether the petroleum industry is competitive or not therefore hinges on market power and freedom of entry at each stage, not in the extent to which firms operate at more than one stage.

Senator Bayh's opening statement at these hearings stresses the degree of concentration in the petroleum of industry as a major issue.[5] I agree that it is a major issue. The statement then goes on to recite the market share of the largest twenty oil companies in production, refining, transportation, and marketing. The Senator then concedes that there are other U.S. industries—many others in fact—that are more concentrated. But, the Senator

---

[2]Bork, R. H., "Vertical Integration and Competitive Processes," in Weston and Peltzman, eds., *Public Policy Towards Mergers,* Pacific Palisades, Calif., 1969; Liebler, W. J., "Toward a Consumer's Anti-Trust Law: The Federal Trade Commission and Vertical Mergers in the Cement Industry," *UCLA Law Review,* Vol. 15, No. 4, June 1968; Peltzman, S., "Issues in Vertical Integration Policy," in Weston and Peltzman, op. cit.; Spengler, J.J., "Vertical Integration and Antitrust Policy," *Journal of Political Economy,* 58, (1950); Schmalensee, R., "A Note on the Theory of Vertical Integration," *Journal of Political Economy,* 81, March-April 1973; and Warren-Boulton, F.R., "Vertical Control and Variable Proportions." *Journal of Political Economy,* 1974, vol. 82, no. 4.

[3]Edwards, C.D., "Vertical Integration and the Monopoly Problem," *Journal of Marketing,* vol. 17, (1953); and Mueller, W.F., "Public Policy Toward Vertical Mergers," in Weston and Peltzman, op. cit.

[4]Edwards, op. cit., p. 404.

[5]Bayh, op. cit., p.2.

tells us, "concentration in the oil industry must not be weighed against concentration in other industries."[6] But what else could an objective person possibly weigh it against?

The impact of the relatively modest degree of concentration in the oil industry is said to be "highly negative."[7] No evidence is offered to support this statement. If it were true, however, it would mean that the impact of concentration in the bulk of the American economy is highly negative, or worse. The attack on the modest levels of concentration in the petroleum industry must therefore be regarded as an attack on American industry itself.

But what would happen to the degree of concentration if a vertical divestiture were accomplished? Nothing! If firms are disassembled vertically there is no effect on the concentration at each stage. Exxon as it stands today is the largest crude producer in the United States. Exxon Production, the crude producer created by divestiture, would be the largest crude producer in the United States with the same market share as before. Indeed, the parade of statistics showing the shares of each market held by the twenty largest companies at *each* stage would not be changed one iota by vertical divestiture. Concentration at each stage would remain as it is now—modest—and competition would remain as it is now—aggressive. Thus, the argument that vertical divestiture would enhance competition is unfounded.

Is No Other Industry so Completely Vertically Integrated?

To answer this question requires a definition of vertical integration that permits comparisons between different industries. Three measures have been proposed. In Appendix A I explain why two of these measures must be rejected and why one measure, although imperfect, does have some validity. This is the ratio of the "net income" (y) of a firm to its sales (s), where "net income" is defined to be the sum of wages and salaries, profits before taxes, and interest on debt. This measure, originally proposed by Professor M.A. Adelman,[8] is in fact a measure of *backward* integration only, but it is the best we have. It is not clear that a measure of *forward* integration can be defined that would be useful for comparing different industries.

---

[6] *Ibid.*, p.3.

[7] *Ibid.*, p.3.

[8] Adelman, M., "Concept and Statistical Measurement of Vertical Integration," in *Business Concentration and Public Policy*, National Bureau of Economic Research, Princeton (1955).

Application of this y/s measure to American industry has been undertaken by Adelman (op. cit.) and by Gort.[9] Adelman's conclusions are displayed in Table I below taken directly from his 1955 article. (p. 302). They show that the petroleum industry is the second least integrated industry of the nineteen manufacturing industry groups. Separate calculations from corporate reports for the same year on 183 large corporations confirm this finding. Of the nineteen manufacturing industries petroleum emerges as the third least integrated.

Calculations similar to Adelman's were made by Gort, except that Gort used the ratio of value added to shipments for the year 1954. It is

TABLE I

Ratio of all Corporate Income to all Corporate Sales by Manufacturing Industry Groups, 1919

(dollars in millions; ratios in per cent)

Industry Group	Wages and Salaries	Profits before Taxes	Interest Paid	Total Income	Sales	Ratio of Income to Sales
Food and kindred products	$4,103	$1,600	$ 71.2	$5,775	$36,167	16.0
Tobacco manufacturers	218	250	20.6	488	1,714	28.5
Textile mill products	3,131	596	31.6	3,761	10,602	35.5
Apparel and related products	2,086	142	7.4	2,235	7,896	28.3
Lumber and lumber products (except furniture)	970	228	7.6	1,204	3,061	39.4
Furniture and fixtures	1,218	97	6.6	1,320	3,082	42.8
Paper and allied products	1,496	547	22.6	2,066	5,301	39.0
Printing and publishing	2,444	249	13.3	2,707	6,067	44.6
Chemicals and allied products	2,504	1,475	38.7	4,017	13,355	30.0
Petroleum and coal products	2,041	2,446	126.8	4,614	18,450	25.0
Rubber products	785	181	10.1	977	3,088	31.6
Leather and leather products	900	83	5.6	988	2,750	35.9
Stone, clay, and glass products	1,421	522	8.7	1,952	3,917	49.8
Iron and steel and their products	6,123	2,042	83.1	8,253	19,921	41.4
Nonferrous metals and their products	1,604	477	28.2	2,109	5,587	37.8
Machinery (except electrical)	4,635	1,305	21.9	5,962	13,139	45.4
Electrical Machinery	2,496	629	16.6	3,140	8,466	37.1
Transportation equipment	4,426	2,199	16.0	6,642	18,963	35.0
Miscellaneous manufacturers	1,366	290	18.3	1,673	3,229	51.8

Source: Census of Mineral Industries: 1939. Bureau of the Census; Statistics of Income for 1946, Bureau of Internal Revenue; Quarterly Industrial Financial Report Series for 1946 and 1949. Federal Trade Commission and Securities and Exchange Commission; Census of Manufacturers: 1947. Bureau of the Census; National Income Supplement, 1951, Survey of Current Business. Department of Commerce.

[9]Gort, M., *Diversification and Integration in American Industry,* National Bureau of Economic Research, Princeton (1962). Gort prefers another measure to Y/S, but his preferred measure is irreparably flawed. See Appendix B.

unclear to me from reading Gort how faithful Gort's measure is to Adelman's definition. Table II reproduces table 30 from his book.[10] It shows petroleum to be the least vertically integrated of the thirteen industries, and by a rather wide margin.

These results may come as some surprise to oil men who often seem to regard their industry as highly vertically integrated. But a simple list of important contributions to the value of petroleum products that are usually or frequently not made by so-called integrated firms will serve to clarify the issue. Oil companies rarely build their own refineries, tankers, pipelines, or gasoline stations. Yet in a capital intensive industry depreciation of these items forms a significant part of the sales dollar. Also some equipment is leased rather than purchased, eliminating the rate of return as well as the depreciation component. For example, production departments frequently lease drilling rigs. Bonus payments and royalties form an important part of the sales dollar but accrue to the original owners of the petroleum resources, as a return to the efforts of "nature," not to the oil companies.

Both the Adelman and the Gort data show that larger firms do not tend to be more vertically integrated than smaller firms.[11] This is true for the petroleum industry and most other industries studied by them. This confirms research on the physical measures of vertical integration in the petroleum industry by Livingston and by McLean and Haigh.[12] Livingston found that the twenty largest domestic refiners in 1960 had an average ratio of crude production to refinery runs of 49.7 percent, while of the next twenty-five largest refiners, eighteen published appropriate data and their average ratio was 44 percent. McLean and Haigh show that in 1950 the largest eighteen refiners had a production-refining ratio of 50.0%, the ten next largest refiners had a ratio of 59.8%, and the fifteen next largest had a ratio of 21.2 percent. Still smaller refiners averaged somewhat higher than 21 percent.

Thus, in the petroleum industry integration from refining into crude remains at a fairly constant level until we move past the largest thirty firms or thereabouts. The top 28 firms (those with capacities of 30,000 b/d or greater) accounted for 87 percent of refining capacity in 1950. Very small (5,000b/d or less) refiners had smaller production-refining ratios than the larger firms, but higher ratios of service station sales of gasoline to gasoline

---

[10]*Ibid.*, p. 83.

[11]Adelman, op. cit., p. 82ff., Gort, op. cit., p. 84.

[12]Statement of Morris Livingston before the U.S. District Court for the Northern District of California, Southern Division, in the case of U.S.A. vs. Standard Oil Co. (Indiana), Civil No. 40212; and McLean and Haigh, *The Growth of Integrated Oil Companies,* Harvard University Press. 1954.

TABLE II
Ratios of Value Added to Shipments, 589 Manufacturing Companies Grouped on the Basis of Industry and Employment Size, 1954

Primary Industry of Company	Ratios for Size Classes[a]										Industry Mean	Coefficient of Variation (per cent)
	(4)	(4)	(12)	(10)	(10)	(10)	(10)	(10)	(10)	(10)		
Food products	.209	.356	.309	.349	.404	.422	.377	.419	.342(8)		.364	43.1
Textile mill products	.339	.395	.386	.406	.455	.346	.402	.447(6)			.399	25.8
Paper products	.452	.367	.379	.436	.409(9)						.406	23.4
Chemicals	.553	.513	.496	.438	.529	.512	.404				.492	30.1
Petroleum and coal	.179	.145	.239	.147(7)							.193	56.5
Rubber products	.434	.468	.440(4)								.447	17.7
Stone, clay, and glass products	.617	.583	.577								.586	16.2
Primary metals	.370	.359	.338	.512	.481	.492					.436	28.2
Fabricated metal products	.446	.497	.554	.503(7)							.516	20.7
Machinery[b]	.479	.551	.554	.562	.572	.561	.654	.611	.580	.763(8)	.594	21.5
Electrical machinery	.535	.526	.445	.565	.571	.516					.522	23.4
Transportation equipment	.339	.529	.508	.475	.492	.476	.492(4)				.481	24.3
Instruments	.583	.582	.659(10)								.625	16.6

Source: Special census tabulation.

[a] Included are all multiestablishment companies in the specified industries with total employment of 2,500 and over, except for six companies for which data could not be shown for reasons of disclosure of individual company information. Numbers in parentheses indicate the number of companies represented in the class. The first class consists of the largest four, the second, the next four, etc. Numbers in parentheses in the body of the table show the number of companies in a cell where the numbers differ from those in the column head.

[b] Except electrical.

yields. While backward integration was less for very small refiners, forward integration was actually greater.[13]

The fallacy of associating vertical integration with monopoly power can be illustrated from the Adelman and Gort statistics. A well-known textbook on the economics of industry properly asserts that "Among our major manufacturing industries, textile production comes as close as any to meeting the formal requirements of pure competition."[14] Adelman's figures show textiles 40 percent more integrated than petroleum and Gort's show it 100 percent more integrated than petroleum. Furthermore, Gort's data show that the smaller textile firms are typically more vertically integrated than the larger ones.

To push the point to its extreme, if one wishes to see the epitome of an integrated firm one merely has to drive to the nearest small farmer's roadside fruit and vegetable stand!

If we take the Adelman and Gort figures at face value and if we were to accept the view that vertical integration is bad, then the Congress has its divestiture priorities all wrong. Before it starts forcing divestiture on the petroleum industry it ought, at the least, get the rest of the U.S. manufacturing industry down to the same level of integration as petroleum. To do this would require the average U.S. manufacturing firm outside of petroleum to divest itself of assets and employees accounting for 33 percent (using Adelman's figures) or 60 percent (using Gort's) of its operations.

Are There Cost Savings From Vertical Integration?

Vertical integration means nothing more than substituting internal organization for the market. A firm always has two decisions to make for each product:

(1) to buy it or to make it;

(2) to sell it or to process it further.

When a firm chooses to make or to process further it vertically integrates. It does so because it is less costly to internalize than to use the market.

I defer to few in my appreciation of the social utility of markets. Nevertheless there are conditions where markets are inferior to internal organization.

---

[13]McLean and Haigh, op. cit., p. 43.
[14]Weiss, L. *Economics and American Industry,* J. Wiley and Sons, New York 1961, p. 121.

The first condition is where transactions costs are high, a point originally developed by Coase.[15] The second condition is where information is available more quickly and/or more cheaply to the integrating firm than to outsiders, a point raised by Adelman[16] and developed by Arrow.[17] Most businessmen defend vertical integration on grounds of supply or market reliability, or costs of capital and reduction of risk. As we shall see, these points are valid but are more properly subsumed under the two conditions just given.

Market exchange is costly. It is especially costly when the contractual arrangements entered into by the parties can not adequately guarantee what each party wants, as is common in the petroleum industry. Indeed, it may be impossible to write for firms to arrive at a useful contractual arrangement.

By the costliness or impossibility of "contractual arrangements" I mean to include the problem of formulating any rule of behavior that prescribes detailed courses of action to be adopted in the face of complex future contingencies. Thus the "contractual arrangement" includes far more than the kinds of contracts known in everyday life. It includes any rule laid down in advance that would formally describe all the necessary adjustments in operations that would be made by each party in the future. Such a "contract" in many instances would be inordinately expensive, enormously time consuming, or even impossible to achieve. In general, the greater the complexity and uncertainty, the more costly it will be to devise a contractual arrangement that would adequately specify all future contingencies affecting the parties and adequately specify what each party must do.

Often, it is to avoid these problems that firms integrate. Unfortunately, some of the older economic literature (and some not so old) associated vertical integration with purely technical or engineering considerations and therefore assumed very narrow limits on vertical economies. For example J. Bain's well-known textbook *Industrial Organization*[18] (of which I possess a 1968 edition) states that:

the cases of clear economies of integration generally involve a physical or technical integration of the processes in a single plant. A classic case is that of integrating iron-making and steel-making to effect a saving in fuel costs by eliminating a reheating of the iron before it is fed to a steel furnace. Where integration does

---

[15]Coase, R., "The Nature of the Firm," *Economica* (Nov. 1937), 4; and Coase, R., "The Problem of Social Cost," *Journal of Law and Economics*.

[16]Adelman, op. cit., pp. 318-320.

[17]Arrow, K., "Vertical Integration and Communication," *Bell Journal of Law and Economics,* Vol. 6, No. 1, Spring 1975.

[18]New York, (1968).

not have this physical or technical aspect—as it does not, for example, in integrating the production of assorted components with the assembly of those components—the case for cost savings from integration is generally much less clear.[19]

Bain admittedly based these conclusions on "miscellaneous scraps of evidence" while noting the "lack of systematic research endeavor."[20] Unfortunately this narrow and highly conjectural view has influenced a number of policy makers.

The more modern view, stemming in large part from Coase[21] is summed up by Williamson:

In more numerous respects than are commonly appreciated the substitution of internal organization for market exchange is attractive less on account of technological economies associated with production but because of that may be referred to broadly as "transactional failures" in the operations of markets for intermediate goods.[22]

It appears that some Senators and staff still retain the older, narrow view associating vertical integration solely with technical considerations, as evidenced by their concept of an efficient-sized firm. In defense of their proposed cut-off points for the size of integrated operations permihted under the divestiture bill, Senators Nelson, G. Hart, P. Hart, and Abourezk offer the argument that the most efficient size of a refinery is 150 to 200 thousand barrels per day.[23] But the optimal sized *plant* is largely a technical concept. The optimal sized firm, vertically and horizontally, is an economic concept. (It is peculiar that no senator ever offers a bill banning refineries less than 150 thousand barrels per day if that is really the minimum efficient size.) To determine the optimal-sized firm requires economic and financial information far beyond that required to determine the optimal-sized plant. Furthermore, what is optimal in one place is sub-optimal in another. Many refineries would become suboptimal in size if moved 100 miles from their present site.

Under what circumstances are contractual or market costs likely to become so costly as to lead to economically motivated internalization or integration? At least two are important:

---

[19]*Ibid.,* p. 381.

[20]*Ibid.,* p. 381.

[21]Coase, op. cit.

[22]Williamson, O., "The Vertical Integration of Production: Market Failure Considerations," *American Economic Review,* Vo., LXI, No. 2, May 1971, p. 112.

[23]Attachment of letter to Senate colleagues from Senators J. Abourezk, G. Hart, P. Hart, and G. Nelson, (mimeo.), p. 6.

First, when the investments associated with performance of the contract are long-term. When investments are short-term, contractual problems or mistakes can be continuously corrected and sequentially improving contracts can be arranged with the same or other parties. When the investments are long term one may never get a chance to correct a contractual imperfection.

Second, when the investments associated with the agreement are highly specific and have an extremely low value in alternative uses.

Both circumstances arise, for example, if a refinery is built to handle a specific type of crude. The refinery is a long-lived investment. It may be that costs can be lowered by designing it specifically for a certain type of crude, but this makes it more vulnerable to any contractual performance problems that should arise since the alternative sources of the particular crude must be narrower than the crude market as a whole.

Failure to allow a firm to integrate vertically by owning its crude supply or the gathering system and pipeline for this crude force the firm to build a less specific and higher cost refinery (in other words a less vulnerable one) since there may be no contract that can satisfactorily replace ownership and direct control.

Some transactional costs of using the market can be seen when there is a contract dispute. Each side of the dispute has an incentive to haggle up to the point where the marginal cost of haggling (including litigation) equals the expected marginal benefit. But haggling is a zero-sum game; what one party gains the other loses. The haggling costs are therefore a net loss to the two parties collectively and to society as a whole. If the parties to the dispute were departments within the same organization a general manager would perceive the waste involved in the intraorganizational haggling and settle the dispute quickly by arbitrary fiat. This may be less equitable to one of the departments but it will usually be less costly to the firm.

A specific example of contracting problems in the petroleum industry is given by Standard of Ohio's attempts to arrange satisfactory long-term supplies of crude oil without actually integrating into crude production.[24] After the dissolution of the Standard Oil trust in 1911 Standard Oil Company (Ohio) was left as a small refiner and marketer operating within the state of Ohio and without crude production. "During the 1920s Sohio lost a large share of the Ohio market" and "by 1928 the company's competitive and economic position had become so precarious that a new management

---

[24]McLean and Haigh, *The Growth of Integrated Oil Companies*, Harvard University Press, 1954, pp. 239ff.

and an entirely new board of directors was placed in charge of the company's affairs."[25] In 1930 the new management attempted to solve its crude supply problems. It entered into a long-term contract for crude supplies with Carter Oil Company sufficient to meet all its refining needs. It further entered into an agreement with Standard Oil Company (New Jersey) and the Pure Oil Company to build a crude trunk line from the source of the Carter crude in Oklahoma to Illinois, where the crude could then be moved to Sohio refineries via existing common carrier pipelines. The agreement called for paying posted (market) prices for the crude plus fixed charges for purchasing and gathering services.

Two problems arose subsequent to the agreement. First, Sohio management concluded shortly after the initiation of the arrangement that the fixed charges for purchasing and gathering services were too high. It spent the early and middle 1920's attempting to reduce the rates with only partial success. Second, prolific crude fields were developed in the late 1930's in Illinois and the price of that crude delivered to Ohio refineries was lower than the cost of the Oklahoma crude. This made the crude Sohio contracted for non-competitive in Ohio, although presumably competitive in the southwest. "The situation became so difficult that Sohio was compelled to inform the Carter Oil Company that it could no longer comply with provisions of the crude oil purchase contract. Fortunately, Carter did not seek the legal recourse available to it under the contract and permitted Sohio to withdraw from the arrangement.

"In retrospect it appears therefore that Sohio's effort to assure its crude supplies by means of the long-term contract in 1930 eventually created more difficulties for the company than it solved."[26]

The contractual difficulties arose for Sohio because it did not anticipate in the contract the *possibility* of two events. First, crude prices plummeted in the 30's and the gathering and purchasing charges were in *fixed* not *percentage* terms. To quote the Sohio management: "at the present price of crude, it represents approximately 23 percent of the value of the crude itself—a rather ridiculous amount or percentage for a brokerage fee to bear to the cost of the product. . ."[27] Second, the temporary cheap supplies of nearby crude made the Oklahoma crude non-competitive in Ohio. (If Sohio had owned the crude outright it could have simply held production back for future use, or sold the crude locally without the high gathering and purchasing charges. Under the contract neither option was available.)

---

[25] *Ibid.*, p. 240.
[26] *Ibid.*, p. 246.
[27] *Ibid.*, p. 244.

The contract provided for neither contingency and was thus, in retrospect, incomplete. (Subsequently, Sohio embarked on a program of integration backward into crude. Under the terms of its recent agreement with BP it will become a crude-rich integrated company with enormous Alaskan production.)

A second condition favoring vertical integration is that knowledge can often be communicated faster and more cheaply within an organization than between two firms through the marketplace. This point originates with Adelman[28] who believes that vertical integration often occurs in rapidly growing or changing industries where the perception of what upstream or downstream facilities are required occurs much earlier to the integrating firm than to potential entrants into the new markets.

If we start with an industry in its earliest years, when it is an innovation, it is at first adapted to and fills a niche in the existing structure of markets and of factor supply. It is essentially a rearrangement of known and available resources. Few can discern its large possibilities for growth and for pushing the capacity of supplying industries and firms. The railroads were originally feeders to canals and turnpikes, and, later, pipelines and trucks were considered as feeders to railroads; the automobile was a rich man's toy; wireless transmission of signals was intended for ship-to-shore telegraphy; and many other examples might be given.

As the firms and their industry grow, they do so under the forced draft of demand chronically in excess of supply at prevailing prices. This economic tension is transmitted to the factor markets as the firms bid not only for increasing amounts but for changing composition of factors. As larger quantities are needed, some factors become relatively scarce and substitution must be resorted to, often by painful trial and error. Economies of scale now appear, as Stigler rightly insists; my point is that they appear unforeseen and generally lagging behind a keenly felt need. A sluggish response will often force the growing firm to provide its own supplies and/or marketing outlets.[29]

This motive for vertical integration has been extended from the case of a rapidly changing industry to the more general and omnipresent case of firms facing uncertain shifts in supply and demand conditions by Nobel Laureate Kenneth Arrow.[30] So long as these shifts can be communicated within an organization faster and more cheaply than through the market the economy of vertical integration exists.

Perhaps the best example of this motive for integration in the petroleum industry is the case cited by Adelman above: oil pipelines. The knowledge of where and when a crude pipeline ought to be built must occur

[28]Adelman, op. cit., pp. 318-320.
[29]Adelman, opt. cit., p. 319.
[30]Arrow, op. cit.

to producer-refiner intent on transporting crude supplies before it occurs to anyone else. The producer-refiner can plan his pipeline and his refinery in parallel. Other potential suppliers of pipeline services obviously do not have access to the same detailed information day by day in the planning process that the refiner himself has. Even if a producer-refiner should choose to communicate his plans each day to a number of potential pipeline companies this would be a more costly and less timely approach than simply keeping its own transportation department in close touch with its producing and refining departments.

This communications or planning motive for integration is greatly reinforced by the transactions cost motive in the case of pipelines. An oil pipeline is among the longer-lived and most specific investments one can make. Once built it can move liquids between point A and point B. That is all it can do. If one builds a pipeline on the basis of a contractual arrangement and later finds the arrangement faulty the error would not be correctible and would prove extremely costly.

For this reason crude oil pipelines are almost never built by anyone but integrated companies. Non-integrated pipelines—crude or product—have been the exception. Even in the twenties and thirties when the rapidly expanding pipeline industry offered ostensibly high rates of return to attract new investments hardly any non-integrated companies chose to enter the industry and the building of new lines was left almost entirely to integrated companies.

Lest one believe that there was anything artificial or contrived about these arrangements we have only to look at the sorry experience of non-integrated oil pipelines created by the forced divestiture of Standard Oil in 1911. Arthur Johnson, at the conclusion of his massive two-volume history of U.S. oil pipelines,[31] summarizes the divestiture consequences:

> *Although the 1911 decision eventually added to the number of independent, integrated companies, it could not—and did not—end the interdependence of pipelines and refiners. None of the refining companies divorced from the combination remained without pipelines of their own two decades later, and most had found it necessary to integrate backward sooner than that. The pipeline companies separated from the combination found themselves just as dependent on Standard companies' patronage as before the dissolution. Because initially the dependence was reciprocal, they made few changes in operating practices and rates. This policy, plus the changing location of oil production and consumption*

---

[31]Johnson, A. M. *The Development of American Petroleum Pipelines: A Study in Private Enterprise and Public Policy, 1862-1906,* Cornell U. Press (1956); and Johnson, A. M., *Petroleum Pipelines and Public Policy, 1906-1959,* Harvard U. Press (1967).

centers, contributed to the decline or demise of most of the independent disaffiliated pipeline companies by the early 1930's.

Limited disintegration of the most powerful element in the oil industry by antitrust action, then, failed to produce a viable, independent pipeline sector.[32]

As mentioned earlier, businessmen do not usually couch their arguments for vertical integration in terms of contractual or communication problems. Typically, they will think in terms of the importance of reliable supplies, assured markets, the reduction of risk, and lower financing costs. Yet, while seemingly different, the businessman is saying the same thing as the economist. When the businessman says he must acquire an upstream supplier to assure reliable supplies he is saying (in our language) that it is impossible to write an ironclad and complete contract with an upstream supplier that gives him the assurances he needs to run his plant efficiently, or that no upstream company has acquired the knowledge as to exactly what he requires and is not likely to do so in the near future. In brief, because of the impracticability of perfect contracting or the lack of communication of his needs, it is cheaper and more timely for the businessman to do it himself.

The lower risks and reduced costs of capital often cited as an advantage of vertical integration also stem from transactional advantages of the integrated firm. The integrated firm can be viewed as a chain of business entities that are better able to enter into long-term complete contracts, while the non-integrated firm can be viewed as one of a chain of business entities that is constrained to deal more often in spot markets because of contractual problems. Possessing long-term assurances on the terms of the supply of its raw materials and the demand for its product each department of an integrated firm can plan for and realize a less variable level of output and less variable unit costs in the face of fluctuations in demand and supply at each stage of the market. Knowing with more certainty its future level of operations permits the integrated firm to

(1) incur lower average costs since knowledge of future rates of operation generally permits more specialized (less flexible) facilities; and

(2) incur smaller variations in levels of output and hence smaller variations in average unit cost.

This second advantage results in less variable profits and hence a less risky investment for the stockholders and bondholders of the integrated firm.

---

[32]Johnson, *Petroleum Pipelines . . . ,* p. 471.

As an example of the way in which lower and less variable costs can be achieved by integration consider the matter of inventories. Because fluctuations in demand are smaller and because information about market conditions in the downstream operations can be communicated to and from upstream operations more quickly than through the market the integrated firm need hold a lower quantity of stocks than its non-integrated counterparts. This lower level of inventories means

(1) lower carrying costs of inventories per unit of sales; and

(2) smaller fluctuations in inventory values as crude and product prices vary and hence smaller variations in unit sales cost.[33]

The lower variability of operations of integrated refiners is strongly confirmed in by the survey of McLean and Haigh. In 1950 "the typical integrated refining company was able to maintain refinery runs equal to 81.6 percent of its operating and shutdown capacity whereas the typical non-integrated company was able to maintain refinery runs equal to only 54.3 percent of its operating and shutdown capacity."[34]

Most significant, McLean and High find that integration is a far more decisive factor in determining operating rates than size. ". . . although the larger refining companies typically had higher levels of refinery runs than did the smaller ones, the differences among companies of different sizes were significantly less than the differences between the companies in the integrated and non-integrated groups . . . moreover . . . the differences *between* successive size groups were characteristically less than the differences between the integrated and nonintegrated companies *within* each size group."[35]

Another attempt to reduce the variability of operating rates is sought in the marketing operation of some integrated firms. In the highly competitive and volatile gasoline market firms often sell gasoline to service stations which feature convenient location, credit, and other consumer services. This availability of gasoline with service is advertised and greater customer loyalty is sought. By appealing to "regular customers" cross-elasticities of demand among different gasolines are reduced. The reduced volatility of sales created by this approach enables the firm to operate at less variable

---

[33]Although lower inventory/sales ratios are possible for integrated firms they may in fact choose larger inventories in order to further smooth the levels of operations. My point is that for a given degree of "smoothness" in operating rates inventories will tend to be lower for the integrated firm. On the choices available and the advantages of integrated firms, see McLean and Haigh, op. cit., pp. 312-318.

[34]*Ibid.*, p.40.

[35]*Ibid.*, p. 40., italics in original.

rates and therefore to reduce operating costs and reduce the variability of operating costs, thereby making profits less erratic and lowering investor risk. With competition among many companies adopting this approach the benefits of lower operating and capital costs are passed on to the consumer in the form of lower prices.

Integrated refiners seem to have adopted this approach more commonly than non-integrated refiners, according to the 1950 survey of McLean and High. The typical integrated company converted 43.4 percent of its refinery runs to gasoline and naphtha whereas the typical non-integrated company secured a gasoline and naphtha yield of only 27.0 percent. Again, "the variations in the typical ratios among different sizes of refinery companies were less than between integrated and non-integrated companies. . . . many of the nonintegrated refiners have elected to concentrate on specialty products, other than gasoline, where the lack of well-recognized brand names is not a handicap to them."[36]

My theory of the risk-reducing aspect of vertical integration has the following empirical implications:

(1) output rates of integrated firms fluctuate less than those of non-integrated firms,

(2) unit final sales prices of integrated firms fluctuate less than those of non-integrated firms;

(3) integrated firms attempt to differentiate their products and advertise more than non-integrated firms.

(4) profits of integrated firms fluctuate less than those of non-integrated firms;

(5) investors regard integrated firms as less risky than non-integrated firms and offer capital at a lower cost to integrated firms than to non-integrated firms.

From the foregoing arguments and evidence one might form the impression that vertical integration is always economically superior to non-integration. That is not the case. The arguments made above are general and, in general, integration in the petroleum industry is presumed to be superior. Nevertheless, there are many special circumstances in which the benefits of integration can be realized without actual integration. Also, like all good things integration has its costs, and the benefits of integration are subject to diminishing returns. Beyond some point further integration may yield no reductions in unit costs or further stability in profits. Indeed, as will be

---

[36]*Ibid.*, p. 41.

shown below, integration from refining backward into crude will, beyond a certain point, make a firm less stable.

Perhaps the most important situation in which refinery integration into crude or transportation yields no benefits that are not already realizable without integration is the case of what might be called "geographical advantage." Often a small oil field is discovered lying under an existing market. If the size of the market is smaller than the producing rate of the field a refinery equal to the size of the market will be built to use the local crude, the excess crude being transported to the next closest refinery. The local refinery is assumed to be below the optimal scale of refineries. Thus, only one refinery will be built locally to handle the local crude.

This local refinery has no motivation to integrate. Its supply of crude is assured. Its market is assured. The next closest refinery, which is purchasing at least some of the same crude, cannot bid away the local refinery's crude supply or its customers unless it is so much more efficient that it can pay the transport cost *to* and *from* its refinery and still offer more for the local crude or undercut the local refiner's product price.

While a larger refinery will be more efficient than a smaller one (up to about 150,000 bpd, as noted before) the existence of many small crude fields and markets distant from large refineries coupled with the high cost of moving small volumes of oil suggest that it will be common for the local refiner to have an enormous transportation or geographic advantage over the nearest competing refineries. In all such circumstances the local refiner has no need to integrate into production or marketing to achieve the transactional efficiencies of an integrated firm.

A second and very similar case is where the local crude supply is smaller than the local market. In this case the local refinery will be built to handle all of the local crude. The remaining part of the market will be supplied from outside. The costs of product from outside will set the local product price. The local refiner will have no control over that. However, the local refiner will be in a position to influence the local crude price. Since he can acquire the local crude to some extent on his own terms he can always compete in the local product market and sell all of his output, backing out some non-local product if necessary. Again, the local refiner has an assured supply and an assured market and can plan accordingly. He can thus achieve many of the efficiencies of integration without actually integrating.

An example of the first type of local refiner with geographic advantage was the Shallow Water Refining Company.[37] The company owned a very

---

[37]McLean and Haigh, op. cit., pp. 633-639.

small (3000 bpd) refinery located in western Kansas. The nearest competing refinery was in Wichita, 200 miles away. The transportation advantage over this refinery was 1.5 to 2 cents per gallon, which amounted to a 58¢ to 77¢ per barrel advantage on refinery runs. The total cost of refining per barrel, even for so small and inefficient a plant, averaged 54.7¢ per barrel. With crude oil at the local fields selling at the same price for all refiners, there was no way for outside refiners to undersell Shallow Water.

Shallow Water did not own or lease any marketing facilities. The output of the refinery was transported overwhelmingly by outside truck haulers. The company owned no pipelines. Significantly, the stockholders of Shallow Water did own the pipeline company that supplied about one-third of its crude, but this was not integrated into the operations of the refining company. Quite possibly the motive here was to get the pipeline built quickly (see Adelman above, p. 18), and obviously not to coordinate refining and pipeline operations. Some of the remaining crude was brought in by railroad and some by company trucks. Only after ten years of operation (1937-1946) did the company enter into any crude oil producing activities. Entry on a relatively small scale apparently assured the firm that production for some pools would be maintained as the natural rate of decline proceeded. In general, "Its strategic location assured the company that whatever crude oil was available in the area would be diverted to the refinery."[38]

Ashland Oil and Refining Company, operating in the Kentucky-West Virginia region during the 1920's and 1930's provides a similar example.[39]

There are no data available that show with any precision the extent of non-integration due to "geographical advantage." However, some data put together by Cookenboo[40] bear upon the question. Cookenboo classified refineries as "market-oriented," "crude-oriented," or at "nodal" transshipment points. He then classified refiners as "independent" or "major" and observed the relationship between these classifications. Unfortunately the major-independent classification is of little use for our purposes (if indeed it is useful for any purposes other than political rhetoric). Nevertheless, it is probably true that the bulk of the non-integrated refinery capacity is in the "independent" category. Cookenboo finds that 60 percent of "small independents" capacity is purely "crude-oriented," while only

[38]*Ibid.*, p. 638.

[39]*Ibid.*, pp. 639-641.

[40]L. Cookenboo, *Crude Oil Pipelines and Competition in the Oil Industry,* Harvard University Press, (1955).

12 percent of "major" capacity is.[41] This is consistent with the existence of many small non-integrated "geographically advantaged" companies among the "small independents." (It does not *prove* that much of the non-integrated capacity is "crude-oriented" or "geographically advantaged" because, while "non-integrated" tends to imply "small independent," "small independent" does not necessarily imply "non-integrated.")

Since it has been my primary purpose to explain the benefits and motivations of vertical integration I have neglected two important questions:

(1) Why petroleum companies don't integrate into some activities; and

(2) Why petroleum companies normally do not integrate fully into their integrated activities.

The answer to the first question consists of several parts. First, it is obvious that some parts of the industry do not involve long-lived or specific investments. Offshore drilling rigs, for example, are highly mobile. They can be used for relatively brief periods in one location and then be moved on to another location. Offshore drilling rigs are therefore commonly rented rather than bought. Second, the activity into which the petroleum company considers integrating may only be efficiently performed by a firm that performs many other tasks unrelated to the petroleum industry.[42] For example, firms that build and design refineries also build and design other industrial facilities. There are no pure refinery-building firms,—just engineering and construction firms that build a wide range of facilities. (A firm that built only refineries might find itself totally unemployed at times. The construction business is sufficiently erratic as it stands without further destabilizing demand by narrow specialization.) Thus, if the integrated firm were to efficiently enter the refinery construction business it would have to acquire or create a construction company. This would take the oil company far afield from its areas of expertise and know-how. The diseconomies of managing greatly differing businesses would set in. Third, the potentially integrated business may be one that the firm has only irregular use for. For example, seismographic work may be required only on particular occasions. It will commonly be cheaper therefore to hire a firm that serves many

41Cookenboo, op. cit., p. 52.

42M. Canes, "The Vertical Integration of Oil Firms," American Petroleum Institute (May 1975), mimeo, p. 25.

clients and finds itself highly employed than to set up a seismographic division that cannot be used productively on a regular basis.[43]

Even when a petroleum company integrates into a particular activity it normally does not integrate fully; that is, the average operating rates or capacities of the production, refining, marketing, and transportation sectors, are not perfectly equated. As elaborated above, the transactional advantages of integration are equivalent to the advantages of perfect long-term contracts as opposed to using the spot market. The advantages of long-term contracts are, in turn, the cost savings yielded by the ability to plan with greater certainty regarding the future and to specialize facilities with regard to inputs, outputs and the level of operations, plus the lower capital costs associated with more stable operating rates, sales revenue and profits.

But trading in spot markets has its advantages, too. It permits greater flexibility and enables the firm to take advantage of changing profit opportunities at different times and places by shifting purchases and sales among markets. Thus, the firm must always balance the benefits of long-term as opposed to spot trading. We must suppose that in general the benefits of each approach diminish as we employ that approach more and more. At some point a balance is struck that optimizes profits and risk. A priori we cannot say where that balance will occur for each firm.

Consider the case of refining-production integration. Often, it happens that a refiner integrates into production rather than the other way around. That is, the refiner is highly motivated to acquire an assured crude supply, while the crude producer is relatively less concerned about acquiring assured markets. The reason for this is partly a function of the nature of each business and partly a function of the institutions created in the production area. The failure to use crude oil production capacity now means that crude must be sold later, that cash inflow is postponed, and therefore that the present discounted value of the crude is reduced. The failure to use refinery capacity leads not only to this postponement of cash flow, but also to a deterioration in the refinery unrelated to its use. Refineries depreciate with age as well as use, while crude oil capacity depreciates (depletes) almost only with use. Thus, by the nature of the activity the refiner is more highly motivated to operate his plant near capacity levels of utilization.

The institutions of market demand prorationing and rateable take laws in effect assure an individual producer that he will produce a "fair" share of

---

[43]The firm could offer the services of its seismographic crews for sale to other firms when not in use, but the value of their crews to competing firms may be perceived as considerably lower than the value of the services of an independent firm.

the total crude produced in a state. Market demand prorationing allocates production among producers so as to prevent some producers from displacing the production of others. Rateable-take laws ensure that gathering lines acquire crude from producers in proportion to their production and thus assure that once produced the crude oil will be sold. While these institutions do not work perfectly they do reduce enormously the fluctuations in demand for the crude oil of individual producers. There is no comparable institution for refiners.

Thus, it is refiners who will be more interested in acquiring long-term assurances of crude supplies while the motivation of producers to integrate forward into refining is less. How far will a refiner choose to integrate into production? This would seem to depend upon a number of factors, including:

(1) the location of the refineries relative to crude sources and transport facilities;

(2) the specificity of crude used;

(3) the propensity of management to assume risks;

(4) the capabilities of management in spot-trading.

Even when all these factors are known the magnitude of integration could not be predicted well if integration is attempted through exploration as opposed to acquisition of proved reserves. The same dollar investment in integration via exploration may yield very different quantities of crude capacity and have different degrees of realized integration.

The uncertainty of exploration is itself a deterrent to integration. The acquisition of assured crude supplies through exploration is a riskier activity than refining. Thus, acquisition of crude via exploration decreases the risks to the refining department of an integrated firm but this is offset to a degree by the fact that the overall firm is undertaking more riskier investments in the producing department. At low levels of integration into crude the reduction of risk and costs in refining will probably more than offset the added riskiness of investments in production. As the level of integration grows the incremental cost and risk advantages to the refining department will decline while the incremental risks incurred in production will remain high. (Incremental risks in production could decline somewhat with the magnitude of exploration if diversification is practiced.)

Focussing on risk alone a refiner at 100 percent self-sufficiency in crude only increases the riskiness of the firm when it expands crude production beyond that point. Indeed, the trade-offs may be such that the riskiness of the firm is at a minimum long before 100 percent self-sufficiency is reached.

If one looks at the statistics on integration of refiners into production one finds that the different choices made by firms in varying circumstances plus the varying degrees of success realized in exploration programs result in widely varying self-sufficiency ratios (crude production divided by refinery runs). For the 22 domestic refiners listed in Table III the average ratio is 53.2 percent. But individual firms vary from 0 to 149 percent. Eight of the 23 firms have ratios of 20 percent or less. All but two of the remaining firms have ratios between 47 and 96 percent. (Skelly has a ratio of 110 percent; Getty, 149 percent). Thus, the pattern seems to be that firms barely integrate at all (those 20 percent or less), or integrate from about 50 to 100 percent.

Table III also indicates the varying degrees of integration into pipelines. As with integration into crude, some companies are far more integrated into pipelines than others. But, by and large, they are not the same companies. The four companies with the highest ratios of crude production to refinery runs—Getty, Skelly, Husky, and Kerr-McGee—are integrated into pipelines only to a trivial extent. It is true that those companies that are heavily integrated into pipelines—Cities Service, Continental, Marathon, and Standard (Indiana)—are also substantially integrated into crude. But the reverse is not true. The simple linear correlation between the indexes of integration into crude and into refining is only .14, indicating an almost total lack of correspondence overall.

Earlier I stated that the benefits of integration were of two sorts: (1) lower average costs of operations and (2) lower capital costs. I have made no attempt in my research thus far to quantify the effects of of integration on capital costs. An equation has been estimated that relates investment risk to its principal determinants, including firm size, capital structure and integration. From this equation it is possible to measure the extent to which integration reduces investment risk and therefore capital costs.

The starting point for this analysis is a good measure of investment risk. Possible measures included the so-called "beta coefficient" derived from financial theory and the various quality ratings assigned to stocks and bonds by advisory institutions such as Moody's and Standard and Poor. My research thus far points to the use of the stock ratings as the most relevant and useful measure for our purposes. Standard and Poor rates common stocks primarily, but not exclusively, on the basis of investment risk from

TABLE III

Stock Rating, Size, Capitalization, Crude Oil Integration, and Pipeline Integration Data for Twenty-Two Domestic Refiners

COMPANY	STANDARD & POOR'S STOCK RATING[a]	TOTAL ASSETS[b] (in millions of dollars)	COMMON STOCK-HOLDER'S EQUITY/CAPITALIZATION[c] (in percent)	REFINING SELF-SUFFICIENCY[d] (in percent)	PIPELINE INTEGRATION INDEX[e]
American Petrofina	3	263	68	20	0
APCO	4	151	54	15	0
Amerada Hess	4	1,378	50	20	1
Ashland	4	1,275	46	13	14
ARCO	2	4,629	75	58	17
Cities Service	2	2,495	71	88	44
Clark	4	206	59	2	15
Commonwealth	5	382	46	0	0
Continental	2	3,250	64	59	44
Crown	5	115	55	2	2
Getty	3	2,182	82	149	1
Husky	4	281	54	96	1
Kerr McGee	3	807	70	92	1
Marathon	2	1,514	70	78	29
Murphy	4	568	41	68	2
Phillips	2	3,270	66	49	20
Shell	1	5,172	69	64	17
Skelly	2	748	88	110	3
Standard (Indiana)	1	6,182	76	47	26
Sun	2	2,980	70	48	15
Tesoro	4	157	72	17	0
Union	3	2,696	65	77	13
AVERAGE	**3.0**	**1,850**	**64**	**53**	**12**

NOTES: (a) 1975 S & P stock rating converted to numerical index by the following rule: A+ = 1, A = 2, A− = 3, B+ = 4, B = 5, Source: S & P Stock *Guide* (December 1975).

(b) Net assets, December 31, 1972 as given by Moody's *Industrials*, 1973, various pages.

(c) Common stock plus retained earnings plus capital surplus divided by net assets minus current liabilities times 100, December 31, 1972. Source: Moody's *Industrials*, (1973).

(d) 1972 Domestic crude production divided by 1972 refinery runs times 100. Source: Kerr-Rice Chemical Service, (1973); Moody's *Industrials*, (1973).

(e) Barrel-Miles of trunk line crude and product traffic in owned pipelines (jointly-owned pipeline traffic prorated on basis of ownership share) divided by 10,000 times average daily refinery runs. Source: Barrel Miles data from special study by Oil and Gas *Journal* Staff; refinery run data: same as above.

A+, the highest rating, to C, the lowest rating for a firm not in reorganization. (The definition and criteria for Standard and Poor stock ratings are given in Appendix B.)

It is an axiom of economic and financial analysis that higher investment risks imply higher rates of return to stockholders and bondholders. Precisely how much higher equity capital costs become when spot ratings decline could not be found in the financial literature. I have therefore undertaken some research on this question but no quantitative conclusions are available yet.

Table III supplies the raw data for our analysis. It is generally believed that size contributes to financial stability and lower risk. We have therefore included the 1972 net assets of each petroleum refiner as a potential explanatory variable. Capital structure is also believed to be important and we have thus considered stockholder's equity as a percentage of capitalization. Pipeline integration was measured by the index given and defined in Table III. Integration into crude is a more complex matter. We have already indicated that beyond some point further integration probably makes a firm more risky as the inherent riskiness of the crude producing sector overwhelms the risk reducing effects of integration. In other words integration into crude has a V-shaped effect on risk: at first reducing risk and then raising it. To capture this effect I constructed the following two variables:

SSF equals the crude integration index if that index is 50 percent or below and equals 50 percent if the index is 50 percent or greater;

SSR equals the crude integration index if that index is 50 percent or greater and equals 50 percent if the index is 50 percent or less.

Thus, SSF measures the effect of integration into crude up to 50 percent and ignores any further integration, while SSR measures the effect of integration beyond 50 percent and ignores integration up to 50 percent.

My choice of 50 percent as the point at which the *average* domestic refiner minimizes risk is merely a guess. I have not experimented with other figures to find the particular percentage that makes the equation work best. I would stress that the point of lowest risk will be different for each firm and that firms are not interested in simply minimizing risk, nor should society want all firms to minimize risk.

The following equation was estimated by applying ordinary least squares to the date in Table III:

$$\text{SPR} = 6.5 - .0018 \text{ TA} - .044 \text{C} - .026 \text{ SSF} + .011 \text{ SSR} - .015 \text{ PI},$$
$$\quad\quad\quad (-2.4) \quad\quad (-4.8) \quad (-3.6) \quad\quad (2.3) \quad\quad\quad (-2.0)$$
$$R^2 = .92, \quad F = 39,$$

vhere SPR is the S & P stock rating in the metric given in Table III; TA is total assets or net assets; C is stockholders equity as a percentage of capitalization; SSF and SSR are as defined above; and PI is the index of pipeline integration. The numbers shown in parentheses below each coefficient is the corresponding t-statistic.

The coefficients and the t-statistics tell us that each of the explanatory variables is a significant determinant of the S & P rating. The equation is to be interpreted as follows:

• Other things constant, each additional billion dollars of assets raises a firm's stock rating by about two-tenths of a risk class;

• Other things constant, an increase of ten percentage points in stockholder's equity increases a firm's stock rating by almost half of an S & P class;

• Other things constant, increased integration *up to the 50 percent benchmark* into crude reduces risk: a ten percentage point increase in self-sufficiency raises the S & P rating about one-quarter of a class;

• Other things equal, increased integration *beyond the 50 percent benchmark* raises risk: a ten percentage point increase in self-sufficiency lowers the S & P rating about a tenth of a class;

• Other things equal, an increase of ten percentage points in the pipeline index raises the S & P rating by about one-sixth of a class.

Taken together the five explanatory variables account for 92 percent of the variation in stock ratings. If the scores predicted by the equation are rounded to the nearest whole number (as the S & P index is given) then 19 of the 22 companies' ratings are predicted exactly correct by the equation and the other three are off by one class each.

To explain in less technical terms the effect of each variable the following comments are offered:

• If two firms were otherwise identical but one firm had five billion dollars more assets, the larger firm would probably rate one class higher;

• If two firms were otherwise identical but one firm had twenty percentage points less debt in its capitalization, the more conservative firm would rate one class higher;

• If two firms were otherwise identical but one firm had 50 percent self-sufficiency while the other firm had no crude production the more self-sufficient refiner would rate more than one class higher;

- If two firms were otherwise identical and one firm was 150 percent self-sufficient while the other was only 50 percent self-sufficient, the firm with relatively more crude production would rate one class lower;

- If two firms were otherwise identical but one firm had no pipelines while the other had the highest pipeline integration of the 22 refiners, the more integrated refiner would have a rating about two-thirds of a class higher.

In general terms, the most important conclusion is that all these factors combined seem to determine the overwhelming bulk of the differences in ratings or risk among domestic refiners. More surprising is the conclusion that size is not nearly so crucial as degree of integration and capital structure. For example, if Standard of Indiana, the largest company in our sample, were to exchange its pipeline and production assets for more refining assets and shift its capital structure to that of Murphy Oil, it would remain just as large but would fall from A+ to B+ in the S & P ratings according to our equation.

All of the discussion thus far has dealt with equity capital. Obviously an equation like that we computed to explain stock ratings could also be computed for bond ratings. But the equation for bond ratings would be more complex and I have had not had time to construct it. While a stock rating depends on the general riskiness of the company a bond rating depends on that *plus* the specific terms of the bond issue in question: the rights of bondholders, the guarantees offered them, the specific assets backing the bonds, if any. I believe such an equation can be constructed and that it would also show that vertical integration reduces the risk to bondholders other things constant. With regard to the connection between bond rating and cost of debt, it is well known that higher rated bonds offer lower yields, as can be observed in any issue of the Federal Reserve Bulletin. For example, the October 1975 issue, p. A28, shows that September 1975 Baa rated corporate bonds cost their issuers 16 percent more than Aaa rated bonds.

A major problem in making predictions of the consequence of divestiture from my equations is the difficulty in calculating for each company the value of assets in each sector and therefore I cannot predict the size of the remaining refining entities. More serious, however, is the fact that the equation predicts stock ratings only for refiners, it does not predict ratings for producers or pipelines or marketers. I would conjecture that each of the latter would be far riskier and have higher capital costs than a refiner of comparable size and capital structure. Thus, any consequences predicted for the remaining refining entities would be more severe for the producing, pipeline, and marketing entities.

My judgement with respect to pipeline companies is supported by the experience of the split-up pipeline companies after the 1911 Standard Oil divestiture and by the current rates of return achieved by non-integrated pipeline companies. In May 1963 *Moody's Transportation Manual* lists only two non-integrated oil pipeline companies, Kaneb and Mid-America (later MAPCO). Another non-integrated company, Williams Bros. (later Williams Cos.) had substantial pipeline investments which it greatly increased in 1966 with the purchase of the Great Lakes Pipeline system. Over the period 1964-1974 Williams Cos. earned its stockholders the highest average annual rate of return of all the Fortune 500: 37.4 percent, while MAPCO earned 21.5, and Kaneb 12.4 percent. The average for all Fortune 500 companies was 1.8 percent. Since there has been no apparent flood of capital into the pipeline industry by non-integrated companies (including the three cited here) one must conclude that the cost of capital to non-integrated pipelines is substantial.

That producing entities are riskier than refining entities is supported by our equation which shows that firms that integrate beyond 50 percent tend to have lower stock ratings. Table V supports this point more directly. It compares those six smallest refining companies from Table III with self-sufficiency less than 20 percent with the six largest producing companies. As much as possible therefore we are comparing pure refining companies with pure producing companies. The average size of refiners and the producers is about the same. (At any rate the size difference observed would have no perceptible effect on stock rating according to our equation.) The average S & P stock rating is identical for the two groups. But the producers have far stronger capital structures. According to our equation, if the refiners had had the capital structures the producers had their ratings would have been six-tenths of a rating class higher. Since they in fact had the same rating one infers that a producer identical in size and capital structure to a refiner would probably have a stock rating about six-tenths of a class lower.

Thus, the impact of divestiture on capital costs for the producing and pipeline entities after divestiture is likely to be greater than for the refining entities (and probably far greater in the case of pipelines).

We have not dealt at all in this analysis with the five U.S. international companies: Exxon, Gulf, Mobil, Socal, and Texaco. Undoubtedly, the analysis applies to them but it would be improper for purposes of estimating our equation to pool together primarily domestic firms with firms whose production and refining lie mostly outside North America. Nevertheless, the impact estimated for Shell and Standard of Indiana would probably apply equally to the international companies after divestiture.

TABLE IV

**Size, Capital Structure and Stock Rating
of Producers and Refiners**

REFINERS

Company	Total Assets (in millions of dollars)	Stockholder's Equity as a percentage of Capitalization	S & P Stock Rating
American Petrofina	263	68	3
APCO	151	54	4
Clark	206	59	4
Commonwealth	382	46	5
Crown	115	55	5
Tesoro	157	72	4
AVG. REFINER	**212**	**59**	**4.17**

PRODUCERS

Aztec	80	81	5
Consolidated	69	58	6
General American	222	100	4
Louisianna Land	406	66	2
Superior	572	62	3
Reserve	87	72	5
AVG. PRODUCER	**239**	**73**	**4.17**

Source: Table III or same sources as Table III

The immediate effect of a vertical divestiture would be a reduction in the wealth of the stockholders and bondholders of the affected companies. This would occur for two reasons. First, since the new entities are more risky than the old, potential buyers of their shares and bonds would offer less in the marketplace for any given stream of dividends and interest payments. Stock prices and bond prices would fall. Second, the future stream of earnings would decline because of higher operating costs and thus income growth and prospective dividend and interest payments would be retarded, again lowering the share and bond prices.

After the permanent once-and-for-all capital loss suffered by current stockholders and bondholders, the capital costs of the new entities would continue higher. Over the longer term this rise in the capital costs of the bulk of the petroleum industry could only mean a rise in consumer prices, reduced consumption of petroleum, and reduced investment in producing, refining, transportation and marketing. In the stock market and on corporate balance sheets this would show up as higher rates of return to stockholders of petroleum companies. But these stockholders would feel no wealthier. They would on average be indifferent as between the lower rates of return on the less risky investments without divestiture and the higher rates of return on the more risky investments with divestiture. Thus, while consumers would pay more for oil after divestiture, stockholders of oil companies would be no better off. What consumers would lose in higher prices, no one would gain. Vertical divestiture of the petroleum industry would be a deadweight loss to society.

Is Vertical Integration Confined To Large Privately Owned American Companies?

The answer is no. Facts cited above indicate that small and medium-sized American companies are commonly integrated. The numerous easily observed instances of vertical integration throughout the world by both private and government-owned petroleum companies suggests that it is a common way of doing business abroad as well as at home. If one insists that vertical integration exists for the purpose of monopolization as opposed to its inherent economies then one is implicitly arguing that not only American but numerous foreign private and government-owned companies are engaged in the same monopoly game.

The list of foreign privately-owned petroleum companies with a significant degree of vertical integration include:

Attock Oil Co. Ltd. (England
Berry Wiggins & Co. Ltd. (England)
Canadian Hydrocarbon Ltd. (Canada)
"Delek" The Israel Fuel Corporation Ltd.
Husky Oil Ltd. (Canada)
Maruzen Oil Co. Ltd. (Japan)
National Refinery Ltd. (Pakistan)
Pacific Petroleums Ltd. (Canada)
Petrofina S.A. (Belgium)
Wintershall Aktiengesellschaft (Germany)
Royal Dutch/Shell Group

Vertically integrated petroleum companies that are entirely or largely owned by foreign governments include:

British Petroleum Co. Ltd (BP)
Compagnie Francaise des Petroles (CFP) (France)
Entreprise de Recherches et d'Activites Petrolieres (ERAP) (France)
Ente Nazionale Idrocarburi (ENI) (Italy)
Iraq National Oil Co. (INOC) (Iraq)
National Iranian Oil Co. (NIOC) (Iran)
Neste Oy (Finland)
Norsk Hydro A.S. (Norway)
Oesterreichische Mineralolwervaltung A.G. (OMV) (Austria)
Petroleo Brasileiro S.A. (Petrobras) (Brazil)

Petroleos Mexicanos (PEMEX) (Mexico)
Societe Nationale pour la Recherche, la Production, le Transport, la Transformation, et la Commercialisation des Hydrocarbure (SONATRACH) (Algeria)
Venezolana Del Petroleo (CVP) (Venezuela)
Veba A. G. (Germany)

According to Professor Neil Jacoby at least 50 integrated oil companies entered the international market over the period 1953-1972.[44]

It is unclear why so many government-owned companies would be vertically integrated if the sole purpose of integration is to achieve a monopoly. If government wants a monopoly, it can merely create one at a single stage: production, refining, transportation or marketing. Monopoly at any one stage would give the government monopoly power with regard to the entire industry.

Not only do government-owned integrated oil companies exist in large numbers and size, but there is a strong movement in some countries for government to encourage the merger of non-integrated companies or to directly merge non-integrated government companies. Recently, the West German government through its 40% interest in Veba A. G. has merged Deminex (a government sponsored and subsidized group of overseas production companies), Aral A. G. (a large retail marketer), Gelsenberg A.G. (an integrated oil, petrochemical and nuclear power company), with the old Veba company (a producer-refiner).

The Japanese government is pushing ahead with plans for inducing the merger of non-integrated refining and marketing companies.[45] The plans would involve the merger of 29 companies into two or three concerns according to the Ministry of International Trade and Industry. Kyodo Seikyu Co., a large oil wholesaler, began merger talks last October with six refining companies that jointly account for 18 percent of Japan's refining capacity.

Apparently the West German and Japanese governments' assessment of vertical integration is very different from that of the sponsors of vertical divestiture in the U.S.

---

[44]Neil H. Jacoby, *Multinational Oil,* Macmillan, New York (1974), p. 120.
[45]*The Wall Street Journal,* Nov. 17, 1975, p. 6.

Are Small Non-Integrated Firms Squeezed Out of The Industry by Integrated Firms?*

This is one of the very few questions for which a specific answer or theory had been proposed. De Chazeau and Kahn[46] advanced the theory that vertical integration does in fact permit a "squeeze" to be placed on non-integrated refiners. Their argument can be summarized as follows:

A firm that had crude production equal to its refinery output would be indifferent to the price of crude oil for a given product price. Its total revenues would be the same regardless of the crude price and, given its costs, its profits would be the same. However, crude production was favored by the tax system. Higher crude prices would mean a greater value to the depletion allowance and, thus, lower taxes. Thus, for any product price and profit before taxes, a greater profit after taxes would be realized by taking minimum earnings on refinery operations and maximum earnings in crude production.

Few refiners have complete self-sufficiency in crude production. But even if they had a fairly high degree of self-sufficiency, it can be shown arithmetically that they would benefit from a rise in crude prices even if product prices remain unchanged. When the depletion allowance was 27.5 percent, a refiner with 77 percent self-sufficiency or higher would benefit from higher crude prices even if product prices remained unchanged. If only a part of the crude price increase were passed on in the product price, a correspondingly lower degree of self-sufficiency would suffice to make the crude price increase profitable. (The FTC's report on the petroleum industry succeeded in proving the impossible: that the reduction in the depletion allowance increases the incentive to higher crude prices.)[47]

Thus, an artificially high crude price and artifically low refining margin would exist. This would make it difficult for refiners that were not integrated to survive and discourage entry into refining since the refiner must also be a crude producer.

This artificial price structure would obviously imply that crude production would be more profitable than refining, and therefore both crude producers and highly self-sufficient refiners would be more profitable than less integrated refiners. In fact, de Chazeau and Kahn show that from 1947 to 1957 security prices of producers and highly self-sufficient refiners substantially outperformed less integrated refiners. Also, from 1946 to 1955 accounting profits on total invested capital were higher for producers than for refiners.[48]

---

*Some of the material used in this section has been reported to this committee by me on an earlier occasion. See my testimony before the Special Subcommittee on Integrated Oil Operations, Committee on Interior and Insular Affair, U.S. Senate, 21 February, 1974.

[46]Melvin G. de Chazeau and Alfred Kahn, *Integration and Competition in the Petroleum Industry* (New Haven: Yale University Press, 1959), pp. 221-229.

[47]This is due to an arithmetic error. See Preliminary Federal Trade Commission Staff Report on its investigation of the Petroleum Industry (Washington, 1973), Appendix B. I am grateful to my former colleague, Richard Mancke, for pointing this out and the fact that when the arithmetic is corrected, the argument collapses.

[48]de Chazeau and Kahn, op. cit., pp. 321-332.

The de Chazeau and Kahn argument is not sustainable in logic or in fact. It is true that artifically small refining margins would drive nonintegrated refiners out of the business. However, they would also drive integrated refiners out of the refining business. If the refining business is unprofitable, it is unprofitable to everyone. The argument requires integrated refiners to continue investing in activities that yield subnormal earnings and thus not to maximize the total profits of the firm. The rational integrated firm would cease investing in refineries and invest in super-profitable crude production. Indeed, anyone, whether refiner, producer, or outside the oil business, would want to invest in production and avoid refining until each sector's rate of return became normal and equal.

But, it will be counter-argued, this is a conspiracy, and even though it is not rational for the individual firm to build refineries, the group must build them and so they will be built. Adding the assumption of conspiracy does make the argument more logical, but it makes it even less realistic. If a cartel is requiring its members to invest in unprofitable activities, then it must divide this burden among the firms in some equitable manner. But, in fact, refining and production activities—that is, unprofitable and profitable activities—are shared very unequally among large firms. Getty's ratio of crude oil production to refinery runs in 1972 was 149 percent. Standard of Ohio's ratio was 7 percent. How does Getty induce Standard of Ohio to keep sinking money into refineries? For this cartel to work, literally billions of dollars of bribes would have to be paid among the top twenty or so companies. No evidence has been presented thet this happens. To my knowledge, no one has suggested that it happens.

What about refining and producing profits? Everyone knows that producing is more profitable than refining. As with so many things everyone knows, this is untrue. During the period examined by de Chazeau and Kahn (1947-1957) crude prices rose 64 percent. During the same period spare capacity in refining rose from 4.9 percent to 10.1 percent. It would certainly be surprising if stock prices of producers had not performed better than those of refiners.

Economic theory suggests that production and refining should be equally profitable in the long run, although they may certainly differ in the short run. Therefore, over the long run producers should earn rates of return similar to refiners, and refiners with relatively large crude production should earn rates of return similar to less integrated refiners, adjusted, of course, for any differential risk in these activities.

Looking at Table V we find only two producers for the period 1953 to 1972, and they earned 9 percent. Fourteen refiners averaged 11.3. It would be hard to say profitability was significantly different given only two observations on producers. In any case it certainly contradicts the de Chazeau-Kahn thesis which requires that the producers do better than the refiners. When we turn to the 1960-1972 data, we find eleven producers averaging 5.3 percent, much lower than the twenty-one refiner average of 12.5 percent.

To compare profitability of more integrated and less integrated refiners, I have plotted the rates of return against the so-called "self-sufficiency ratio," the volume of crude production divided by refinery runs. Figure 1 shows the 1953 to 1972 period, and Figure 2 shows the 1960 to 1972 period. In both cases there is an absence of correlation. The most profitable firms include crude-poor and crude-rich refiners.

While the de Chazeau-Kahn or "squeeze" thesis never had validity, it could not today even be offered seriously. For it is clear that the thesis depends upon two crucial premises: the depletion allowance and the control of domestic prices by means of market demand prorationing and the Mandatory Oil Import Program. All of these institutions are dead (or, more properly, in the case of market demand proportioning, dormant).

Have small firms been deterred from entering the refining business? The FTC has explicitly stated that barriers to entry into refining are "overwhelming" and that "there has been virtually no new entry into the industry."[49]

It is difficult to find a good yardstick for ease of entry, but perhaps the simplest approach is just to count how many firms have entered and relate the number to the size of the industry. The Bureau of Mines survey of refineries for 1972 indicates that thirty-one refiners had capacities of 50,000 barrels per day or greater. In 1951 the number was twenty. Nine of these thirty-one companies were not in the refining business in 1950 and ten of the fourteen newcomers (three 1950 companies merged with others in the top twenty) entered by building totally new capacity—not by purchasing existing refineries.[50] While it is hard to construct an absolute standard for ease of entry, the fact that 30 percent of the larger refiners in 1972 were not in the refining business in 1950 does not suggest "overwhelming" barriers to entry.

---

[49]Testimony of James T. Halverson of the Federal Trade Commission before the Subcommittee on Antitrust and Monopoly of the Senate Judiciary Committee, 27 June 1973, pp. 21-25.

[50]National Petroleum Refiners Association, Washington Bulletin, 29 June 1973, p. 2.

Table V

OIL INDUSTRY STOCKHOLDERS' AVERAGE ANNUAL RATE OF RETURN[a] AND STANDARD & POOR'S 500 STOCK COMPOSITE INDEX, 1953—72 AND 1960—72

Refiners	1953–72	1960–72	Producers	1953–72	1960–72
Domestic			**Domestic**		
American Petrofina	—	18.5%	Aztec	—	8.9%
Ashland	13.8%	13.6	Baruch-Foster	—	0.9
Atlantic Richfield	12.8	14.6	Consolidated	—	4.9
Cities Service	10.5	9.7	Crestmont	—	− 4.8
Clark	—	19.0	Crystal	—	4.8
Commonwealth	—	11.8	Felmont	—	8.7
Continental	9.0	6.9	General American	8.9%	11.5
Crown	—	9.0	Louisiana Land	—	13.7
Getty	12.3	16.0	Superior	9.0	8.9
Husky	—	11.4	Westates	—	5.5
Kerr-McGee	14.6	18.3			
Marathon	9.7	10.2	Average	9.0%	6.3%
Murphy	—	10.5			
Phillips	9.4	7.8	**Canadian**		
Reserve	—	− 5.2	Canadian Export	—	6.4%
Shell	9.9	6.8	Canadian Homestead	—	24.9
Skelly	10.2	12.5	Canadian Superior	—	14.3
Standard (Indiana)	11.7	15.3	Dome	21.4%	32.0
Standard (Ohio)	15.4	16.1	Home	—	15.8
Sun	7.1	9.4	United Canso	—	20.3
Union	11.1	12.8			
			Average	21.4%	19.0%
Average	11.3%	11.7%			
			Overseas		
International			Asamera	—	37.5%
Exxon	11.6%	10.7%	Belco	—	4.7
Gulf	12.3	8.9	Creole	—	5.2
Mobil	13.3	15.3	Occidental	—	23.8
Standard (Cal.)	11.4	10.2			
Texaco	13.7	9.7	Average	—	17.8%
Average	12.5%	11.0%			
Canadian					
Gulf Oil of Canada	—	11.1%			
Imperial Oil	12.4%	17.2			
Pacific Petroleum	—	12.3			
Average	12.4%	13.5%			

Standard & Poor's 500 Stock Composite Index

1953–72	15.6
1960–72	12.8

[a]Annual rate of return that would yield same increase in value over the period as realized price appreciation with dividends reinvested. Figures shown are averages of three rates of return based on three alternative price assumptions: (1) Stock purchased at initial year's high, sold at final year's high, with all dividends reinvested at succeeding year's high, (2) stock purchased at initial year's low, sold at final year's low, with dividends reinvested at succeeding year's low, and (3) stock purchased at initial year's closing price, sold at final year's low, and (3) stock purchased at initial year's closing price, sold at final year's closing price, with dividends reinvested at succeeding year's closing price.

Figure 1

PROFITABILITY AND "SELF-SUFFICIENCY" OF FOURTEEN REFINERS, 1953-1972

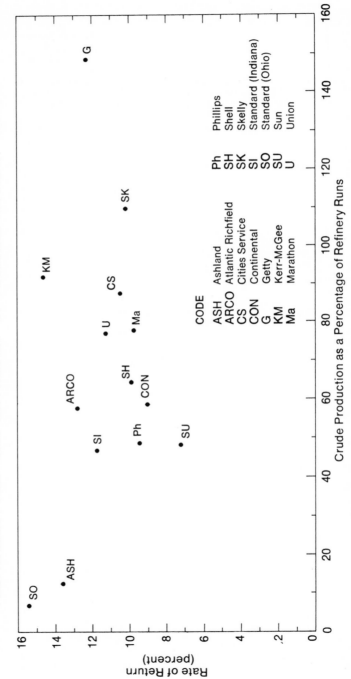

CODE

ASH	Ashland	Ph	Phillips
ARCO	Atlantic Richfield	SH	Shell
CS	Cities Service	SK	Skelly
CON	Continental	SI	Standard (Indiana)
G	Getty	SO	Standard (Ohio)
KM	Kerr-McGee	SU	Sun
Ma	Marathon	U	Union

Source: Profit data is from Table B-1; self-sufficiency data is from *Rice/Kerr Chemical Service* (Laguna Beach, California, November 1972).

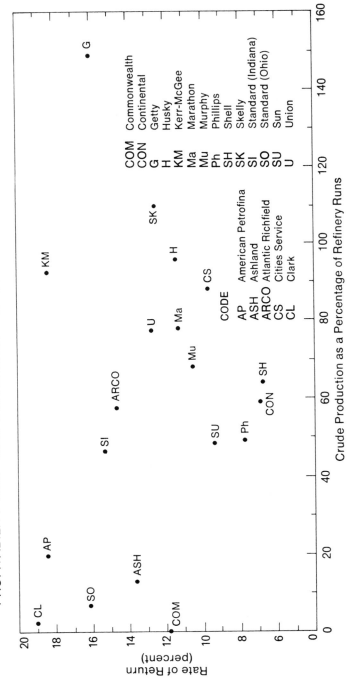

Figure 2

PROFITABILITY AND "SELF-SUFFICIENCY" OF NINETEEN REFINERS, 1960–1972

Rate of Return (percent)

Crude Production as a Percentage of Refinery Runs

CODE

AP	American Petrofina
ASH	Ashland
ARCO	Atlantic Richfield
CS	Cities Service
CL	Clark
COM	Commonwealth
CON	Continental
G	Getty
H	Husky
KM	Kerr-McGee
Ma	Marathon
Mu	Murphy
Ph	Phillips
SH	Shell
SK	Skelly
SI	Standard (Indiana)
SO	Standard (Ohio)
SU	Sun
U	Union

Source: Profit data is from Table B-1; self-sufficiency data is from *Rice/Kerr Chemical Service* (Laguna Beach, California, November 1972).

A recent report of the Federal Energy Administration *Trends in Refinery Capacity and Utilization* (June 1975) suggests that entry by so-called independent refineries will not only accelerate, but actually surpass the expansion of major integrated companies. Planned new refineries, expansions and reactivations from 1975 to 1979 were reported as follows:

Percent of Planned New Capacity[51]

	"Majors"	"Independents"
1975	41	59
1976	51	49
1977	54	46
1978	33	67
1979	0	100

While these plans may not always work out they do not suggest that "independent" companies believe they are being squeezed out.

Has The Petroleum Industry Reaped Monopoly Profits as a Consequence of Vertical Integration?

We have already seen that integration by refiners into producing does not result in an overall higher level of profits thus contradicting the "refining squeeze" thesis. What about the overall level of profits in the petroleum industry? Do they indicate the presence of monopoly rents? What about the integration of refiners into pipelines? Does pipeline ownership by refiners enhance their profits? These are the questions we now turn to.

The overall level of profits in the petroleum industry up to 1972 were shown in Table V. A more recent tabulation I made for this Committee in testimony on August 6, 1974 takes these profit data up to mid-1974. Table VI shows these later data, while figures 3 & 4 shows some of the findings in the bar chart form. These figures and charts confirm the earlier results. An investment of $1,000 in the American international oil companies, or 14 domestic refiners, or 2 domestic producers whose stock was listed on the major stock exchanges would have left the investor worse off than an investment of $1,000 in the S & P 500 Stock Composite Index. Oil company

[51]op. cit., pp. 7-10.

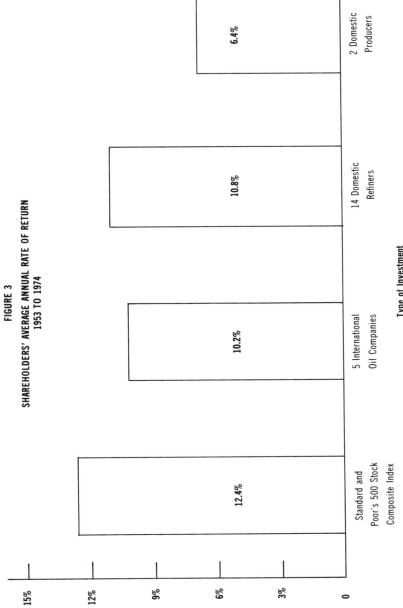

FIGURE 3

SHAREHOLDERS' AVERAGE ANNUAL RATE OF RETURN

1953 TO 1974

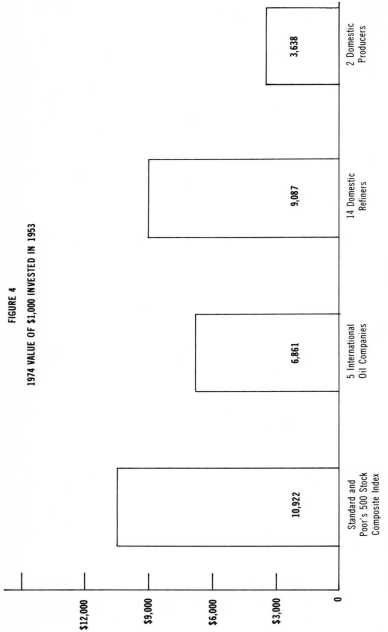

FIGURE 4

1974 VALUE OF $1,000 INVESTED IN 1953

stockholders have not reaped monopoly profits. Indeed, they have fared somewhat worse than the average owner of common stock. How have stockholders fared where companies integrated into pipelines? It is widely argued, particularly before and within the Congress, that control of pipelines enables their owners to charge exorbitant tariffs or to deny access to non-integrated firms, thus enhancing their profits. If this thesis is correct we should expect to find that refiners that were highly integrated into pipelines earned above-normal rates of return for their stockholders.

TABLE VI

Stockholders' Annual Averate Rate of Return*

Standard & Poor's 500 Stock Composite	1953-74	1960-74
	12.4%	8.3%

Domestic Refiners	1953-74	1960-74	Domestic Producers	1953-74	1960-74
American Petrofina	—	18.4	Aztec	—	5.8%
Ashland	11.4	8.4	Baruch-Foster	—	0.3%
Atlantic Richfield	13.3	14.2	Consolidated	—	7.3
Cities Service	9.3	7.2	Crestmont	—	−3.5
Clark	—	14.1	Crystal	—	5.5
Commonwealth	—	14.0	Felmont	—	4.9
Continental	8.8	5.9	General American	7.5%	8.1
Crown	—	8.9	Louisiana Land	—	6.8
Getty	13.0	16.6	Reserve	—	−5.3
Husky	—	10.5	Superior	5.3%	3.2
Kerr-McGee	15.0	16.0	Westates	—	6.6
Marathon	8.8	8.6			
Murphy	—	7.8	**Average of Domestic**		
Phillips	10.3	8.3	**Producers:**	**6.4%**	**3.6%**
Shell	8.0	4.6			
Skelly	9.4	10.7	Internationals		
Standard (Indiana)	11.3	13.1			
Standard (Ohio)	15.5	15.4	Exxon	10.0%	8.7
Sun	6.1	7.3	Gulf	9.8	5.5
Union	10.3	11.0	Mobil	9.4	9.4
			Standard (Cal.)	8.9	6.2
Average of Domestic			Texaco	10.6	5.3
Refiners:	**10.8%**	**11.1%**			
			Average of		
			Internationals:	**10.2&**	**7.0%**

* Annual rate of return that would yeild same increase in value over the period as realized price appreciation with dividends reinvested. Stock purchased at initial year's closing price, sold at final year's closing price, with dividends reinvested at succeeding year's closing price.

The main counterthesis is obviously that pipeline ownership does not confer monopoly power and is not rewarded by monopoly profits. If the counterthesis is correct there should be no correlation between returns to investors and pipeline control.

A second and stronger counterthesis would argue that firms that control pipelines will provide *lower* returns to their stockholders because ICC regulation and the Elkins Act Consent Decree place limitations on the net income and dividends on pipelines to levels below normal rates of return on production, refining and other investments. Thus, pipeline ownership would lower a firm's overall returns on capital.

The returns to stockholders are measured here by the annual rate of return that would give a stockholder the same change in wealth as realized by stock price appreciation plus reinvested dividends over the period 1953 to 1972.

Table VII shows the rates of return of nineteen domestic refiners over the period 1960 to 1972 and computed indexes of pipeline ownership. The ownership index is equal to the barrel-miles of 1972 trunkline traffic carried by each firm divided by the firm's 1972 average daily refinery runs. Where a firm owns a pipeline jointly with others, traffic is allocated to the firm on the basis of its ownership share. The firms are classified into three distinct groups based on their pipeline ownership: a "low" ownership group consisting of firms whose indexes range from 0 to 3, a "medium" ownership group with indexes between 13 and 29 and a "high" ownership group of two firms each with indexes of 44.

The low implicit rate of return on oil pipelines does not necessarily suggest that firms building them have made mistakes. Many of the pipelines built are likely to have been lower risk ventures than the typical investment of a petroleum company and for that reason less rewarding. (Often these lower risks have been achieved through joint ventures.) High risk, high rate of return pipelines may not have been built because the Interstate Commerce Commission and the Elkins Act Consent Decree do not permit rates to be charged that yield high rates of return. This has great significance for public policy because it means that a whole class of pipelines whose construction would have reduced oil transportation costs and lowered product prices have not been built. In a forthcoming book on oil pipelines I expect to show that regulation of pipelines has probably thwarted the construction of new pipeline capacity and resulted in higher prices to consumers of oil products.

The conclusions of our study of profits and integration are thus threefold:

(1) the petroleum industry as a whole does not earn profits beyond the normal rate of return;

(2) petroleum refiners that integrate into production are not more profitable than petroleum refiners that do not integrate into production (they do tend to have lower costs but these savings are computed through to the consumer);

(3) petroleum refiners that integrate into pipelines are less profitable than petroleum refiners that do not integrate into pipelines.

The analysis of profits therefore contradicts any thesis that integration causes "squeezes" and higher profits for integrated refiners.

TABLE VII

Profitability and Pipeline Ownership
of 19 Domestic Refiners

Company	Index of Pipeline Ownership 1972 (0000Deleted)	Stockholders Rate of Return 1960-1972 (in percent)
American Petrofina	0	18.5
Commonwealth	0	11.8
Getty	1	16.0
Husky	1	11.4
Kerr McGee	1	18.3
Murphy	2	10.5
Skelly	3	12.5
Low Pipeline Ownership Group	1	14.1
Union	13	12.8
Ashland	14	13.6
Clark	15	19.0
Sun	15	9.4
Atlantic Richfield	17	14.6
Shell	17	6.8
SOHIO	17	16.1
Phillips	20	7.8
Standard of Indiana	26	15.3
Marathon	29	10.2
Middle Pipeline Ownership Group	19	12.6
Cities Service	44	10.5
Continental	44	9.0
High Pipeline Ownership Group	44	9.8

Source of Pipeline Data: Oil and Gas Journal, special study on 1972 ownership of crude and product trunk pipelines.

APPENDIX A

Three measures of vertical integration have been proposed for the purpose of comparing different industries. Gort, in his *Diversification and Integration in American Industry,* Princeton (1962), measures vertical integration by computing the ratio of employment in a firm's "auxiliary" activities to the total employment of the firm. "Auxiliary" activities are defined as activities other than the "major" activity, which was defined to be the activity in that industry with the largest employment. This measure should be rejected on three grounds. First, while there are purposes for which one may usefully define "activities" in a given industry and compare firms within the industry with regard to their integration into various "activities", one cannot compare "activities" in one industry with "activities" in another industry. The definition of an activity is completely arbitrary. One is inevitably comparing apples and oranges and economic theory suggests using prices or values to handle such comparisons, an approach that Gort implicitly rejects. Second, employment is only one factor of production. In some industries, especially petroleum, capital is equally important. But the contributions of capital are ignored by Gort. Third, what is a "major" activity for an industry doesn't always work out to be a "major" activity for each firm in the industry. For example, some petroleum companies in Gort's study had more employees in production than in refining even though refining was defined to be the "major" activity for the industry.

A measure proposed by Adelman (op. cit.) is the ratio of inventory to sales. Adelman's preference here would be goods in process, thus measuring the length of the production chain as compared to the value of the final product. While this measure might have some merit for comparisons within an industry it is hard to see how different industries could be compared. One of the important determinants of inventory levels, both for finished goods and goods in process, is the variability of demand. Industries with more variable demand would choose larger inventories. But what would this choice have to do with integration?

The other measure proposed by Adelman and used here is the ratio of income to sales. The deficiency in this as a measure of overall integration is that sales are taken as given and then we work back to find out how much the firm contributed to those sales. As a measure of backward integration this is fine. But unless all the firm's sales are to final consumers (as opposed to other firms) we have arbitrarily stopped the firm's potential forward integration. If the products of the firm are sold to other firms for still more value to be added the firm is, to the extent of the value added by downstream firms, unintegrated forward. To measure both forward and backward integration consistently we would have to take as our denominator, not the sales of the firm, but the sales of all the products to which the firm contributed some value. Thus, a gallon of gasoline might be used to deliver steel to a fabricating plant. The value of all of the steel products (and the products of these products and so forth) derived from that steel must be counted in the final sales generated by the firm. For any basic industry, such as steel or petroleum, the denominator is likely to approach the whole gross national product. Clearly, this is not where we want to go but it is where logic forces us to go if we are to be consistent in measuring forward and backward integration. Stopping anywhere short of this in measuring forward integration is clearly arbitrary.

My solution, if it can be called that, is to acknowledge that we possess, for purposes of meaningful industry comparisons, only a measure of backward integration.

APPENDIX B

Earnings and Dividend Rankings for Stocks

The relative "quality" of common stocks cannot be measured, as is the quality of bonds, in terms of the degree of protection for principal and interest. Nevertheless the investment process obviously involves the assessment of numerous factors—such as product and industry position, the multifaceted aspects of managerial capability, corporate financial policy and resources—that make some common stocks more highly esteemed than others.

Earnings and dividend performance is the end result of the interplay of these factors, and thus over the long run the record of this performance has a considerable bearing on relative quality. Growth and stability of earnings and dividends are therefore the key elements of Standard & Poor's common stock rankings, which are designed to capsulize the nature of this record in a single symbol. The rankings, however, do not pretend to reflect all other factors, tangible and intangible, that also bear on stock quality.

The point of departure in arriving at these rankings is a computerized scoring system based on per-share earnings and dividend records of the most recent ten years—a period long enough to measure significant time segments of secular growth, to capture indications of basic change in trend as they develop, and to encompass the full peak-to-peak range of the cycle. Basic scores are computed for earnings and dividends, then adjusted as indicated by a set of predetermined modifiers for growth, stability within long-term trend, and cyclicality. Adjusted scores for earnings and dividends are then combined to yield a final score.

Further, the ranking system makes allowance for the fact that, in general, corporate size imparts certain recognized advantages from an investment standpoint. Conversely, minimum size limits (in terms of corporate sales volume) are set for the three highest rankings, but the system provides for making exceptions where the score reflects an outstanding earnings-dividend record.

The final score for each stock is measured against a scoring matrix determined by analysis of the scores of a large and representative sample of stocks. The range of scores in the array of this sample has been aligned with the following ladder of rankings:

A+	Highest	B+	Median	C	Marginal
A	High	B	Speculative	D	In Reorganization
A−	Good	B−	Highly Speculative		

Standard & Poor's present policy is not to rank stocks of most finance-oriented companies such as banks, insurance companies, etc., and stocks of foreign companies; these carry the three-dot (. . .) designation. NR signifies no ranking possible because of insufficient data.

The positions as determined above may be modified in some instances by special considerations, such as natural disasters, massive strikes, and non-recurring accounting adjustments. And in the oil industry, for example, "cash flow" is taken into account to avoid distortions that might be caused by differences in accounting practices.

Because of the special impact of regulation on earnings and dividends of public utilities, special parameters have been devised for this group, and such factors as capital structure, operating rates, growth of potential service area, regulatory environment, and rate of return are considered. These scorings are not to be confused with bond quality ratings, which are arrived at by a necessarily altogether different approach. Additionally, they must not be used as market recommendations; a high-score stock may at times be so overpriced as to justify its sale, while a low-score stock may be attractively priced for purchase. Rankings based upon earnings and dividend records are no substitute for analysis. Nor are they quality ratings in the complete sense of the term. They cannot take into account potential effects of management changes, internal company policies not yet fully reflected in the earnings and dividend record, public relations standing, recent competitive shifts, and a host of other factors that may be relevant to investment status and decision.

Source: Standard and Poor's *Stock Guide*, December 1975.

Myers examines the rate of return on investment in oil pipelines and finds that this rate is no higher than the cost of attracting capital to that industry. From this evidence, there is no "fat" that could be eliminated with divestiture. Further, non-integrated oil pipelines would bear higher costs of capital or less access to funds than integrated. Because of this, such pipelines would be more expensive to build and operate.

8

PIPELINES: THE COST OF CAPITAL

STATEMENT OF STEWART C. MYERS*, MASSACHUSETTS INSTITUTE OF TECHNOLOGY, TO THE SPECIAL SUBCOMMITTEE ON INTEGRATED OIL OPERATIONS OF THE SENATE COMMITTEE ON INTERIOR AND INSULAR AFFAIRS— FEBRUARY 20, 1974.

This statement is a brief and general analysis of the financial implications of breaking up the integrated oil industry into separate production, refining, transportation and marketing segments. Special attention is given to the probable effects of separation on oil pipelines.

The statement answers the following questions:

1. Is it financially feasible to have a viable petroleum industry that is not vertically integrated?

The answer to this question is clearly yes. The question is not *whether* a separated oil industry could attract capital, but *how much it would cost*. The more relevant questions are:

2. Are there financial advantages to vertical integration that will be lost

---

* Associate Professor of Finance, Sloan School of Management, Massachusetts Institute of Technology

if separation is enforced? Does a vertically integrated industry enjoy a lower cost of capital or more convenient access to funds?

3. What is the probable effect of separation on the cost and availability of funds to the oil pipeline industry specifically? Are financial problems likely to arise during the transition from integrated to separate status?

The answer to question (2) and (3) is also yes. There are some financial advantages to vertical integration which would be lost under separation, although I cannot offer a quantitative estimate of these advantages for the oil industry generally or the oil pipeline in particular. However, recent average rates of return to capital in the oil pipeline industry have not been high, and it is not likely that they could be reduced without restricting the industry's ability to attract capital. Whether existing rates of return are sufficient to attract new capital if the industry is separated depends on how it is regulated after separation.

Of course, the financial impact of separating oil pipelines from the integrated oil companies depends on how the separation is effected. I was not able to analyze alternative strategies in detail, but even a general review identifies several financial problems in the transition from integrated to separate status. I do not mean to imply that these problems are insuperable, but that they should be taken into account if separation is seriously considered.

Financial Feasibility of a Non-integrated Oil Industry

The financial feasibility of a non-integrated oil industry is not really in question. Separation will not reduce the *demand* for gasoline, fuel oil, petrochemicals, etc., and, if the markets are left to do their work, supply will follow. If separation leads to shortage at current end-product prices, the prices will rise until profit prospects are favorable enough to attract the needed capital into production, refining, transportation and marketing; supply will meet demand, albeit at a higher final price. If supply responds to demand in a free market, the industry is by definition financially feasible.

A non-integrated oil industry would be financially infeasible only if separation were accompanied by some government action that restricted profits to levels so low that new capital could not be attracted. But this failure would be the result of stupid public policy, not of separation per se.

The real question is not *whether* a non-integrated oil industry could attract capital, but *how much it would cost* to attract the capital necessary to build the capacity to satisfy final demand.

Of course, we would not expect all the customary financing procedures of a vertically integrated industry to survive the shift to a non-integrated structure. Thus, it may be perfectly correct to point out an existing procedure as "infeasible" without integration. It is also relevant to point out transitional problems in changing procedures. But since procedures can change, the most fundamental question is not feasibility, but whether the rate of return necessary to attract capital to a vertically integrated industry increases or decreases if that industry is split up.

Vertical Integration and the Cost of Capital

The "cost of capital" for an industry may be defined as the minimum expected rate of return necessary to attract new capital to the industry. Of course, there are many ways to measure "rate of return," and to each corresponds a particular definition of the cost of capital. The most appropriate definition of rate of return for present purposes is:

$$\text{Rate of Return} = \text{ROI*} = \frac{\text{After-tax Operating Income}}{\text{Total Assets}}$$

The corresponding definition for cost of capital is:

$$\text{Cost of Capital} = \rho^* = r(1 - T_c)\frac{B}{V} + k\frac{S}{V}$$

This is just a weighted average of the current borrowing rate, after tax, and an expected rate of return sufficient to compensate equity investors for the time value of money and for the business and financial risks they bear. Specifically:

$r =$ current long-term bond rate

$T_c =$ the marginal corporate income tax rate

$B/V =$ the ratio of debt outstanding (B) to the firm's total market value (V).

$k =$ the expected rate of return necessary to attract new equity capital

$S/V =$ the ratio of the value of the firm's outstanding stock (S) to the firm's total value.

To repeat, a firm or industry will not attract new capital unless its investment opportunities offer an expected rate of return (ROI*) equal to or in excess of the cost of capital (ρ^*).[1]

Factors determing the cost of capital.—There are two fundamental determinants of the cost of capital:

---

[1]This requires a minor qualification. A firm *could* invest in assets yielding a ROI* less than ρ^*, but the result would be a capital loss for the firm's owners. Thus, while it may be feasible to attract capital for low profit investments, no rational firm would do so.

Figure 1

Weighted Average Cost of Capital as a Function of Business Risk and Financial Leverage

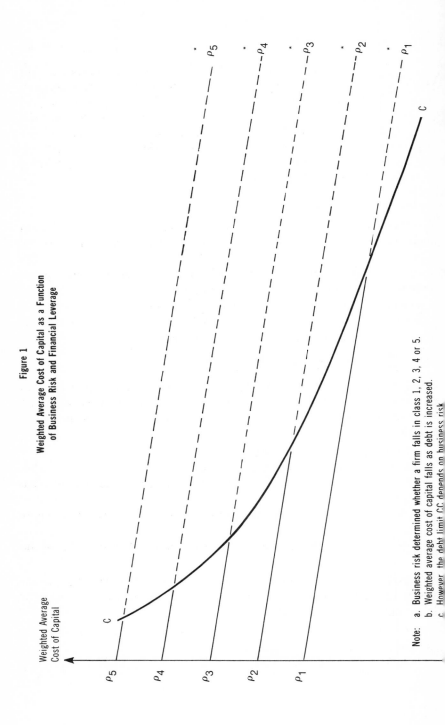

Note: a. Business risk determined whether a firm falls in class 1, 2, 3, 4 or 5.
b. Weighted average cost of capital falls as debt is increased.
c. However, the debt limit CC depends on business risk

1. The *business risk* of the assets acquired. This is the risk stockholders bear even if the assets are financed entirely with equity. (Stockholders also bear financial risk in proportion to the amount of debt financing employed.)
2. The additional *debt capacity* created by the asset acquired. In other words, there is an advantage to debt financing, so a firm can afford to accept a lower ROI* from an asset to the extent that it contributes to the firm's debt capacity.

The relationship of the cost of capital to business risk and debt capacity is shown in Fig. 1. For simplicity, the figure is drawn on the assumption that firms can be grouped into five classes on the basis of business risk—i.e., their risk level under all-equity financing. Class 1 has the lowest business risk, class 5 the highest. Business risk determines ρ, the cost of capital under all-equity financing. Then, given ρ, the weighted average cost of capital is a declining function of financial leverage.

Of course, the firms with high business risk are not likely to have much capacity for carrying debt. Low risk firms, which enjoy a low cost of capital even under all-equity financing, obtain an extra benefit from their ability to operate at high debt ratios. In the figure, this is shown by assuming that firms are restricted to the solid part of their cost of capital curves. If all firms used their debt capacity to the fullest, their costs of capital would all lie on the steeply declining curve, which passes through the cost of capital curves at the debt limits.

Vertical integration and debt capacity.—The problem now is to determine how vertical integration increases or reduces business risk and debt capacity. The effect of vertical integration is clearer in the case of debt capacity.

Debt is limited by the probability of "trouble"—i.e., the more debt issued, the greater the probability that the firm's future earnings and asset values will not cover the fixed liabilities. At some point this probability rises to a level that is unacceptable to lenders, stockholders and/or management.

How soon this point is reached obviously depends on the predictability of the firm's future aggregate earnings, and aggregate value. This predictability is increased by vertical integration, for the same reason that the return on a portfolio of stocks is more predictable than the return on any of the individual stocks comprising the portfolio. Fluctuations in returns on individual securities "cancel out" in a portfolio. Likewise, fluctuations[2] in

---

[2] I am not suggesting that production, refining, transportation and marketing are totally independent. Obviously, there is a common element underlying fluctuations in earnings and asset values at the different stages. But these fluctuations are by no means perfectly correlated.

earnings or asset values in production, refining, transportation and marketing tend to cancel out within a vertically integrated firm. Consequently, the aggregate debt capacity of the parts is less than that of the whole. Vertical integration, by increasing debt capacity, reduces the cost of capital. This is a financial advantage that would be lost if the integrated oil industry is split up.

The impact of vertical integration on debt capacity and the cost of capital is due to diversification, not size per se. Size is a *convenience* in financing—there are economies of scale in security issues for example. However, in the present case, the extra convenience is a second-order effect, since most of the separate firms resulting from splitting the vertically integrated oil companies could not be considered "small."

Vertical Integration and Business Risk.—The other determinant of the cost of capital is business risk. In order to isolate its effect, assume all-equity financing and consider an investor owning shares in a vertically integrated firm. Then the relevant question is whether the risk borne by the shareholder is increased by breaking up the firm, so that the original shares are replaced with a *portfolio* of the shares of the separate companies.

Economic theory provides no clear answer to this question. The effect of splitting up a vertically integrated industry is to replace centralized control and coordination with decentralized control aided by intermediate markets. Therefore, the impact of vertical integration on risk depends on how well the intermediate markets do their job. If the markets are active, efficient and complete, then they probably provide *more* information than management of vertically integrated firms could obtain from internal sources. But if markets fall short of this ideal, limits on information hamper planning and probably increase risk. If this is so, we could say that vertical integration decreases business risk.

I have not been able to reach a clear-cut conclusion in this issue, since I have no way (without a much more detailed study) of predicting what sort of intermediate markets would develop if the vertically integrated oil companies were separated.

Summary.—To summarize, the effect of vertical integration on debt is positive and the effect on business risk unclear. The safest prediction is that vertical integration *decreases* the cost of capital—an advantage that will be lost if the integrated oil companies are split up.

This conclusion applies to the *average* cost of capital for the production, transportation, refining and marketing segments. We cannot say anything about particular segments' costs of capital without further analysis. In this statement I would like to concentrate specifically on the oil pipeline industry.

Table 1
Contribution of Oil Pipelines to Major
Oil Companies' Assets and Revenues, 1971

Firm	Revenues (1000's)		Assets (1000's)	
	Pipelines	Overall	Pipelines	Overall
Standard Oil, N.J.	98,286	18,700,631	318,917	11,930,428
Texaco	80,468	7,529,054	195,245	7,222,947
Standard Oil, Ind.	88,478	4,054,293	169,780	3,964,347
Mobil	84,797	8,243,043	287,486	4,425,202
Shell	72,867	4,591,238	156,195	3,272,214
Standard Oil, Calif.	40,106	5,143,256	103,305	4,399,757
Gulf	70,237	5,940,002	209,378	5,793,065
Atlantic Richfield	78,043	3,658,437	294,519	3,100,119
Totals	613,282	57,859,954	1,734,825	44,108,079
Proportions	1.1	100.	3.9	100.

Source: Pipelines: ICC Transport Statistics in the U.S., Part 6.
Overall: Moody's Industrial Manual, 1972

Financial Characteristics of Oil Pipelines

In order to analyze the effects of separation on oil pipelines, it is necessary to give a brief review of their relevant characteristics.

Importance of Oil Pipelines to the Oil Industry.—Oil pipelines account for a relatively small part of total oil industry assets and revenues, as is shown by Table 1. They are nevertheless critical to the industry, since pipelines are by far the most economical means of large-scale overland transportation for crude oil and products, and they are large in absolute terms. In 1971 interstate oil pipelines reporting to the ICC had assets of $4,951 million, revenues of $1,249 million, and moved 7,797 million barrels of crude oil or products for 2,484 billion barrel-miles.[3]

Most oil pipelines are owned and operated by firms active in other segments of the oil industry. The oil pipelines analyzed in this study are common carriers, but most of these are simultaneously an integral part of oil companies' production, refining and distribution systems.

---

[3]Industry data are taken from ICC Transportation Statistics, Part 6, unless otherwise noted.

Capital requirements.—Oil pipelines are extremely capital intensive. Capital costs (depreciation, interest and profit) typically account for well over half of total costs. So long as pipelines operate at less than design capacity, the out-of-pocket cost of shipping another barrel is low.

Pipelines also require *long-term* commitments of capital. Typical design lives are longer than 30 years. Needless to say, once a pipeline is in the ground, it stays there—the salvage value is minimal if the line is taken up. This obviously exposes pipeline investment to certain risks. If an oil field dries up sooner than expected, or if refining locations are shifted, then there may be no way to recover the initial investment.[4]

Competition.—Despite the economies of scale, the industry is not dominated by a few extremely large pipeline owners. Table 2 shows that the degree of concentration of revenues by ownership in oil pipelines is about the same as in other segments of the oil industry. The table does not show that the pipeline segment is any less competitive than the others.

Competition among oil pipelines is of course somewhat impeded by a natural market segmentation. A line from New Mexico to California is not in competition with a line running from Louisiana to Illinois, any more than a refinery in Illinois competes with one in California. On the other hand, there is free entry into any segment, since the ICC cannot require certificates of convenience and necessity, and there are many market segments, for example Louisiana to the Chicago area, in which several lines are in direct competition.

Financing.—Present financing patterns in the oil pipeline industry are interesting in two respects, both of which are evident in Fig 2. First, there is considerable variation in the debt ratio from pipeline to pipeline. (Ratios of short to long-term debt also vary widely.) Second, many pipelines have remarkably high debt ratios—ratios of debt to total assets of .8 or .9 are not uncommon.

It is tempting, but wrong, to infer a similarly wide variation in pipelines' costs of capital. The cost of capital depends on debt *capacity*: the fact that a major new pipeline is financed with 90 percent debt does not imply that the pipeline generates $.90 of debt capacity per $1.00 invested. A substantial part of the debt represents a transfer to the pipeline of the pipeline owner's credit. This is customarily done by means of throughput agreements between the pipeline and its owners.

---

[4]In some cases new uses can be found for old lines, for example reversals of flow in the lines, shifts from crude to product transportation or vice versa, or extension of the oil line to new fields or markets. But these options for rescue are by no means generally available.

Table 2

Concentration Ratios for Major Segments of the Oil Industry

Segment — Measure	Proportion Accounted for by Major Firms			
	8 largest		20 largest	
Production				
Net crude production (1969)	50.54		70.21	
Domestic Proved Reserves (1970)	63.88		93.55	
Pipelines (1971)[a]	Among all owners	Among oil co-owners	Among all owners	Among oil co-owners
— Barrel-miles	57.01	52.83	88.65	77.27
— Revenues	50.84	49.72	82.63	71.02
— Assets	51.97	45.45	79.94	64.68
Refining (1970)				
Crude capacity	58.07		86.15	
Gasoline capacity	58.78		87.38	
Marketing				
— Gasoline sales (1971)				
(in gallons)	52.83		76.82	

[a]Concentration of ownership

Source: ICC Transportation Statistics (Part 6), 1971.

Preliminary Federal Trade Commission Staff Report on its Investigation of the Petroleum Industry. Prepared for Committee on Interior and Insular Affairs, U.S. Senate, 1973.

The Association of Oil Pipelines supplied a tabulation of pipeline ownership.

In other words, it is wrong to assume that oil pipelines' existing financing patterns could persist if the pipelines were separated from the integrated oil companies. A vertically integrated firm has a certain amount of aggregate debt capacity, but it need not allocate this to assets in proportion to the assets' contribution to this capacity. If the firm is split up, however, then each asset has to stand on its own.

Problems in Measuring Oil Pipelines' Costs of Capital.—The lack of correspondence between pipelines' debt ratios and their debt capacities poses an obvious problem in measuring their capital costs. Another problem is that most pipelines are subsidiaries of other companies, so that their shares are not publicly traded. (Usually cost of capital estimates are based partly on an examination of the level and volatility of the firms' stock prices.)

A Comparison of Average Rates of Return in the Oil Pipeline Industry to Cost of Capital Estimates for Other Industries.

The problems noted just above make it difficult to analyze the impact of separation on oil pipelines' costs of capital, except for the statement that these costs should rise for the oil industry generally in the absence of vertical integration. Some insight can be gained, however, by comparing actual average rates of return in the oil pipeline industry and inquiring whether these rates of return would be sufficient to attract capital if the industry were separated.

Accordingly, this section contains a brief review of oil pipelines' rates of return and a comparison to cost of capital estimates for other industries.

Oil Pipelines' Rates of Return.—There are 98 oil pipelines regulated by the ICC and included in the ICC's 1971 Transport Statistics for the U.S. (Part 6). For each of these firms, ROI* was calculated as

$$\text{ROI*} = \frac{\text{After-tax operating income}}{\text{Net total assets}}$$

After-tax operating income was first calculated as

$$\begin{matrix}\text{Income after} \\ \text{interest} \\ \text{and taxes}\end{matrix} \quad + \quad \text{Interest} \quad - \quad \begin{matrix}\text{Tax shield} \\ \text{provided by} \\ \text{interest}\end{matrix}$$

Since interest was not separately reported by the ICC, interest payments were estimated by multiplying an average long-term bond rate (8 percent) times total liabilities (excluding equity) for that year. The tax rate was assumed to be 50 percent. This procedure will overestimate ROI* somewhat, since the bond rates used will be higher than actual embedded interest costs.

It was possible to compute ROI*'s for all 98 pipelines in 1971. The results are shown in histogram form in Figure 3. The mean ROI* was 9.4 percent and the median 8.4 percent. (The difference between mean and median is largely due to one outlying observation, Crown Rancho's ROI* of nearly 70 percent.) Perhaps the most striking aspect of Figure 3 is the degree of variation across firms. Evidently this is an industry in which some firms do very well after the fact, but some do very poorly—which is at least circumstantial evidence of high risk.

One somewhat unusual aspect of the ICC Transport Statistics is that all income is reported under so-called "flow through" accounting. That is, the tax benefits of accelerated depreciation and the investment tax credit are flowed through to income in the year in which they occur. This is in contrast to "normalized" accounting, in which these benefits are not credited to income but recorded as a deferred charge. For a growing firm which is accumulating deferred taxes, a switch from normalized to flow-through accounting will increase after-tax operating and ROI*.

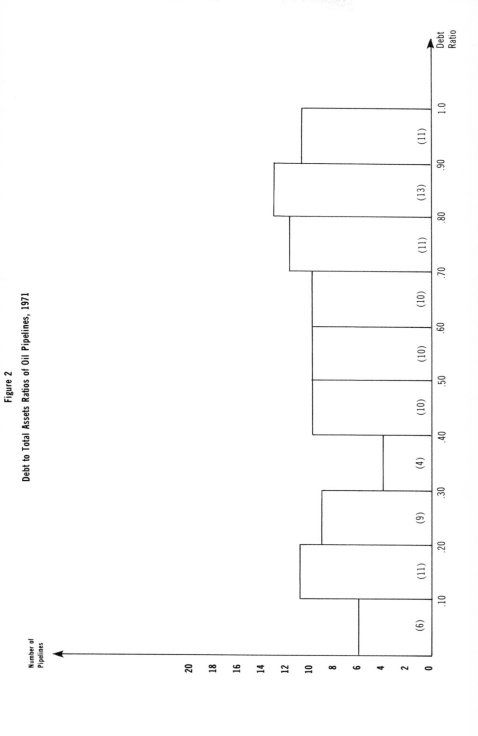

Figure 2

Debt to Total Assets Ratios of Oil Pipelines, 1971

Figure 3

Distribution of Rates of Return (ROI*) in the Oil Pipeline Industry
— 1971, Flow-Through Accounting

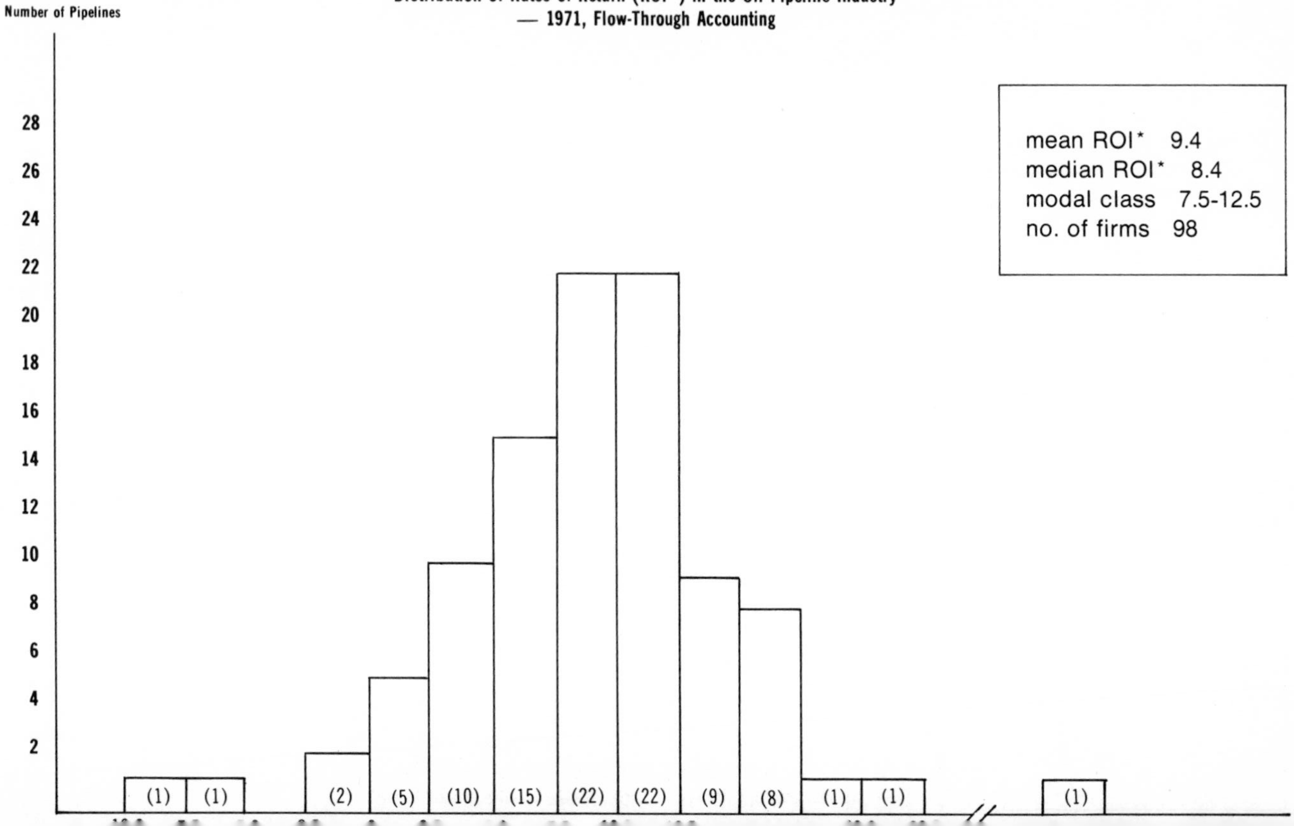
Number of Pipelines
28
26
24
22
20
18
16
14
12
10
8
6
4
2
(1)
(1)
(2)
(5)
(10)
(15)
(22)
(22)
(9)
(8)
(1)
(1)
(1)
mean ROI* 9.4
median ROI* 8.4
modal class 7.5-12.5
no. of firms 98

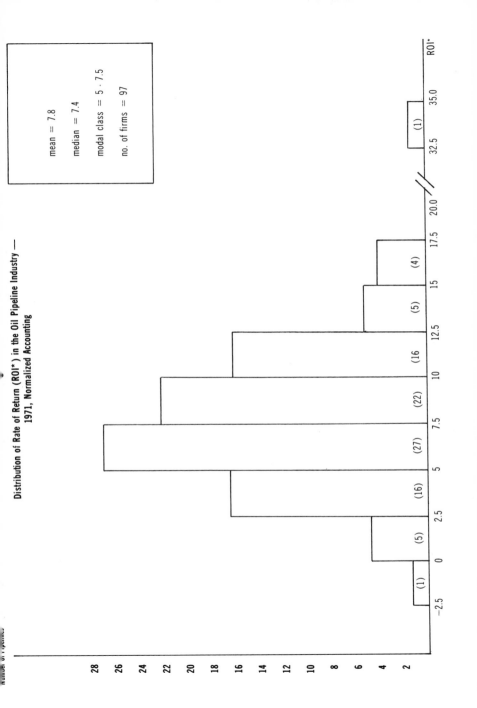

Distribution of Rate of Return (ROI*) in the Oil Pipeline Industry —
1971, Normalized Accounting

mean = 7.8

median = 7.4

modal class = 5 - 7.5

no. of firms = 97

Although no one can say that one or the other of these two procedures is right, it is relevant to present the oil pipeline ROI*'s on a normalized basis. This is done in Figure 4.[5] As would be expected in a growing industry, the effect of normalized accounting is to reduce the ROI*'s: the mean and median drop to 7.8 and 7.4 percent, respectively. The dispersion about the mean is somewhat less when ROI* is calculated on a normalized basis, but there is still a substantial spread between winners and losers.

In short, the ICC's specification of flow-through accounting, instead of normalization, has made the industry appear to be more profitable. It also has the effect of making the industry appear riskier, insofar as risk can be judged from Figures 3 and 4.

The figures just presented are *unweighted* averages of ROI*'s. A weighted average ROI* can be simply calculated as the ratio of *total* industry operating income, after tax, to *total* net assets for the industry. This weights each firm's ROI* according to its contribution to net industry assets.

	Weighted Average ROI*	Unweighted Average ROI*
Flow-through accounting	8.7	9.4
Normalized accounting	7.7	7.8

Since the weighted averages are below the unweighted ones, we can reject the view that large pipelines are more profitable, on a book basis, than small ones. If anything, the evidence supports the opposite conclusion.

Lack of time made it impossible to calculate all of the ROI*'s just presented for all ICC regulated pipelines in previoss years. However, the 1971 figures are not unusual. This is shown by Fig. 3, which presents weighted average ROI*'s (flow-through accounting) for each of the years 1955-71.

Table 3

Weighted Average Rates of Return
for Interstate Oil Pipelines, 1955-71

Flow-Through Accounting

Year	Rate of Return	Year	Rate of Return
1955	8.1	1964	8.4
1956	9.1	1965	8.5
1957	8.2	1966	8.7
1958	7.5	1967	9.2
1959	8.5	1968	8.8
1960	8.0	1969	8.9
1961	8.3	1970	9.5
1962	9.2	1971	8.7
1963	8.0		

Source: ICC Transport Statistics (Part 6), various years.

[5]One of the 98 pipelines had to be dropped from this calculation because of missing data.

Evaluation — A T & T and the Federal Communications Commission.

The average ROI*'s just presented do not "look high," but this impression is worth very little in itself. The critical question is whether the ROI*'s indicate unfairly high average returns, that is returns in excess of the cost of capital.

In many regulated industries it is possible to obtain a direct measure of $\rho*$, the cost of capital, defined as the minimum acceptable expected rate of return (ROI*) on new investment.

A T & T is a natural subject for comparison, since a great deal of effort and analysis have been devoted to estimating its cost of capital and determining the rate of return that should be allowed by the FCC. The most recent round of investigation ended with the FCC's "Decision and Order" of November 22, 1972, in which it settled on 10.5 percent as a fair return on A T & T *equity*. This may be taken as the Commission's best estimate of k, the necessary return to equity capital. (Remember that $\rho*$, the overall cost of capital, is a weighted average of debt and equity costs.) This figure is one of the most important final results of a long proceeding (beginning in 1970) in which several witnesses presented independent estimates of k, based on the market behavior of A T & T stock and a wide variety of other securities.

What does the 10.5 percent figure imply for the overall cost of capital $\rho*$? Using A T & T's average debt cost (7.25 percent) and debt ratio (39 percent)[6] we have:

$$
\begin{aligned}
\text{Cost of capital} \\
\text{implied by} \quad &= \quad \rho* = r(1 - \tau)B/V + k\,(S/V) \\
\text{FCC decision} \\
&= \quad .0725(1 - .5)\,.39 + .105(.61) \\
&= \quad .078
\end{aligned}
$$

These figures are remarkably close to the simple or weighted average ROI*'s calculated for the oil pipeline industry under normalized accounting. (A T & T and the FCC also use normalized accounting.) In view of this, it is hard to see how the average pipeline return could be viewed as unfairly high. One would have to argue that the oil pipelines have, on the average,

---

[6]The debt cost and debt ratio are calculated at pp. 70-72 in S. C. Myers, "A T & T Cost of Capital Study," prepared Testimony, FCC Docket 19129, 1971.

lower business risk or generate *more* debt capacity per dollar of net property than A T & T.[7]

Natural Gas Pipelines and the Federal Power Commission.—Table 4 shows the equity rates of return allowed gas pipelines by the Federal Power Commission in all cases settled during 1972-74.[8] We can infer a value for ρ^* by the same procedure used for A T & T. For Pacific Gas Transmission, for example, we have

$$
\begin{aligned}
\rho^* &= r(1 - T_C)\frac{B}{V} + k\frac{S}{V} \\
&= (.08)(1 - .5)(.716) + .1146(.284) \\
&= .0612
\end{aligned}
$$

This uses the same interest rate (8 percent) used to calculate the oil pipeline ROI*'s. The same procedure was used for the other 17 settlements noted in Table 4.

The average ROI* allowed by the FPC during this period was 6.66 percent. At first glance this appears somewhat lower than the oil pipeline ROI*'s. However, Table 4 also shows that the average ratio of equity to total capitalization for the gas pipelines was only 35.4 percent.

Now, a given ROI* is fair if it is approximately equal to ρ^*, the cost of capital. But ρ^* is a function of two things, business risk and the debt capacity generated by the firm's assets. Thus, the fact that the 6.66 percent ROI* allowed by the FPC is less than the 7.7 to 7.8 percent ROI* earned by the oil pipelines does not mean that the oil pipelines' returns are unfairly high. It is clear from Figures 3 and 4 that oil pipelines face considerable business risk—risk more typical of unregulated industry than of a tightly regulated industry such as the gas pipelines. Thus, I doubt that oil pipeline assets could support a debt ratio as high as the gas pipelines'.

It is interesting to calculate what a fair ROI* would be for the gas pipelines if they were financed at a more normal debt ratio—40 percent debt and 60 percent equity, for example. Assume for purposes of argument that 6.66 percent is fair given 64.6 percent debt. That is, assume $\rho^* = 6.66$.

---

[7]The fact that some pipelines have extremely high debt ratios does not imply that this debt is actually supported by the pipeline assets. As was pointed out above, the high debt ratios are made possible by a transfer of debt capacity from the pipeline owners, via throughput agreements.

[8]I wish to thank the Office of Economics, Federal Power Commission, for compiling these figures on short notice.

Then ρ^* at 40 percent is approximately 7.9 percent.[9] Thus, even if we assumed that the oil and gas pipeline industries had the same business risk, but that the oil pipeline assets could be financed only with 40 percent debt, in the absence of throughput agreements, then the FPC's decisions would imply a cost of capital for the oil pipelines of approximately 7.9 percent.

Table 4

Rates of Return Allowed by the Federal Power Commission, 1972-73[a]

Company	Docket No.	Percent Common Equity	Rate of Return on Equity	Imputed Cost of Capital[b]
1. Pacific Gas Transmission	RP71-98	28.4	11.46	6.12
2. Cities Service Gas Company	RP71-106	64.3	9.26	7.38
3. Great Lakes Gas Transmission	RP71-102	17.33	14.0	5.73
4. Natural Gas Pipeline	RP71-125	34.05	11.75	6.64
5. Texas Gas Transmission	RP72-45	34.06	11.55	6.57
6. Trunkline Gas Company	RP72-23	29.25	12.14	6.38
7. Colorado Int. Gas Co.	RP72-4	33.10	12.35	6.76
8. United Gas Pipeline	RP71-41	36.4	11.4	6.77
9. Southern Natural Gas	RP72-91	43.82	10.95	7.05
10. Southwest Gas Corp.	RP72-71	29.8	12.7	6.59
11. Algonquin Gas Transmission	RP72-110	40.9	11.09	6.9
12. United Gas Pipeline	RP72-75	42.9	11.625	7.27
13. Columbia Companies	RP71-18	40.67	11.41	7.01
14. McColloch Int. Gas	RP72-119	30.00	11.66	6.30
15. Natural Gas Pipeline	RP72-132	38.05	11.75	6.95
16. Midwestern Gas Transmission	RP72-52	37.23	11.17	6.67
17. Michigan Wisconsin	RP72-118	38.11	11.46	6.84
18. Great Lakes Transmission	RP73-74	18.84	14.12	5.91
Averages	....	35.4	. . .	6.66

Source: Office of Economics, Federal Power Commission
[a]Listed in order of date of settlement.
[b]Calculated using an 8 percent interest rate for debt and preferred and a 50 percent marginal corporate tax rate.

---

[9]We can use the following equation to calculate the approximate shift in ρ^* if debt is changed from 64.6 to 40.0 percent of total assets:
$$\rho^* = \rho(1 - T_c(B/V)),$$
where ρ = ρ^* under all-equity financing
T_c = the marginal corporate tax rate
B/V = the debt ratio
Give 64.6 percent debt, we have
$$\rho^* = 6.66 = \rho(1 - .5(.646)), \rho = 9.84$$
Thus, at a 40 percent debt ratio, $\rho^* = 9.84(1 - .5(.4)) = 7.87.$
This formula is not exact, but it is an acceptable approximization for present purposes. See S. C. Myers, "Interactions of Corporate Financing and Investment Decisions—Implications for Capital Budgeting." *Journal of Finance*, March 1974.

Summary.—These comparisons provide no evidence that average ROI*'s of oil pipelines are out of line. Pipeline profitability for 1971 was almost exactly the same as contemporary estimates of A T & T's cost of capital. It was approximately one percentage point greater than the average cost of capital implied by recent FPC decisions concerning gas pipelines, but this can be accounted for by the gas pipelines' high debt ratios.

It is more difficult to draw conclusions about oil pipelines' future ability to attract capital. The problem here is to determine whether pipelines' business risk is generally equal to or greater than that of A T & T and the gas pipelines. (It is hard to believe that it is less, for reasons explained below.) If the business risk is equal, then pipelines' ROI* must equal their costs of capital, on the average. Consequently:

1. Pipelines could continue to attract capital without a general increase in rates.
2. However, there is no "fat" that could be eliminated as a by-product of separation.
3. If separation increases business risk or reduces pipelines' debt capacity, then a general increase in rates will be required to attract necessary capital into the industry.

If, on the other hand, pipelines' business risk is greater, then pipelines' costs of capital must be higher than the rates of return actually being earned. In this case rates of return must be expected to rise regardless of whether separation occurs, unless the integrated oil companies are somehow forced to subsidize the pipelines.

Actually, oil pipelines probably have greater business risk than A T & T or the gas pipelines, judging from the following evidence:

1. The distribution of pipeline ROI*'s around the mean is remarkably wide, as can be seen in Figures 3 and 4.
2. Pipelines require large capital outlays but have low salvage values, which makes them vulnerable to geographic shifts in crude supplies and markets.
3. Point (2) applies to gas pipelines as well. But oil pipelines are in no way protected from the threat of competitive entry, while new gas pipelines cannot enter without a certificate of convenience and necessity from the FPC. Likewise, A T & T has a legal monopoly over most of its business.
4. Finally, A T & T and the gas pipelines are subject to the traditional procedures of utility regulation, which prevent rates of return much in

excess of the cost of capital, but also allow price increases when the rate of return falls below the cost of capital. Basically, these traditional procedures allow utilities to shift risk to their customers. This has obviously not happened in the oil pipeline industry, as is clear from Figures 3 and 4.

This still leaves the question of whether separation *per se* would have any effect on oil pipelines' costs of capital. If this means simply a change in ownership, without any change in tariffs, operating procedures, throughputs, etc., the effect would probably be minor. However, it is difficult to imagine a change in ownership not leading to other changes as well. Precisely what these changes may be will depend on the ground rules under which the separation is effected. The real question is "how would the industry be reorganized after separation?" This is difficult to answer, but one can make a start at least by considering how separation and reorganization might occur.

Effects of Separation

It is best to start by considering separation with no other changes. "No other changes" assumes, among other things, continuation of current throughput agreements and the availability of similar agreements to pipelines built in the future. In this case we can project past experience with relative confidence. Nothing would be changed from the viewpoint of lenders, since the industry's "natural" debt capacity would continue to be augmented by throughput agreements. The only change would be the source of equity capital.

At first glance this appears to be an easy way out, since it gives at least the appearance of separation, and continuation of the status quo would minimize any financial difficulties. However, there are problems which lead me to doubt that this status quo could be maintained.

First, it is not clear whether the throughput agreements would have to be renegotiated if the oil pipelines were separated from their present parents. If they are renegotiated, the effect will be to raise embedded interest costs, since old debt will have to be refinanced at today's interest rates. The increased interest payments will have to be absorbed by pipeline customers and/or the oil companies.

However, if the throughput agreements do remain binding, the effect will be to force the present owners to continue to bear much of the pipelines' business risk after giving up the possible rewards of equity ownership. Present throughput agreements absorb business risk because they are one-way streets: pipelines are guaranteed revenues to service debt, but they have no obligation to reserve capacity strictly for the firms guaranteeing throughput. If tenders exceed capacity, pipelines' obligations as common carriers prevent them from meeting any firm's capacity demands in full. In other words, the throughput agreements' only function is to support pipeline subsidiaries' debt. This is common in many industries, but I know of no cases in which a firm supports—without special compensation—the debt of another independent firm.

For these reasons, I conclude that the present system of throughput agreements cannot survive separation. Oil companies may be legally bound to continue present throughput agreements, but they will not voluntarily enter into new ones.

There are three alternatives to the present system. The first is to retain the status quo except for the absence of throughput agreements of any kind. Then pipelines would be in the position of railroads, which post point-to-point tariffs, provide capacity and hope the demand materializes. In my judgment, this would reduce pipelines' debt capacity, increase their business risk, and consequently increase their cost of capital. Under this alternative there is no way that new pipeline capacity would be built without an increase in industry rates of return.

Under the second alternative, these risks would be partially absorbed by long-term contracts between pipelines and shippers. Basically, the shippers would absorb the pipelines' business risk in exchange for guarantees of available capacity and cost. (Presumably this cost would be lower than for intermittent shippers.) The problems with this alternative are clearest if we consider a pipeline having 100 percent of capacity under long-term contracts. Such a carrier could not be a common carrier, since it has no capacity available for new or intermittent shippers. If pipelines are to remain bona fide common carriers, long-term contracts must allow enough reserve capacity to meet these shipper's needs. But one of the costs of maintaining a significant reserve capacity is increased business risk and reduced debt capacity. The higher the reserve, the less likely it is that the pipeline industry could attract capital without an increase in average rates of return.

The third alternative is to regulate oil pipelines by the traditional procedures of utility regulation, under which gas pipelines are regulated now. (Note, however, that gas pipelines are not common carriers.) These procedures tend to lower capital costs by providing protection from competitive entry and stabilizing the rate of return. If oil pipelines' rates of return were stabilized, then new capital would probably be attracted without any significant increase in industry rates of return.

Whether this is sound public policy is a broader issue than can be addressed here. But note that the only way traditional regulatory procedures can reduce the risk borne by pipeline owners is to transfer that risk to pipeline customers. This is accomplished by setting prices such that the rate of return *after the fact* remains approximately equal to the cost of capital. That is, after the fact returns are to some extent guaranteed regardless of whether economic conditions turn out to be more or less favorable than expected. The feasibility of this guarantee for common carriers in turn would require restrictions on competitive entry. It is hardly evident that these changes are desirable in an industry where there is no present evidence of unfairly high average rates of return.

Conclusions

My conclusion is that the second alternative is the most sensible organization for the industry if separation is enforced. That is, pipelines would be allowed to enter into long-term contracts with shippers, but required to maintain enough reserve capacity to serve intermittent shippers. The base provided by the long-term contracts would enhance pipelines' debt capacity and reduce their business risk. Although it is difficult to make definitive statements about the industry's cost of capital under this alternative (vs. the status quo), it is probable that industry rates of return would have to rise to attract the necessary capital.

Swenson argues that shipper-owned oil pipelines possess significant financing advantages over other pipelines because of lower risks involved. According to him, because each shipper-owner agrees to provide a certain percentage of total throughput and to guarantee a percentage of any cash deficiency incurred by the pipeline, both financial and business risk are minimized. In Swenson's view, such long-term commitments both have allowed the financing of most of the oil pipelines built to date and will be necessary to finance planned new lines.

9

VERTICAL INTEGRATION INTO PIPELINES

STATEMENT OF GARY L. SWENSON*, FIRST BOSTON CORPORATION, BEFORE THE SUBCOMMITTEE ON ANTITRUST AND MONOPOLY, COMMITTEE ON THE JUDICIARY, UNITED STATES SENATE—JANUARY 30, 1975

Mr. Chairman and Members of the Committee:

I appreciate the opportunity to be here today at the invitation of Senator Philip A. Hart. My name is Gary L. Swenson. I am a Vice President and Director of The First Boston Corporation, a major New York City investment banking firm. The First Boston Corporation's basic activity is raising new capital for major U.S. and foreign corporations and governments. In this regard, we develop financing programs for corporate and public entities, in addition to performing the traditional underwriting and sales services for competitive bids and negotiated underwritten public offerings of securities. First Boston is also a major factor in sales and trading of all types of marketable corporate and government securities. The knowledge of markets gained through these activities is integral to pricing and selling debt and equity issues. During the five-year period 1970 through 1974, our firm

*Senior Vice President and Director of the First Boston Corporation

has been one of the leading investment banking firms on Wall Street, having managed or co-managed a total of $73 billion of publicly-offered securities issues.

We have also been involved in the sale of pipeline debt securities totalling over $600 million, including Dixie Pipeline Company, Explorer Pipeline Company, Interprovincial Pipe Line Company, Lakehead Pipeline Company, Inc., Marathon Pipe Line Company, and Trans Mountain Pipeline Company Ltd. Currently, First Boston is financial advisor to LOOP (Louisiana Offshore Oil Port), a proposed $700 million superport, and Seaway Pipeline, a $200 million crude oil pipeline. As a result, I think we are qualified to express opinions with respect to financing oil pipelines. I will confine my remarks to this area.

There have been basically four forms of ownership of crude oil and petroleum product pipelines. In three cases, ownership of the pipeline is by companies who intend to transport product through the line. The fourth case is ownership by the public. These four forms of ownership can be summarized as follows.

First, the most widely used form involves ownership of the pipeline by two or more oil companies (shipper-woners) who intend to transport product through the line. The financeability of these pipelines is based upon the credit of the shipper-owners. In most cases, this credit is transferred to the pipeline via a throughput and deficiency agreement.

Second, ownership of 100% of the pipeline by a shipper-owner oil company. Here the financing is generally provided directly by the parent company or in some way supported by the parent. Information based upon the ICC reports of the oil pipelines indicates that, from 1963 through 1973, 303 pipeline financings have raised $2.24 billion using these two methods of ownership.

Third, ownership of an undivided interest of assets in a pipeline system by two or more shipper-owners. In this method, each oil company directly provides his share of the capital necessary to the pipeline system. The Trans Alaska Pipeline System and Capline are examples of oil pipelines built on this basis.

Fourth, ownership by the public. Here the financing is based on the pipeline's own credit and assets. Throughput and deficiency agreements from oil companies are not available to support these financings. By way of contrast, the number of independently-financed oil pipelines has been relatively small. From 1963 through 1973, our sources indicate that 19 pipeline financings have raised approximately $75.7 million using this method. Examples are mid-America Pipe Line Company, Kaneb Pipe Line Company, and Buckeye Pipe Line Company.

The financeability of the second and third form depends directly on the credit of their parent company owners. Therefore, I will direct most of my remarks to the financeability of the first form, pipelines owned by more than one shipper-owner, versus the fourth form, pipelines owned by the public.

In the shipper-owned pipeline, the typical throughput and deficiency agreement provides that the shipper-owners, who may number as many as 20, will ship or cause to be shipped their respective percentages of the total amount of shipments required to meet the pipeline's obligations. However, if, for any reason, the pipeline has a cash deficiency on the date when principal or interest on the debt falls due, each shipper-owner will immediately advance its pro rata share of the pipeline's cash deficiency as prepaid transportation. This pro rata share cash payment is generally adjusted among the shipper-owners based on the volume of their respective shipments.

The tariff per unit shipped, which is filed with the Interstate Commerce Commission, is designed to provide revenue sufficient to meet operating expenses, discharge all obligations, and provide a reasonable return on assets. Included in this is depreciation which is equal to the amounts necessary to repay all debt obligations. The rights of the shipper-owners to use the pipeline are, of course, subject to the common carrier obligations of the pipeline to handle products of others at the same rates. Thus, nonshipper-owners can use the pipeline without bearing the risks of ownership and without bearing the long-term financial obligations.

In most shipper-owned pipelines, the obligations of the shipper-owners under the agreement are several, not joint. This means that if one shipper-owner defaults in meeting his share of a deficiency, there is no legal manner in which lenders can recover the deficiency from the nondefaulting shipper-owners. However, if the nondefaulting shipper-owners do not cover the deficiency, the lenders may force the pipeline company into bankruptcy. Consequently, there is a strong incentive for the nondefaulting shipper-owners to make arrangements to cover the deficiency. To my knowledge, there has never been a bankruptcy of a shipper-owned pipeline.

The availability of financing for the shipper-owned pipeline generally has depended upon lenders accepting the throughput and deficiency agreement as support for the pipeline's obligations. Additional conditions required by the lenders include that the shipper-owners who enter into the throughput and deficiency agreement are creditworthy and that the obligations under the throughput and deficiency agreement cannot be changed before the debt has been retired without the consent of the lenders. This financing technique has enabled shipper-owned pipelines to have obtained funds that might not otherwise have been available and to have borrowed these funds at a lower cost than would otherwise have been possible. It allows utilization of the oil companies' known long-term requirement to move product and their generally high-quality credit as support for raising capital. The effect has been to reduce financing costs of oil pipelines and encourage investment in oil transportation and distribution facilities.

In my experience, most shipper-owned pipelines, that are not wholly-owned subsidiaries, have been financed 90% debt and 10% equity. This is possible generally because of the high-quality credit provided by the throughput and deficiency agreement entered into by the oil company shipper-owners. Of the shipper-owned pipeline issues that have been rated by the two major bond rating agencies, all have been rated single A or better by both Moody's Investors Service, Inc. and Standard & Poor's Corporation. It is important to receive single A ratings or better because ratings by these agencies are relied upon as indicators of investment quality by fixed-income investors. These ratings are broadly used as a guide when making investment decisions. The highest quality rating is Aaa by Moody's and AAA by Standard & Poor's and in today's market such a rating enables a borrower to issue debt securities at an interest rate of about 1.00% below the single A rate. If a debt issue is rated Baa/BBB, which is one grade below the single A rating, the interest cost would probably be 1%-2% higher and it is doubtful that large amounts of Baa/BBB securities could be sold in today's markets. First Boston's records show 86 issues (over $4.0 million each) totalling $8.4 billion of single A or better rated industrial issues marketed publicly during 1974. Conversely, according to our records, only two issues totalling $125 million of Baa/BBB or lower rated industrial issues were marketed publicly during 1974. This is because some investors are required by law to invest a large percentage of their debt portfolios in single A-rated or better securities. In addition, many investors as a matter of policy restrict their debt investments to single A-rated or better securities.

The ratings of debt securities issued by the shipper-owned pipelines have generally averaged about one grade below the weighted average of the shipper-owners' ratings (see Exhibit A). Since pipelines are highly leveraged financially, it is clear that their ratings have been awarded with heavy emphasis on the sponsorship of the shipper-owners. In my opinion, it would be difficult to obtain a single A rating for debt securities issued by a new pipeline project where substantial leverage is contemplated without the support of a throughput and deficiency agreement or a guarantee by creditworthy companies. The risks, as seen by the rating agencies and investors, of building a new pipeline without the shipper-owner sponsorship would fall into three general categories: political risks, financial risks, and business risks.

The political risks include environmental, condemnation, litigation, and regulation or control of profitability. Although these risks are inherent in most businesses, they are of particular concern to investors where there is little or no diversification.

The financial risk is increased as the amount of debt used to finance the pipeline is increased. Therefore, a new publicly-owned pipeline would require a greater percentage of equity investment and a lesser percentage of debt. If things go well and the pipeline is profitable, increased leverage increases an equity investor's return on investment. However, increased leverage increases risk and enhances probability of financial difficulty if things go wrong and the line is unprofitable. Consequently, leverage is seen by debt and equity buyers as an additional risk. Therefore, a new independent pipeline, without the support creditworthy shipper-owners, would find it difficult to obtain a single A rating unless leverage is reduced. This would, of course, require a greater equity investment. Historically and currently, equity capital is more expensive than debt capital. The many uncertainties of today's economy has given debt and equity investors the desire to reduce their risks. According to our records, during 1974 there was only $262 million of new equity issues sold publicly for established industrial companies. To my knowledge, no significant amount of equity capital was raised in the public markets for newly-formed companies. In a shipper-owned pipeline, a throughput and deficiency agreement or guarantee shifts the risk from the debtholder to the shipper-owner. The shipper-owner also contributes the equity capital and therefore also assumes the equity risk.

Business risk represents all of the operating and economic risks facing any company. As an independent entity, investors are concerned about the risks of competition from other pipelines, other modes of transportation, the possibility of shipments drying up, or loss of markets at the delivery point. The business risk is lower for the shipper-owner because he usually has, or has access to, a source of supply and knows his own long-term requirements to ship product through the line. Based upon my observations, it appears that shipper-owners have attempted to equate ownership in the pipeline to projected usage. For example, if a shipper-owner intends to use 15% of the capacity of the pipeline, they usually own about 15% of the

EXHIBIT A
Credit Ratings of Selected Pipeline Projects and Their Participants

Name	Participants (Parent)	Shares Owned	%	Moody's Rating[1]	Moody's Weight[4]	Standard & Poor's Rating[1]	Standard & Poor's Weight[4]
Explorer	Gulf	5,850	26.69%	Aaa	160.14	AAA	160.14
	Shell	5,700	26.00	Aaa	156.00	AAA	156.00
	Texaco	3,500	15.97	Aaa	95.82	AAA	95.82
	Sun	2,060	9.40	Aa	47.00	AA	47.00
	Continental	1,690	7.70	Aa	38.50	AA	38.50
	Cities Service	1,490	6.80	A	24.20	A	24.20
	Phillips Petroleum	990	4.52	Aa	22.60	AA	22.60
	Apco	640	2.92	Ba	5.84	B	2.92
		21,920	100.00%		550.10/5.50		547.18/5.47
Colonial	Standard Oil (Indiana)	5,155	14.32%	Aaa	85.92	AAA	85.92
	Atlantic Richfield	569	1.58	Aa	7.90	AA	7.90
	Cities Service	5,033	13.98	A	55.92	A	55.92
	Continental	2,717	7.55	Aa	37.75	AA	37.75
	Mobil	4,136	11.49	Aaa	68.94	AAA	68.94
	Phillips Petroleum	2,556	7.10	Aa	35.50	AA	35.50
	Texaco	5,138	14.27	Aaa	85.62	AAA	85.62
	Gulf	6,040	16.78	Aaa	100.68	AAA	100.68
	Union	1,430	3.97	A	15.88	AA	19.85
	Standard Oil (Ohio)	3,226	8.96	A	35.84	AA	44.80
		36,000	100.00%		529.95/5.30		542.88/5.43
Plantation	Exxon	62,260	48.83%	Aaa	292.98	AAA	292.98
	Standard of California	34,593	27.13	Aaa	162.78	AAA	162.78
	Shell	30,647	24.04	Aaa	144.24	AAA	144.24
		127,500	100.00%		600.00/6.00		600.00/6.00
Dixie	Standard Oil (Indiana)	5,072	12.00%	Aaa	72.48	AAA	72.48
	Atantic Richfield	1,000	2.38	Aa	11.90	AA	11.90
	Atlantic Richfield	2,100	5.00	Aa	25.00	AA	25.00
	Cities Service Company	2,100	5.00	A	20.00	A	20.00
	Continental	1,701	4.05	Aa	20.25	AA	20.25
	Exxon	4,643	11.00	Aaa	66.00	AAA	66.00
	Mobil	2,100	5.00	Aaa	30.00	AAA	30.00
	Phillips Petroleum	6,103	14.53	Aa	72.65	AA	72.65
	Shell	2,321	5.53	Aaa	33.18	AAA	33.18
	Texaco	2,100	5.00	Aaa	30.00	AAA	30.00
	Gulf	7,651	18.22	Aaa	109.32	AAA	109.32
	Transcontinental Gas	1,499	3.57	Baa	10.71	BBB	10.71
	Allied Chemical	3,610	8.60	A	34.40	A	34.40
		42,000	100.00%		535.89/5.36		535.89/5.36
Wolverine	Union	6,032	26.00%	A	104.00	AA	130.00
	Mobil	4,872	21.00	Aaa	126.00	AAA	126.00
	Texaco	3,944	17.00	Aaa	102.00	AAA	102.00
	Clark	2,552	11.00	—	—	—	—
	Marathon	2,320	10.00	A	40.00	AA	50.00
	Cities Service	1,856	8.00	A	32.00	A	32.00
	Shell	1,624	7.00	Aaa	42.00	AAA	42.00
		23,200	100.00%		446.00/5.01[3]		482.00/5.42[3]
Olympic	Shell	10,875	43.50%	Aaa	261.00	AAA	261.00
	Mobil	7,375	29.50	Aaa	177.00	AAA	177.00
	Texaco	6,750	27.00	Aaa	162.00	AAA	162.00
		25,000	100.00%		600.00/6.00		600.00/6.00
Yellowstone	Continental	16,400	40.00%	Aa	200.00	AA	200.00
	Exxon	16,400	40.00	Aaa	240.00	AAA	240.00
	Husky	2,460	6.00	—	—	—	—
	Union	5,740	14.00	A	56.00	AA	56.00
		41,000	100.00%		496.00/5.28[3]		496.00/5.28[3]

[1]At time of initial financing.
[2]Public issue 3-1/2% due 1986 was financed on own credit.
[3]Weighted Average derived by dividing by 100 minus the respective percentage of the unrated company.
[4]Assumes AAA = 6, AA = 5, A= 4, BBB = 3, BB = 2, B = 1.
[5]With a 10% equity maintenance agreement.

FIB—9/11/74

% AAA	% AA	% A	% Baa & Below	Rating on Oustanding Debt	Standard & Poor's	Form of Security
				Moddy's		
68.66[1]	21.62	6.80	2.92	A	A	Throughput and deficiency agreement
56.86	16.23	26.91	—	A	AA	Throughput and deficiency agreement
100.00[1]	—	—	—	A[2]	A[2]	None[2]
56.83[1]	31.49	13.60	3.57	NR	AA	Throughput and deficiency agreement[5]
45.00[1]	—	44.00	11.00	A	A	Throughput and deficiency agreement
100.00[1]	—	—	—	NR	NR	Throughput and deficiency agreement
40.00	40.00	14.00	6.00	NR	NR	Throughput and deficiency agreement

pipeline. Furthermore, in many cases, when a shipper-owner no longer needs the service of a particular pipeline, they have sold their interest.

In my opinion, the debt ratings of future issues of many existing pipelines would be lowered if the shipper-owners did not provide the back-up created by the throughput and deficiency agreement or guarantees. With respect to the feasibility of obtaining throughput and deficiency agreements or guarantees of companies who use the pipelines but are not owners, it has been our experience that corporations have been unwilling to commit their credit unless they have a voice in the management of the facility and are provided with low-cost service over a period of time that corresponds to the length and magnitude of their financial commitment. Almost all shipper-owners are publicly-owned oil companies and should not undertake guaran-tees or financial risks without an expectation of a reasonable earnings return.

The total cost of capital to a business enterprise depends upon the amount of debt versus the amount of equity (the debt to equity ratio) as well as upon the costs of the debt and equity components. I have just dis-cussed how oil pipelines reduce the cost of debt and equity as well as the amount of equity investment by having throughput and deficiency agree-ments, guarantees or some similar form of sponsorship. I will now show that a decline in the debt to equity ratio (less debt and more equity) would also increase the difficulty of obtaining financing.

Due to the risks involved, investors would require a high return on their equity capital. I am aware of approximately $8.6 billion of new pipeline joint projects now planned for the domestic United States (see Exhibit B). If we attempted to finance without the backup of the shipper-owners and we assumed a 50% debt and a 50% equity ratio, nearly $4.5 billion each of equity and debt would have to be raised. I believe these estimates represent a minimum requirement for new pipeline capital. I am certain that raising long-term debt and equity capital for these projects would be difficult and costly at best and, more likely, impossible.

In conclusion, I do not believe that most of the oil pipelines built to date could have been financed in the long-term fixed-income securities markets without the long-term financial commitments of the single A-rated or better shipper-owners. I further believe that these long-terms commit-ments are needed to finance the new oil pipelines that are being planned.

EXHIBIT B
Liquid Pipeline Joint Venture Projects Planned in Domestic United States

1. Texoma Pipeline

A 459-mile, 30-inch crude oil line from Nederland, Texas through Longview, Texas to Cushing, Oklahoma. In addition to the 30-inch trunkline, the Texoma system includes a 16-inch lateral extending 46 miles to Wynnewood, Oklahoma. The system is currently under construction with operation planned for mid-1975.

Total Project Cost: $122 million.

Participants:

Sun Oil Company	25.0%
Kerr McGee Pipeline Corporation	10.1
Lion Oil Company	3.0
United Refining Company	6.7
Western Crude Oil, Inc.	20.0
Rock Island Refining Corporation	5.0
Texas Eastern Transmission Corporation	5.0
Mobil Oil Company	10.1
Vickers Petroleum Corporation	5.0
Skelly Oil Company	10.1

2. Seaway Pipeline

A 500-mile crude oil line from Freeport, Texas to Cushing, Oklahoma. The project includes a tanker unloading dock at Freeport. The project is still in the planning stage with Right of Way acquisition currently underway.

Total Project Cost: $204.4 million.

Participants:

Phillips Petroleum Company	42.4%
Continental Pipeline Company	15.6
NCRA	12.0
CRA	12.0
Midland Coop	9.0
Diamond Shamrock	7.0
Apco	2.0

3. Seadock

A deepwater VLCC crude oil unloading terminal 30 miles off the Texas Gulf Coast, south of Freeport, Texas. Earliest operation would be early 1979 assuming no further delays.

Total Project Cost: $750 million to $1.0 billion.

Participants: Now equal owners; final ownership will be based on anticipated use.

Continental	Toronto Pipe Line
American	Mobil
Cities Service	Phillips
Crown Central	Shell
Dow Chemical	Texaco
Exxon	

4. Loop

A deepwater VLCC crude oil unloading terminal 19 miles off Louisiana's marshy shore. If a permit were obtained at the beginning of 1976, earliest operation would be early 1979. System will be capable of up to 3.4 million barrels per day.

Total Project Cost: *$925 million*
(LOOP: $700 million;
Capline connecting pipeline: $225 million)

Current Participants:

Marathon	Gulf
TET	Mobil
Clark	Murphy
Union	Tenneco
Amoco	Texaco
Ashland	Shell
Chevron	Sohio
Exxon	

5. Spplitt

A deepwater VLCC crude oil unloading terminal on the Gulf Coast 30 miles south of the beach at the Mississippi-Alabama state line. Also termed "Ameraport," the port would operate as a public utility under state regulations. Plans would be to get the facility into operation by late 1978, a few months ahead of LOOP or Seadock.

Total Project Cost: $170 million.

Participants:
Southern Pacific Pipe Lines, Inc.
International Tank Terminals

6. Colonial Expansion

Two Cases;
Case I   Expand to 1.85 MMBPD with 270 miles of 36" and 40" loops and 200 miles of smaller loops, all between Houston and Baton Rouge.

Case II   Expand to 2.3 MMBPD by looping between Atlanta and Woodbury and additional hp. Also includes Case I.

Total Project Cost: *Case I —$181 million*
Case II—$773 million (Case I plus additional $592 million)

Participants:

Amoco Pipe Line	14.32%
Atlantic Richfield Company	1.58
BP Oil Company	8.96
Cities Service Oil Company	13.98
Continental Pipe Line Company	7.55
Mobil Oil Company	11.49
Phillips Investment Corporation	7.10

Texaco ——————————————————————————— 14.27
Toronto Pipe Line (Gulf) ————————————— 16.78
Union Oil of California ———————————————— 3.97

7. Capline Expansion

Capline has approval to expand its system to 918 MBPD. However, due to the fact that it is an undivided interest system, investment and ownership figures were not released.

8. Champlin Corpus to Pasadena Products Line

Champlin is looking at buying and converting an existing gas pipe line between Corpus Christi and Pasadena, Texas. The line size will probably be around 26-inch. The line will carry products from Corpus to a Pasadena Terminal which will connect Plantation, Colonial and Explorer pipe lines.

Probable Participants:

Champlin	Kerr McGee
Sun	Others

9. Sohio West Coast to Texas Crude Line

Sohio is looking at building new or converting an existing natural gas line for crude oil volumes from the West Coast into Texas. The project is based on surplus becoming available when Alyeska comes on stream. Line sizes under consideration range from 36'' to 42'' for 1/2 to 1.0 MMBPD of crude.

Total Project Cost: Up to $1.0 billion.

10. Alyeska Pipeline

A 789-mile, 48-inch crude oil line from the North Slope of Alaska to a tanker loading terminal at Valdez, Alaska. Estimated operation date is mid to late-1977. Ultimate capacity is 2 MMBPD with an initial step of 112 MBPD.

Total Project Cost: $5.5 billion.

Participants:

Atlantic Richfield Company ————————————— 21.0 %
Standard Oil (Ohio) ————————————————— 49.18
Exxon Corporation ————————————————— 20.00
Mobil Oil Corporation ———————————————— 5.00
Phillips Petroleum Company ————————————— 1.66
Union Oil of California ———————————————— 1.66
Amerada Hess Corporation ———————————— 1.50

11. Beaumont-Port Arthur-Lake Charles Crude Line

A proposed 42-inch crude line from Seadock to Port Arthur/Beaumont, with a 16-inch line on to Lake Charles. Line would be undivided interest; the project is presently on hold.

Total Project Cost: $118.2 million.

Participants:

Continental Pipe Line	Mobil Pipe Line
Cities Service	Texaco Pipe Line
Gulf (Refining)	Sun Pipe Line

12. Caseline

Houston area refiners are looking at a possible line from Seadock into Houston.

Participants

Crown	Shell
Arco	Exxon

Wilson speaks to the issue of what magnitude of capital U.S. oil firms will try to raise over the next decade. He estimates an amount of over $380 billion in 1974 dollars over the eleven-year period 1975-1985. A major part of this capital would have to come from internal company sources, but the industry still would have to increase its debt, its equity base, and its off-balance sheet financing. The introduction of entirely new risks associated with reorganization of the petroleum industry would much reduce the industry's ability to raise capital and thus would retard domestic energy resource development.

10

FINANCING THE OIL INDUSTRY

STATEMENT OF WALLACE W. WILSON*, CONTINENTAL ILLINOIS NATIONAL BANK & TRUST CO. OF CHICAGO, BEFORE THE SUBCOMMITTEE ON ANTITRUST AND MONOPOLY, COMMITTEE ON THE JUDICIARY, UNITED STATES SENATE—JANUARY 22, 1975

Mr. Chairman, and members of the Subcommittee: My name is Wallace W. Wilson. I am Vice President, Energy and Mineral Resources Division, of Continental Illinois National Bank and Trust Company of Chicago, and have been associated with this bank for almost 19 years. My responsibilities have included account administration, financial planning and lending activity for a broad spectrum of the energy industries, including major integrated oil companies, independent oil and gas producers, coal mining companies and joint ventures for the development of synthetic fuels. Prior to joining Continental Bank I was employed as manager of a headquarters engineering staff for a major international oil company, and as Assistant Professor of Petroleum Engineering at the University of Texas. I also served as a research group leader for another international major oil

---

*Vice President, Continental Illinois National Bank and Trust Company of Chicago.

company, and as a staff engineer for a large consulting petroleum engineering firm. My total professional experience with the energy industries spans more than 33 years.

I belong to a number of engineering, professional and honorary organizations related to the production and utilization of energy fuels, and am a member of the Energy Resources Commission of the State of Illinois.

I appreciate very much the opportunity to be here today to discuss some aspects of S.1167, the legislation now under consideration by this Subcommittee, with particular emphasis on how it would impact the future capital needs of the energy industries. The testimony I shall present is based upon my total professional experience and represents my own views, which are not necessarily those of my present employer.

In the course of preparing for my testimony today I studied the presentations of other witnesses who referred to the petroleum industry. I was struck with the observation that representatives of the independent refining and marketing sectors were much less concerned about problems which this legislation is intended to resolve than about their immediate problems with two-tier crude oil price controls and allocation regulations, originally promulgated as part of the effort to halt inflation, and now retained under FEA administration. I certainly concur with the major thrust of this part of the record, namely that most of the current problems of the domestic petroleum industry stem from governmental failure to permit the return to a free market. There is no question that the continuation of the present two-tier crude oil price controls, whereby "old" crude is priced at $5.25 per barrel and so-called "new and released" oil is allowed to find its own price level creates distortions not found in a free market. As you likely know, FEA now has promulgated a new system of "entitlements," which provide for mandatory raw material cost adjustments between refiners such that the competitive advantage of controlling sources of the fixed-price crude oil presumably is shared. In fact, however, the new system merely is a mixture of a tax and a subsidy. The company which, over a period of many years has invested its capital in exploration and the development of oil production facilities, now is compelled to pay for the right to refine some of their own crude oil, and the payment is made to competing refiners who, through individual choice or other circumstances, do not have comparable percentages of their own sources of this lower priced crude oil. I cannot help but observe that this arrangement of piling confiscatory regulations on top of price control regulations, allegedly to stabilize the market, is the very antithesis of fostering competition and efficiency.

Several of the witnesses who have appeared here have alleged non-competitive behavior of one kind or another, assertedly to prevent free access by independents to crude oil, refined products or pipeline transportation. I cannot qualify myself as an expert witness about all of these matters, but would like to make some general observations which I believe my total industry experience justifies.

The petroleum industry is highly capital-intensive; a report released just last November by The Conference Board showed that in 1971, the latest year for which such figures are available, the petroleum industry—including production, refining and pipeline transportation—ranked first in this category with an investment of over $192,000 per employee, compared with about $28,000 for all manufacturing industries. For this reason economies of scale and elements of risk are extremely important, especially in connection with the construction of long-lived assets such as refineries and pipelines. A refinery, for example, is a complex, highly integrated group of process facilities designed for a limited range of crude oil characteristics and sized to operate efficiently at approximately its designated capacity. In order to provide for growth and some flexibility of operation, most plants are oversized when built, and as it later becomes necessary they are expanded in significantly large modules. The net result is that most major refineries have a reasonable amount of surplus productive capacity during most of their producing lives, and this usually is utilized to refine incremental volumes of product for sale under short-term marketing arrangements, to the "spot" market. Independent marketers characteristically operate with product from such sources, currently supplemented with imported refined products.

Domestic refining capacity has grown only slightly since 1970, reflecting growing uncertainties about long-term crude oil supplies here and abroad, environmental constraints on the siting of new facilities, and declining rates of return on the domestic petroleum industry. As the demand for refined products has increased, surplus refining capacity has dwindled and the spot market tightened.

In a free competitive market, capital investment in new refining capacity can be justified only when the operator has an adequate long-term supply of crude oil, the necessary capital or credit to finance the facility, and an assured market for the output. All three factors are mutually dependent and failure to have any one eliminates the need for the other two. This applies to independent refiners as well as to major integrated companies. There is very little that an independent marketer of petroleum products can do to assure a long-term source of products except enter into long-term purchase contracts, either with a refining company having a surplus of capacity above his present market needs or with an entity which can finance additional refining capacity based upon the finaₐₐcial support of the new sales contract.

I believe that many of the problems with which this Subcommittee has been concerned in connection with competition among various components of these petroleum industry can be traced to such economic circumstances as these. Historically oil production, refining and marketing operations in this country have provided opportunities for a high degree of competition between thousands of individuals and companies of all sizes. Circumstances which might lead some to suggest or allege the existence of widespread anit-competitive conspiracies are more readily explained as the highly complex interactions of technical and economic factors, characteristic of the petroleum industry. To put it another way, simplistic explanations of the performance of such a complex industry are more likely to be wrong than right.

Perhaps it would be helpful to elaborate briefly on the inherent complexity of the petroleum industry, since much of the criticism it has sustained stems from widespread misunderstanding of how it operates. Probably no other industry, even aerospace, employs such a high percentage of scientists, engineers, and trained technologists. It has developed a terminology all its own which no doubt adds to some of these problems. Consider, for a moment, only one aspect of drilling a deep well—say to 20,000 feet, about three to four miles. This is roughly comparable with drilling a hole in the sidewalk below a 100 story building, by rotating a string of paper clips to which is attached a 1/4'' bit, suspended out of a window on the top floor of the building. If this sounds difficult let us add the complication of drilling from a floating drilling platform in about 600 feet of water in the North Sea. Thus instead of leaning out of a window on the top floor of a building, we are now in a small rowboat, in 25 feet of very rough water, attempting to accomplish the same result.

There is widespread lack of understanding about how reserves of oil and gas are determined, what the numbers so derived really mean, and their relative accuracy. These are all highly technical subjects, because there is no direct way to inventory the reserves of a producing well, let alone an undeveloped area, and reliance must be placed on such factors as measured reservoir pressure and temperature, the porosity and permeability of the reservoir rock, the chemistry of the fluids, operating conditions, and even the well-head price of the output, which determine the economic limit rate of production that can be sustained. It may be interesting to note that in my own experience no single well ever was plugged and abandoned because it ceased to produce, but rather because the output at prevailing prices was less than its operating costs.

Reserves, then, are inherently difficult to determine because of the nature of the data used in making the estimates. For the same reason, such figures are subject to frequent revision as more data available, later in the productive life of the wells. This also implies that reserves assigned to an area in advance of development are quite speculative and subject to redetermination at later dates. Customarily, reserves determined for producing wells are not additive to estimates for undeveloped areas, because the relative accuracies of the two categories are not comparable.

These limitations on the absolute accuracy of reserves data are accepted routinely within the petroleum industry but give rise to numerous problems with those not familiar with the situation. For example, there have been a number of widely publicized examples of differences in reserves data between those provided by industry sources and others independently determined by the staffs of various regulatory agencies. These differences have been seized upon as representing evidence of a conspiracy to downgrade our ultimate supply, presumably to justify higher unit prices. All of the reported instances which I have reviewed either stem from normal differences in interpreting basic data and the timing of individual studies, or are the result of erroneously adding together several categories of reserves without regard to their state of development. Recent studies to spot check our domestic natural gas reserves by FPC staff and their independent consultants, as a check upon the validity of comparable figures submitted by industry groups, were most enlightening. Whereas the charge has been made in many quarters that industry representatives deliberately understated proven reserves, the FPC data *on a comparable basis* showed slightly lower totals, but well within the normal range of reproducibility. Unfortunately the results of this comparison did not receive anything like the publicity which attended its authorization.

Routine records of various types have been used—or more often misused—by industry critics on numerous occasions, including several that still are of current interest. The United States Geological Survey routinely has collected and reported statistics on numerous aspects of the petroleum industry for many years, including figures on the inventory of wells. These reports include the number of wells that are shut-in, either awaiting service work or pipeline connections, and those about to be plugged and abandoned. In order to understand the order of magnitude of this example, it should be noted that there were about 620,000 producing oil and gas wells in this country during 1972, and in that year over 27,000 new wells were drilled. In 1972 USGS reported about 2300 more shut-in oil and gas wells than in 1971. This reported increase in shut-in wells gave rise to widely-circulated charges by several prominent political figures who claimed the statistics were proof that producers were holding back production in expectation of higher prices. Only recently USGS announced that the reported increase in shut-in wells was only the result of a change in definitions used in its own accounting system, and that no significant change would have been noted under their former reporting procedures. In the meantime, of course, the misuse of the data which were submitted to USGS has created doubts, confusion, and suspicion of some dark conspiracy which in fact does not exist.

Petroleum industry financial records have been misused on numerous occasions to "prove" that international companies pay virtually no federal income taxes. These distorted results usually result from comparing worldwide income with U.S. taxes alone, not with worldwide taxes. The latest figures I have seen reflect a worldwide effective income tax rate of nearly 50 percent, not 6 percent.

Numerous other examples could be cited, but hopefully the point has been made that simplistic analyses of the performance of the petroleum industry often result in erroneous conclusions. It follows that legislation drafted to alleviate presumed inefficiencies or alleged failure to compete should be based upon a solid foundation of established facts and not upon misunderstandings or the unsupported and/or erroneous charges of industry critics.

It is because of my strong convictions about these matters that I was deeply disturbed with the far-reached implications of section 203 (a) (2) of this bill which, assertedly to foster competition, directs the reorganization of the energy industries regardless of a determination of any violation under Title I. As a banker for the energy industries I can think of no more certain way of destroying their capital viability and with it, any hope that this Nation's energy self-sufficiency can be improved significantly during the foreseeable future.

All of us are acutely aware of the shock effect of the recent Arab oil embargo when, for the first time, most Americans were made to realize the inadequacy of our domestic energy fuel supplies. It is beyond the scope of my presentation to attempt even to outline the numerous factors which brought us from an estimated surplus domestic crude oil producing capacity of about 5 million barrels per day in 1956, to virtually no spare productive capacity and a reliance upon over 6 million barrels per day of imported crude oil and products by 1973. The embargo, which disrupted less than one-third of our import requirements, along with the quantum jump in energy prices imposed by the OPEC cartel, created severe dislocations of supply, a significant increase in unemployment and economic reverberations within our economy that still are being experienced.

Of potentially greater long-term significance, however, is the common misconception that the so-called energy crisis became a thing of the past after supplies of imported crude oil and products again returned to normal. In fact, however, the interruption and the hardships it created are merely the leading edge of a more significant long-range energy supply problem which is yet to be experienced. This fundamental problem is that our domestic growth in demand for energy fuels, coupled with higher rates of demand growth throughout the world, threatens to exceed the anticipated free-world supply of petroleum, even at present price levels. This is the motivating factor behind renewed efforts to increase our domestic sources of supply of all types of energy fuels such that, with improved efficiency of utilization, our future reliance upon uncertain foreign sources of supply can be reduced to a manageable level.

Our ability to achieve a higher degree of energy self-sufficiency by expanding domestic sources of supply will depend largely upon how much capital is expended in the effort. There can be no doubt that the failure of the domestic petroleum industry to develop productive capacity more in line with demand growth during the last ten years is more the result of inadequate capital investment than resource insufficiency. The money was not spent for U.S. exploration and development because of inadequate earnings, the gradual erosion of long-established tax incentives, and counter-productive governmental regulations. One of these deterrents, poor earnings, has been eased as a result of higher crude oil prices since 1973, even though over 60% of our domestic crude oil output still is subject to price controls. The result of this fundamental change in economics are now quite apparent; during 1974 drilling increased by about 20% and 1974 capital investment is estimated to have been about 29% above 1973 levels.

During the last two years a number of studies have been made [1] to project the magnitude of capital investment needed to achieve various levels of

---

[1] Selected examples include:
1. *"United States Energy Outlook"*; Privately published by National Petroleum Council, Washington, D.C., December 11, 1972.
2. Testimony of William E. Pelly, Bankers Trust Company, New York, before the Committee on Interior and Insular Affairs, U.S. Senate, March 6, 1973.
3. Testimony of Eugene W. Meyer, Kidder, Peabody & Co., Inc., New York, before the Committee on Interior and Insular Affairs, U.S. Senate, March 6, 1973.

(Footnotes 4, 5, 6, 7, and 8 Continued on next page.)

self-sufficiency in domestic energy resources. These studies are based primarily upon extrapolations of established historic trends, projected to new output objectives by individual energy sectors, including crude oil and petroleum products, natural gas, coal, electrical energy and the related transportation, refining and marketing facilities. They are not all comparable because of differences in assumptions and methodology, but nevertheless they are in good general agreement as to order of magnitude.

I estimate that during the eleven year period of 1975—1985 the domestic petroleum industry will budget about $380 billion, in 1974 dollars, for new capital expenditures. This estimate includes funds for exploration and development of new reserves, refining, transportation, marketing and related activities. It does not include very substantial additional funds needed for debt retirement, dividends, and working capital. This forecast is at the median level of anticipated performance which implies a gradual downturn in imports to approach a level of about 20 percent of total demand by 1985. Capital expenditures are anticipated to increase from the 1974 level, estimated to have been about $19.5 billion, to over $51 billion by 1985, with an annual average for the eleven year period of $34.5 billion. Comparable figures for 1972 and 1973 are $12.7 and $15.0 billion, respectively. It will be noted that the indicated 1974 investment represents a 29 percent increase over 1973, and is 54 percent greater than in 1972.

The sheer magnitude of the numbers in this forecast, and the high rate of growth of capital investment which is anticipated, give rise to a number of important questions. First, and most important, where will the capital funds come from? Unfortunately, absolute answers to this question are not simple nor are they readily available. I have reviewed several private studies addressed to this problem, which show rather clearly that the key ingredient is a continuous pattern of earnings growth, to achieve a minimum rate of return on equity no lower than presently enjoyed. This earnings rate will be essential to attract new equity capital into the business, at an average annual growth rate of around 5 percent per year. A high level of equity growth will

(Continued from preceding page.)

4. *"Financing the Energy Industry"* by Jerome Hass, et al; Unpublished paper, part of The Energy Policy Project (Ford Foundation), Washington, D.C. 1973.

5. *"Capital Investment of the World Petroleum Industry"*; Privately published by Chase Manhattan Bank, New York, December, 1973.

6. *"Capital Requirements of the Energy Industries,"* by Edward Symonds (First National City Bank, New York), Rocky Mountain Petroleum Economics Institute, 1972.

7. *"Path to Self-Sufficiency- Directions and Restraints, Phase I"* Study for Office of Energy Research and Development Policy of National Science Foundation, contract number NSF-C867. Prepared by Bechtel Corporation, August 1974.

8. *"Record Capital Oil Outlays Aimed at Easing Shortages"* by W. A. Bachman; Oil and Gas Journal, February 4, 1974.

be essential because of an anticipated increase in the industry's debt-equity ratio, probably to an average of about 35 percent from the present 25 percent range. In addition, a large additional component of off-balance sheet financing will be required, at least to the extent that credit ratings are not greatly impaired.

In a recent study by Chase Manhattan Bank (reference article 5), referring to the industry's worldwide capital requirements, it was concluded that earnings equivalent to a rate of return on equity of 15 to 20 percent would be essential if the necessary debt and equity capital are to be raised. The continuing study of corporate profitability by First National City Bank of New York shows that petroleum's average rate of return on equity was slightly over 15 percent during 1973, the first year it had achieved this level since 1951; year-end 1974 figures are not yet available. When it is recognized that reported earnings for 1973 and part of 1974 contain large components of non-recurring profits attributable to currency devaluation and inventory valuations, it is obvious that present earnings are not excessive if the task ahead is to be accomplished.

Consideration also must be given to the adequacy of the total U.S. capital market to supply the funds needed for all of the energy industries including, especially, the electric utilities. You no doubt are aware of the very severe financial problems now being faced by investor-owned electric utilities, as a result of substantially higher costs for fuel, construction and operation. Delays in obtaining rate adjustments for these added costs have resulted in depressed earnings, which in turn have limited their ability to raise new capital for expansion to meet growing demand for service. Historically the capital needs of the electric utilities have been slightly larger than for the petroleum industry, and their future capital requirements are of the same order of magnitude. During the last several years these two major components of the energy business, plus coal mining, gas utilities and related distribution industries have required about 25 percent of the total capital available to the private sector of the economy. Forecasts I have seen generally forecast a gradual increase in this percentage to about 33 percent by 1985, assuming, of course, appropriate economic conditions. The growing share of the capital markets anticipated to be utilized by the energy industries suggests that competition for investment dollars will remain at a high level, and funds will be readily available only for those companies and industries which can compete on the basis of past performance, especially rates of return.

Recent events have created uncertainties about some of the economic assumptions used in projecting this trend, especially the financial health of the electric utilities. During the last year alone, major construction projects with budgeted costs in excess of $16 billion have been deferred or canceled. These include over half of the planned nuclear power plants that had been announced by the end of 1973. The long-range implications of this situation are difficult to evaluate. Stretch-outs and outright cancellations of orders for major equipment components no doubt will have a severe impact on suppliers, and anticipated electric generating capacity simply will not be available as scheduled and forecast. Whether it will be possible to catch up with this construction at a later date, to achieve the total capacity anticipated for, say 1985, cannot now be determined. If inflationary pressures continue unabated, deferred projects at the least will require much more than the original capital budgeted for their construction. The problems now faced by the electric utilities, and the long-range implications of their present shortage of capital give us some indication of what would occur if the petroleum industry should encounter similar problems of capital formation.

I would like now to discuss more specifically how a new body of law and regulations, embodying the provisions of S.1167, would affect the domestic petroleum industry's ability to generate the capital needed for their future operations. I have attempted to show the relative magnitude of the funds which will be required during the next eleven years to develop producing capacity in parallel with the growth of demand, with but nominal reduction in our reliance upon imported crude oil and products. The task of raising the huge amount of capital needed will require substantial increases in long-term debt, frequent infusions of new equity, and the maximum possible use of off-balance-sheet financing. Even so, it is anticipated that debt-equity ratios will climb to new highs, and there will be intense competition for capital funds from other sectors of the economy.

In a financial climate of this type the introduction of entirely new elements of risk could have adverse effects upon the capital markets, the results of which are impossible to forecast. As you know, during the last year a number of bills were introduced in the Congress which would impose new severance taxes and phase out or eliminate outright long-standing tax incentives, principally affecting those engaged in critically important exploration and production of crude oil and natural gas. These proposals are being justified on the presumption of excessive profitability following the worldwide increase in oil prices. It is not my intention to comment more specifically on such legislation, but it is suggested that it has created long-range uncertainties which are important factors in the generally depressed equity market for oil company stocks.

The Industrial Reorganization Act, if adopted, would create a new commission and a special judicial system with unprecedented broad powers to impose plans of reorganization upon entire industries. There can be no doubt that the full implementation of this Act would immediately depress the market values of the securities of businesses in the categories enumerated in section 203 (a) (2). I have no doubt that the market for oil company securities would be affected especially severely, because investors and analysts would expect the new commission to assign a high priority to the petroleum industry. Since neither the commission nor the newly established courts would be operating with any precedent in case law it is to be anticipated that complete judicial review of the initial cases would be very lengthy. During the pendency of any such litigation it would be very difficult, if not impossible, for individual companies to sell their securities or to negotiate new arrangements for long-term borrowings. As I indicated earlier in this presentation, any interruptions in the availability of new capital would further complicate the difficult task of reestablishing our domestic self-sufficiency in energy fuels.

Mr. Chairman, we all should be acutely aware of the fundamental changes that have occurred in ownership, structure and the economic and political usage of the enormous petroleum reserves of the Middle East. These recent developments have triggered reactions among still other petroleum exporting nations, which historically have been sources of part of our essential petroleum supplies. Even our friends in neighboring Canada have started to phase out all exports of crude oil to the United States, and very high export taxes have greatly increased the interim cost of imported Canadian crude oil and natural gas. In short, the worldwide operations of the U.S. petroleum industry are undergoing a shakeout of huge proportions.

We must recognize the urgent necessity for encouraging exploration and development of new sources of supply in this country and the construction of such new processing and transportation facilities as these new sources of supply will require. This task will require unprecedented amounts of new capital, on a continuous basis of investment, if we are to do little more than parallel future growth in demand with new supply.

I believe that the passage of this legislation will severely limit the petroleum industry's ability to raise the capital needed for this job. The potential for legal action under the provisions of this will would create great uncertainty about the continuity of individual companies, and this in turn would depress the market values of their securities and limit their access to long-term credits. In the event of prosecution under the provisions of the Act the companies involved no doubt would be prevented from undertaking any new financing, possibly for extended periods of time. In either case capital formation would be severely limited, at the expense of urgently needed resource development.

Mr. Chairman, I appreciate very much the opportunity to appear here today.

Erickson argues that the major premise underlying horizontal divestiture legislation, a lack of competition in the U.S. petroleum industry, is incorrect. Rather, the U.S. energy crisis has been caused by mistaken past policy actions. In Erickson's view, horizontal divestiture would be a further mistake in that it would impede competitive processes in the U.S. energy market and hence would be harmful to the national interest.

11

PUBLIC POLICY AND THE MONOPOLY MYTH

STATEMENT OF EDWARD W. ERICKSON*, NORTH CAROLINA STATE UNIVERSITY, BEFORE THE SUBCOMMITTEE ON ANTITRUST AND MONOPOLY, COMMITTEE ON THE JUDICIARY, UNITED STATES SENATE—JUNE 19, 1975

Thank you very much for this opportunity to present my views on Senate bill 489, a bill to amend the Clayton Act and intended to preserve and promote competition in the energy industry.

As a citizen and an economist, I take the efficiency of resource allocation very seriously. I take equally seriously the existence and enforcement of the antitrust laws to preserve and promote the competitive market mechanism which leads to efficient resource allocation.

S.489 is admirable in its intent. Unfortunately, however, the bill is based upon a mistaken premise. S.489 makes it unlawful for any person engaged in the production and refining of petroleum or natural gas, or both, to acquire, own, or control any interest in other energy businesses such as coal, oil shale, uranium, nuclear reactors, geothermal steam, or solar energy.

---

*Professor of Economics and Business, North Carolina State University.

This language implies the premise that firms engaged in both the production and refining of petroleum or natural gas are contaminated by monopoly; that such monopoly, in turn, contaminates the petroleum and natural gas industries; and that were firms so contaminated to be allowed to enter or continue operations in the proscribed energy businesses, those businesses would themselves in turn bear the stain of monopoly.

This is incorrect. It is incorrect as a statement of fact, and it is incorrect in terms of its logic. The popular belief that the petroleum and natural gas industries are characterized by private monopoly is deep-seated and long held.

Since higher prices are associated with monopoly and since energy prices have risen dramatically, the events of the recent energy crisis have reinforced that belief. Private monopoly power, however, was not responsible for the energy crisis. Sins of omission and of commission on the part of public policy makers played a major role in contributing to the energy crisis.

This is particularly the case with regard to U.S. energy policy. The world energy economy is now a fossil fuel economy. The United States is both the largest producer and consumer of energy. Even under the most optimistic assumptions of what was then the Atomic Energy Commission, fossil fuels will dominate the energy scene until well into the 21st century.

In terms of total energy consumption, oil and natural gas are likely to continue to be the most important fuels; although, as these hearings indicate, there is an increasing emphasis upon coal. The energy supply and demand system is, however, interconnected across fuels and locales. Marginal changes in one part of the system affect results elsewhere.

Some of the factors which have recently contributed to the stress on the system include:*

---

*This compilation is based in part upon the discussion in the editors' introduction to *The Energy Question: Failures of International Policy, Vol. I,*[1] *The World* (Toronto: University of Toronto Press, 1974), edited by E. W. Erickson and L. Waverman. This introduction is appended to my statement. Also appended is. "The U.S. Petroleum Industry." by myself and R. M. Spann.[2] This is Chapter One, pp. 5—24, Vol. II, North America, of The Energy Question. This chapter, together with the initial pages of "Tax Incentives and Crude Oil Supply,"[3] Brookings Paper on Economic Activity, 2: 1974. pp. 449—478 (which I have supplied separately to the Committee) deals specifically with competition in the U.S. petroleum industry.

[1] See 1975 hearings, Subcommittee on Antitrust and Monopoly, Vertical Integration, Part 1, p. 1055.

[2] See 1975 hearings, Subcommittee on Antitrust and Monopoly, Vertical Integration, Part 1, p. 1074.

[3] See p. 419.

1. The delivery and installation of nuclear power plants have not been as prompt as scheduled;

2. Once installed, nuclear power plants have not, in general, had the reliability that was anticipated;

3. Growth in electricity demand, together with the two factors above, have caused power companies to prolong the life of aging, on average less dependable, equipment; use older equipment more intensively than normally would have been the case; and expand effective capacity with fuel intensive internal combustion turbines;

4. Artificially low ceiling prices for natural gas in the United States have created a regulation, induced shortage of natural gas reserves and production:

5. Environmental considerations have delayed the construction of the trans-Alaska pipeline, the availability of oil from that source, and the drilling on the Alaskan North Slope which would indicate the approximate magnitude of the oil and gas reserves there;

6. The maneuvering surrounding the issue of the trans-Alaska pipeline in turn clouded discussions of a Mackenzie Valley pipeline through Canada and delayed intensive exploratory drilling in the Canadian Arctic;

7. Serious environmental problems caused the drilling program in the Santa Barbara Channel to be curtailed;

8. Oil producers in the United States were made very nervous by the deliberations of the Cabinet Task Force on Oil Import Control and left in a state of uncertainty concerning when and how the mandatory import control program would be relaxed, the prospects for the State conservation regulation system under which they were accustomed to operate, and the landed price, source, and volume of foreign oil against which they would have to compete;

9. Price controls in the United States distorted normal economic incentives with regard to the product mix of refinery output, kept the price of crude oil below the market clearing level, initially impeded U.S. ability to compete in the world oil market for artifically diminished supplies and finally evolved into a two-tier price system for "old" and "new" crude oil with various categories of exemptions and incentives;

10. Power plant emissions controls, land reclamation standards, and mine safety laws simultaneously affected the demand and supply conditions for coal;

11. Uncertainty about the future course of the United States oil import program and refinery siting problems caused a hiatus in U.S. refinery construction at a time when substantial new grassroots refining capacity needed to be initiated;

12. The Tax Reform Act of 1969 cut the depletion allowance on oil and natural gas from 27 1/2 percent to 22 percent;

13. Nonprice rationing end-use priority controls to allocate the shortage of natural gas, together with restrictions on the production and use of coal, shifted fuel demands to low-sulphur fuel oils at the same time that refining capacity was becoming more and more pinched;

14. Automobile emission controls caused a decrease in gasoline mileage and an increase in gasoline demand growth;

15. Challenges to the U.S. Bureau of Land Management postponed lease sales and delayed the discovery and development of new oil and gas reserves in the Gulf of Mexico;

16. Alarmists marching to the beat of an imaginary drummer—in the face of new oil and gas strikes in Indonesia, China, Russia, Nigeria, South America, the North Sea, Australia, Alaska, Canada, and elsewhere—proclaimed that the world was in imminent danger of "running out" of fossil fuels;

17. As a result of all of the above factors but the last, the United States became a significant and unexpected source of incremental demand in world refined product and low sulphur crude oil markets; and

18. The United States adopted the role of supplicant in dealing with the oil merchants of the Persian Gulf.

Most of those factors have an effect upon, either or both, supply and demand of one or another energy source. And in general, all those things had effects which moved the demand for energy out and shifted the supply of energy back which made a shortage of energy; an excess demand for energy in the United States which spilled over into the world market; and which contributed to the rapid run-up in prices and the organization of Arab petroleum exporting countries being able to solidify the larger body, OPEC, into a viable cartel.

I think that these factors that I list are perhaps what OMB had in mind with regard to Mr. Wagner's testimony when they suggested he, at least, allude to some other factors which may have been at work.

Now, these are policy problems and the recent and continuing dislocations in the world energy markets are policy-induced, by and large. U.S.

policy is critically important. In the frontispiece on one of the classics in economics, a book that was first published in 1890 in England, by Alfred Marshall, which still is a standard reference work in graduate economics, there appears the little inscription "natura non facit saltum." What that roughly corresponds to is that nature does not proceed by jumps. It is not a result of any physical shortage of oil that we saw the run-up of the world price of oil go from $2 a barrel to $10, $11, $12 a barrel in the recent past. That was a policy-induced situation, not the inexorable result of some physical law.

In my opinion, the Arab oil embargo was a symptom rather than a cause. There were already ample factors at work that caused dislocations in the world energy markets. The cumulative effects of the policy failures listed above created the economic vulnerability conducive to the political use of the oil weapon.

The demonstrated success of the oil weapon has changed the economics of policy planning. And this is particularly the case with regard to trade-offs among security of supply and other policy objectives. It is critically important that we do try and develop a cohesive, sensible, consistent energy policy that moves us towards desirable objectives.

What is especially ironic is, that the mistaken belief that the U.S. petroleum industry is characterized by monopoly contributed so significantly to the impact of the energy crisis; which in turn, reinforced the belief that the U.S. petroleum industry is a monopoly.

The U.S. petroleum industry is competitive. It is inhabited by very large firms but it, itself, is a very large industry, so that is not to be totally unexpected.

Competition is a dynamic process, a process which involves a host of different actors making different bets on the outcome of market processes. S.489 would impede this process. This is where the logic of the bill puzzles me because what it tries to do is to prevent the entry of oil companies into other sectors of the energy industry.

The oil industry is now effectively competitive. In general, the entry of oil companies into those other sectors would have to be regarded as a pro-competitive event. The example that Senator Hansen used earlier this morning of Gulf Oil and the nuclear reactor business, I think, is a perfect case in point of that.

The United States needs a larger domestic energy sector in its economy. Not only is S.489 unnecessary to preserve competition in the energy industries, but in my opinion, at least, it would be harmful to the national interest.

Kauper presents the view of the U.S. Department of Justice towards horizonal divestiture legislation. In that view, there is no demonstrated need for such legislation. Further, the legislation might be harmful to the public in certain situtations. Considering the lack of factual base for the legislation and the potential adverse effects, the Department concludes that it cannot recommend its passage.

12

JUSTICE LOOKS AT ENERGY DIVERSIFICATION

STATEMENT OF THOMAS E. KAUPER*, DEPARTMENT OF JUSTICE, BEFORE THE SUBCOMMITTEE ON ANTITRUST AND MONOPOLY, COMMITTEE ON THE JUDICIARY, UNITED STATES SENATE, OCTOBER 22, 1975

Mr. Chairman and Members of the Subcommittee:

I appreciate the opportunity to appear before this subcommittee this morning to discuss briefly various aspects of the energy industry. Unfortunately, time has permitted me to do little more than to prepare some rather generalized observations regarding S.489 and the problem at which it is apparently aimed.

The letter of invitation requested me to address several issues, one of which is ". . . whether the energy market is a relevant market in terms of interfuel competition. . ." The facile answer, of course, is "it depends." While that may sound a bit flippant, let me try to explain why I believe that is in fact the only responsible answer.

As you know, the process of defining what is a relevant market for antitrust analysis is frequently more difficult than it might seem at first blush.

---

* Assistant Attorney General of the United States, Antitrust Division.

There are two basic elements to relevant market analysis: the products which should be included, and the geographic areas which must be considered. The general formula by which we are guided in defining a product market under the antitrust laws was stated succinctly by the Supreme Court in the 1962 *Brown Shoe* case:

> "The outer boundaries of the product market are determined by the reasonable interchangeability of use or the cross-elasticity of demand between the product itself and substitute for it. However, within this broad market well-defined submarkets may exist which, in themselves, constitute product markets for antitrust purposes. . . . The boundaries of such a submarket may be determined by examining such practical indicia as industry or public recognition of the submarket as a separate economic entity, the product's peculiar characteristics and uses, unique production facilities, distinct customers, distinct prices, sensitivity to price changes, and specialized vendors." 370 U.S. 294, 325.

The application of this standard to the energy area requires considerable care and depends in the first instance on the existence of a sufficient body of factual information. Some persons contend that all forms of primary energy — oil, natural gas, coal, oil shale, uranium, geothermal steam, solar energy and tar sands are sufficiently interchangeable so that it is appropriate to lump everything into one large so-called energy market. Others argue that a more refined analysis indicates that the degree of interchangeability among the forms of primary energy fluctuates depending upon the types of energy being considered and the context of the analysis. For example, it seems reasonably clear that fuel oil, natural gas, coal and uranium are to a considerable extent reasonably interchangeable insofar as the electric power industry is concerned. Of course, there are a wide variety of factors — i.e., transportation costs, environmental restrictions, mine safety costs, nuclear safety and waste disposal, to mention a few — which importantly affect the degree of interchangeability which actually does exist in a given situation in the electric power industry.

Undertaking the kind of analysis required is further complicated by the fact that many of the energy forms mentioned in S.489 — tar sands, solar energy, geothermal energy, oil shale and coal — are usable only if commercially feasible technology can be developed. Whether "reasonable interchangeability of use" or "cross-elasticity of demand" in the antitrust sense will develop with regard to those forms of energy is a question which can only be dealt with today by speculation.

The other dimension of market definition in the antitrust context — geographic market — must also be considered in evaluating what the proper market or submarkets are in the energy field. For example, the marketing of geothermal steam is necessarily limited geographically. Also, the extent to which solar energy may provide an effective alternative to other forms of energy is, of course, affected by location. Its potential is obviously greatest in those portions of the country which have the greatest exposure to the sun.

In sum, it is virtually impossible to make any general statements about what is and what is not the proper market in the energy area outside of a specific factual context. In the abstract, the only responsible answer to your first question is "it depends."

You also asked us to comment on "... whether ownership in various sources of energy by the same firm creates a potentially anticompetitive situation." In a literal sense, the answer must be yes — the "potential" for adverse competitive effects exists. Whether this potential will become actual, or whether there is any realistic possibility of that happening, simply cannot be answered in the abstract. For example, there would appear to be no inherently pernicious antitrust consequences flowing from the acquisition of a solar heating firm in Massachusetts by a Wyoming oil producer. On the other hand, at least serious issues would be raised if a major petroleum company which is also a major natural gas producer achieves prominence in coal, uranium and oil shale, and also embarks upon an active program of acquiring the important patents in solar energy and other of the yet undeveloped fuel processes.

The Antitrust Division has examined a variety of energy cross-ownership situations in the past and will, of course, evaluate any others which arise. The FTC has done a considerable amount of work in this area. Some transactions of this type have taken place in the past without challenge from the antitrust enforcement authorities. Those decisions were based on analysis of particular factual circumstances.

One of the major problems in the energy area — which has handicapped both the antitrust enforcement agencies and the Congress — is the paucity of hard data. For example, recent court decisions indicate that analysis of mergers in the extractive minerals area requires detailed data regarding the ownership and dedication of reserves. Such information is generally almost impossible to obtain in a form which is usable for analysis. We understand that the Federal Trade Commission is in the midst of a major effort to obtain much of this hitherto unavailable material, and the successful completion of the effort may well permit us to reach more informed conclusions regarding cross-ownership of energy sources.

Finally, you asked for our overall views of the proposed legislation. We understand and appreciate the subcommittee's concern that fewer and fewer large corporations may achieve an unhealthy degree of domination of most of the important sources of energy. None of us wants such a situation to occur. The question then becomes how real is the threat and, if it is serious, how best to combat it. At this juncture we do not feel that it is possible to state categorically that the nation will rapidly move toward a highly concentrated energy industry absent the passage of S.489 or similar legislation. While there has been some movement of companies in one portion of the energy field into other sectors of that industry, there is of yet no clear indication that these transactions constitute an important phenomenon with adverse competitive impacts. Accordingly, we cannot conclude that there is a demonstrable need for S.489 or similar legislation.

Given this conclusion, it is important to realize that the proposed legislation might be harmful to the public in certain situations. For example, we all know that the nation has virtually limitless amounts of coal. Given this development of various complex and expensive technologies, it is conceivable that much more of this coal can be exploited than is currently the case. Coal liquefaction and coal gasification are two of the potential means by which greater coal utilization can be accomplished.

The research and development costs required to achieve commercially viable processes are, however, enormous and generally beyond the reach of all by the largest firms. In fact, many of the major oil companies are currently engaged in such research. Should this bill become law, an oil company might well conclude that further expenditure of capital on coal gasification, for example, was unwarranted and the company might abandon a promising effort. Such a result may well be contrary to the public interest.

The situation with respect to oil shale and tar sands is much the same. At present, neither of these energy sources is being exploited to any commercially significant extent. The expense of developing a technology to utilize the Canadian tar sands is such that a consortium of energy companies banded together to make a joint effort. S.489 appears to categorically prohibit any such effort and it is highly questionable whether such a blanket prohibition advances the public interest.

It is, of course, always possible that a joint venture will produce anticompetitive consequences, either actual or potential. I believe that existing antitrust enforcement authority is quite sufficient to allow careful analysis of such situations and, where appropriate, to enjoin their creation or continuation.

In sum, the factual basis for legislation to categorically prohibit cross-ownership of energy sources has yet to be demonstrated. Absent such an analytical base, and considering the potential adverse effects of such legislation, we cannot recommend its passage. If a basis for action is established by careful analysis, we would, of course, reconsider this position.

Moore views horizontal divestiture legislation as an attempt to reduce concentration in the U.S. energy market. He finds that such concentration in fact is low and that divestiture legislation would not much change that concentration. Further, he views the U.S. oil industry as competitive so that oil company development of alternate fuels will be conducted in a competitive manner. He concludes that horizontal divestiture legislation will not advance the public interest and thus should not be undertaken.

13

HORIZONTAL DIVERSIFICATION BY OIL COMPANIES

STATEMENT OF THOMAS GALE MOORE*, STANFORD UNIVERSITY, BEFORE THE ANTITRUST AND MONOPOLY SUBCOMMITTEE, COMMITTEE ON THE JUDICIARY, UNITED STATES SENATE—JUNE 19, 1975

It is a great privilege and honor to be here today. S. 489 is concerned with the competitiveness of one of our most basic and vital industries. It is essential to be eternally vigilant about the competitiveness of our economy. Too often government has encouraged monopoly rather than competition.

But this legislation is misconceived and potentially harmful to competition. S. 489 apparently reflects a bias against oil and gas companies. This industry has become a whipping boy in recent years. It has been pilloried in the press. Much but not all of the criticism is unwarranted and unjustified.

Basically the criticism is the result of the fact that oil companies are extremely large enterprises by any standards. Out of the largest 10 industrial

---

*Director of Domestic Studies Program at Hoover Institution, Stanford University; Senior Fellow, Professor of Economics.

companies in the U.S. 4 are oil companies. In addition as a result of an international cartel of oil producing governments, oil prices have shot up. It has been easy to blame this increase on the oil companies, since they had to increase the prices they charged for their products.

While it is politically popular to denounce the oil firms for higher prices and to point to large profits as signs that competition is not vigorous, the facts do not support that position. Basically the energy industries appear to be highly competitive. Even hostile critics have been unable to find evidence to the contrary. For example, in *A Time to Choose*, the final report by the Energy Policy Project of the Ford Foundation, the authors concluded somewhat reluctantly that "Compared with other major industries, concentration ratios are low, long term profit rates are generally average, and entry moderately free."[1] I say reluctantly because the report is very biased against the free market and particularly the oil companies.

By all the usual standards the oil companies and the energy industry is competitive. In 1970, the four largest crude oil producers in the U.S. sold 30.5 percent of all crude, the four companies with the largest proved reserves had 37.2 percent of all U.S. reserves, in 1972 the largest four refiners produced 33.1 percent of the output, and the largest retailers nationwide sold 29.2 percent of all gasoline. It should be noted that the four largest crude oil producers are not the four largest refiners nor the four largest retailers. In fact the third largest crude oil producer in 1970, Gulf Oil, was the sixth largest refiner in 1972, and the fifth largest seller of gasoline in 1973.[2]

These concentration ratios indicate that the industry is not controlled by a handful of firms. In fact these firms are all quite similar in size. Unlike many other industries no one or two firms dominate. For example the largest firm, Standard Oil of New Jersey, had 9.1 percent of the domestic refining capacity in 1972; the next largest, Texaco, had 8.4 percent, followed by Shell with 8.1 percent. The fifteenth largest, Cities Service, still had 2.1 percent of the capacity.[3] By no sense of the word can this industry be described as monopolistic or even oligopolistic.

A similar but even less concentrated situation exists in natural gas production. The largest four producers had 25.3 percent of the interstate pipeline sales in 1970.[4] The largest producer Exxon, had 9.0 percent of the

---

[1] (Ballinger Publishing Co., Cambridge, Mass., 1974), p. 238.
[2] T.D. Duchesneau, *Competition in the U.S. Energy Industry* (Cambridge, Mass: Ballinger Publishing, 1975), pp. 38-45.
[3] Ibid., p. 44.
[4] Ibid., p. 67.

total while the next largest had 5.6 percent. On the other hand the four largest pipeline buyers of natural gas had 38.5 percent of the market in 1968 down from 45.2 percent in 1961.[5] The market structure on both the buyer and seller side could best be described as competitive, although in earlier years it appears that pipelines might have been able to exert some oligopolistic control on natural gas prices.

Not only is industry structure competitive but performance is consistent with a competitive industry. In the period 1950 to 1973 the average price of gasoline excluding tax in constant dollars declined 32 percent.[6] Over the same period output per manhour tripled.[7] But profits have not been larger than in other sectors of the economy. The average profit rate of the twenty largest oil firms in the 1967-1972 period was 10.8, exactly equal to the average for all manufacturing in the 1967-71 period.[8] Edward J. Mitchell in his book *U.S. Energy Policy: A Primer* reported that he looked at the rate of return to an investor in oil company stock with dividends reinvested over the 1953-72 period and the 1960-1972 period.[9] He argued that if oil companies were earning any monopoly profits it would show up in the rate of return over such a long period. The result was that investors in U.S. oil company stocks did noticeably less well than the stock market as a whole. The attached table gives the average rates. If the oil producers or refiners had been in a position to control the market, the industry would have been more profitable rather than less profitable than other industries.

The objective of this bill is to deal with the expansion of oil and gas companies into other energy fields, thus becoming truly all-round energy companies. There is much to be said in favor of such expansion but before I discuss that, it might be wise to indicate the market structure of the energy industry generally.

This bill can be viewed as an effort to reduce concentration in the energy market generally. But concentration is low in this market. In 1970 the largest four firms in terms of BTU production in the U.S. produced 21.2 percent of all the BTU's. While it is true this level of concentration has increased from an even lower level earlier, mergers have not played a major role. Two of the largest mergers were the purchase of Consolidated Coal by Continental Oil and the purchase by Gulf of Pittsburgh and Midway Coal. If these mergers are subtracted from the energy output of the oil companies,

---

[5]Duchesneau, p. 70.
[6]Ibid., p. 154.
[7]Ibid, p. 156.
[8]Ibid., p. 157.
[9](Washington, D.C.: American Enterprise Institute, 1974), pp. 92-95.

in other words, if these mergers had not taken place, then the four-firm concentration level would not have been 21.2 but 19.9. In other words the effect of these mergers, which have caused so much concern and which have contributed to the support of this bill, has been to increase concentration by 1.3 percentage points.

Average Rate of Return to Stockholder
1953-74 and 1960-72

	1953-72	1960-72
21 Domestic Refiners	11.3	11.7
5 International Refiners	12.5	11.0
10 Domestic Oil Producers	n.a.	6.3
4 Overseas Oil Producers	n.a.	17.8
Standards & Poor's 500 Stock Composite Index	**15.6**	**12.8**

Source: Edward J. Mitchell, *U.S. Energy Policy: A Primer* (Washington, D.C.: American Enterprise Institute, 1974), Table B-1, p. 94.

Thus we have a basically competitive industry—oil—diversifying into related industries. Should this be stopped or rolled back? Certainly there is nothing in the current situation that appears to be anti-competitive. Thomas D. Duchesneau in *Competition in the U.S. Energy Industry* concludes "The general policy conclusion with respect to interfuel competition is that oil entry into coal and uranium has not resulted in monopolization of the nation's energy supplies, and antitrust action to halt further entry and/or require divestiture, is not economically justified on the basis of the current situation."[10] He goes on to say that "An outright ban on the entry of oil firms into coal and uranium probably has little economic justification. Such entry into coal, while posing a danger to interfuel competition, has also had procompetitive effects in several instances."[11]

As Duchesneau points out there may be some advantage to having oil companies move into other energy areas. For example from 1968 to 1970 Consolidated Coal, which is owned by Continental Oil, increased its output 25 percent and developed 17 new mines while industry output actually declined.[12] Thus oil companies seem to be more expansion minded, more able to tap capital markets, and more competitively oriented than established coal companies.

---

[10]Duchesneau, p. 187.

[11]Ibid., 187-188.

[12]T.G. Moore, "Economies of Scale of Firms Engaged in Oil and Coal Production," Appendix 13 of Duchesneau, p. 227.

As a general rule, it is often the outsider that brings innovations and new competitive vigor to an industry. To ban oil and gas companies from moving into other energy areas is more likely to harm competition than to promote it. There is no evidence that oil firms are likely soon to dominate the energy market and if that day does arise then the Justice Department can act under existing antitrust legislation to stop or reverse the trend.

Let me end by pointing out that the major problem with the energy industry has been government control. For years oil import quotas and prorationing were used to raise domestic oil prices and increase the profits of oil producers. Naturally this led to considerable waste and harmed competition. It also reduced the incentive to build domestic refineries thus eventually leading to shortages of refined products. While oil prices were being forced up natural gas prices were being held down. We are now paying for that mistake with shortages which will only grow worse until natural gas is deregulated.

Currently we hold down the price of "old" oil while letting new oil and imported oil sell at the world price. The result is that production of old oil is reduced, and we are increasingly dependent on foreign producers. Our policy is backfiring. Price controls on natural gas are also reducing domestic supplies with the result that pipelines are increasingly buying gas in Canada or elsewhere at prices much higher than they would need to be in an unregulated market—at the same time making us more dependent on foreigners.

The problems with the energy industries originate right here in Washington. They came from government controls. What we do not need is more legislation, more controls, or more bureaucrats running the energy industries. The best thing this committee could do for the public is to recommend the abolition of prorationing, price controls, market allocations, import tariffs and fees for both oil and natural gas.

Moyer documents that several oil companies have entered the coal market in the past decade; either through acquisition of coal companies or through direct acquisition of coal reserves. According to him, the motives for this expansion include a desire to diversify and a desire to have coal available in the event it becomes economic to convert coal into synthetic oil. There is little evidence to date that oil industry entry into coal mining has damaged competition in the coal industry. As a result, divestiture would not be an appropriate policy.

14

OIL COMPANIES IN THE COAL INDUSTRY

STATEMENT OF REED MOYER*, MICHIGAN STATE UNIVERSITY, BEFORE THE SENATE INTERIOR AND INSULAR AFFAIRS SPECIAL SUBCOMMITTEE ON INTEGRATED OIL OPERATIONS — DECEMBER 6, 1973

My name is Reed Moyer, I am a professor at the graduate school of business, Michigan State University.

I have written a book on the coal industry, an economic study, and done a number of studies on various aspects of the coal industry, including some work recently for the Ford Foundation's energy policy project.

I am going to address myself briefly to several aspects of this problem. First, I look at the extent of the oil industry's penetration into the coal industry.

Second, I trace the potential effect of this penetration on competition in the energy sector and present the historical record of its impact.

Third, I evaluate various policy alternatives designed to improve inter-fuel competition.

*Professor of Marketing at Michigan State University, Marketing and Transportation Dept.

First, and this is not in my statement, I think we need to recognize that the coal industry in years past was a fragmented industry made up of a lot of small and reasonably small companies.

Beginning in the 1940's and continuing through the fifties and sixties there occurred a merger movement in the industry.

Firms within the industry combined in intracoal acquisitions. It was not until 1963 that we got the first penetration of the oil industry into coal mining.

The second aspect that tends to be ignored is that there are several large noncoal, nonpetroleum companies that have acquired coal companies, including Kennecott's acquisition of Peabody, among others.

As far as the oil industry's penetration is concerned, they have entered in two ways. First, in recent years several major oil companies have acquired existing operating coal companies through merger or acquisition. There have been four of these mergers.

In addition, a large number of oil companies have acquired substantial undeveloped coal reserves. Some oil companies have begun to develop these reserves by opening up new coal mines.

Both the acquisition of operating coal companies, and the control of large quantities of undeveloped reserves pose potential threats to free competition.

Let's begin then by analyzing the first of these developments—the takeover of coal companies by major petroleum producers.

Exhibits, 1, 2, and 3 summarize the output performance from 1966-72 for the major coal companies acquired by oil producers.

Four of the companies are operating subsidiaries of four major oil companies. These are Consolidation Coal Co., a subsidiary of Continental Oil Co., Island Creek Coal Co., a subsidiary of Occidental Petroleum, Old Ben Coal Co., a subsidiary of Standard Oil of Ohio, and Pittsburgh & Midway Coal Co., a subsidiary of Gulf Oil Co.

In addition, Arch Mineral Co., is principally owned by the Ashland Oil Co., and the H.L. Hunt oil interests.

Exhibit 4 lists some additional companies that produce oil and also operate coal mines, usually through subsidiary operations.

In addition to the ownership of coal companies by oil producers several major coal producers also have some minor oil interests.

These would include the small amount of oil production by Zeigler

Coal Co., Utah International's ownership of Ladd Petroleum, and Pittston Co.'s oil distribution system.

From 1968, the first year when the major petroleum companies controlled their respective coal operations, until 1972, the market share controlled by the oil-dominated coal companies increased very slightly, from 19.3 percent of total output to 19.8 percent.

The output of individual firms varied. Consolidation Coal Co.'s market share from 1966, the year of its acquisition by Continental, to 1972 rose from 9.6 percent to 10.9 percent.

Island Creek's market share, however, declined as did Pittsburgh and Midway's. The Old Ben Coal Co.'s market share has remained fairly constant since its acquisition by Standard Oil Co. of Ohio.

The Arch Mineral case is unique. Begun by coal operators, ownership has since shifted principally to the Ashland Oil Co. and the H.L. Hunt interests. Some of the company's expansion stems from new mine development, but about half of its total output results from the acquisition by Arch of the Southwestern Illinois Coal Co., an Illinois producer.

In addition to entry through merger and acquisition, oil firms have acquired substantial coal reserves. For example, Humble Oil and Refining Co., a subsidiary of Exxon, has acquired several billion tons of coal reserves in Illinois in addition to several additional billion tons in Western States, and has developed an underground mine in Illinois.

Several other oil companies with extensive coal reserves in the West have announced plans for developing some of those reserves to supply coal to electric utilities on long term coal contracts.

A 1970 study to determine the extent of coal mining or coal reserve ownership by oil companies found 11 of the 25 largest firms involved in one way or the other. Since then at least two additional oil firms have acquired coal reserves.

What could motivate the oil companies to enter the coal industry either through acquisition or through controlled reserves?

Oil industry spokesmen offer two motives for expanding into competitive fuels. First is the diversification motive. Many oil company spokesmen have expressed confidence in coal's long run future and see their move into the industry as sound diversification policy.

Second, oil companies are doubtlessly acquiring coal to augment their long term fuel supplies. They are looking to the time when dwindling domestic oil supplies and higher fuel prices will permit the development of synthetic oil from coal.

Critics of the entry of oil companies into coal mining argue that the principal motive for their entry is the attempt to gain monopoly power through control of competitive fuel supplies. This explanation has intuitive appeal, but little, if any, evidence exists to support it.

At this point it might help to assess the potential harm to competition that might flow from the crossing over of companies from one fuel industry into another.

Interfuel acquisitions pose several potential threats. First is the danger of their creating sufficient market power to affect competition adversely. In markets where petroleum markets and coal compete the acquisition of coal companies might reduce the number of sellers of energy in those markets with a corresponding potential increase of market power.

I emphasize that the number of sellers "might" rather than "will" be reduced since the oil company and its acquired coal company may or may not compete in the same geographic markets.

Such interfuel competition exists primarily in the electric utility market where many plants are capable of burning either coal or oil.

If interfuel mergers increase market power, producers in this imperfectly competitive market may restrict output to maintain prices at levels permitting above-normal profits.

Whether or not market power is increased as a result of acquisitions depends to a large extent on the substitutability of fuels in different end-use markets. Let's, therefore, look at the extent of interfuel substitutability in some of these markets.

Each of the fossil fuels is uniquely suited to serve certain end-use markets. Metallurgical coal converts to coke for blast furnace use; natural gas is ideally suited as input for certain chemical products and as a fuel in other manufacturing processes; petroleum, as diesel fuel, supplies the locomotive fuel market and provides gasoline for the Nation's automobiles.

In other end-use markets, however, different degrees of interfuel competition exist. Some of the competition is continuous and is fairly intense; in other cases it is latent or indirect.

Some markets provide the potential for long run competition among fuels, but little scope for competition in the short run.

The home heating market is dominated pretty much by oil and natural gas, and coal's competitive threat exists only in the long run when existing equipment can be replaced.

The situation differs somewhat in the industrial and commercial markets. There, equipment may be designed to burn a single fuel, or it may permit, through conversion, the use of multiple fuels. We have seen a number of these conversions in recent years as industrial plants have sought to reduce SO_2 emission levels.

The biggest scope for interfuel competition exists in the electric utility market. In 1969, almost one-half of the electric generation capacity had multiple fuel capability.

The situation varied considerably from one region to another depending on fuel costs and fuel availability. But coal and oil competed in six of nine major regions of the country.

In some cases, the shift from one fuel to another can be fairly substantial over a short period of time. For example, in New England, oil supplied 58 percent of the electric utility market in 1953, 31 percent in 1956, and 83 percent in 1970. It competes principally with coal as a fuel source in that market.

Another objection to the takeover of the coal industry by the oil industry is the belief that it will retard research and development of synthetic fuels.

The oil companies have substantial investments in existing petroleum production, and it is argued, presumably would be reluctant to obsolesce those investments by developing synthetic oil production techniques.

One study of the effect on the rate of technological change of the oil companies' entry into the coal industry found that, far from deterring R. & D. the acquisitions were thought to accelerate development of liquefaction, gasification, and other energy-related innovations.

This study by Professor Mansfield found that the oil companies might be more likely than the independent coal companies to provide capital and the research capability that the coal companies lacked.

Reviewing the coal industry's R. & D. record, one finds a singular lack of a strong research commitment. The small size of most coal mining firms probably contributes to this condition.

Factors limiting the ability of the oil industry to slow down R. & D. progress in the development of synthetic fuels are the research activities of nonoil companies and the availability on a royalty-free basis of the results of Government-sponsored research in energy.

The National Petroleum Council's recent energy study estimates that a 50,000 barrel per day synthetic liquid fuel plant using coal as input would cost approximately $370 million to construct.

This cost would exceed the financial capability of virtually every independent coal company and would tax the financial ability of the largest non-independent, non-oil-dominated coal producers.

All but the largest coal producers would be hard pressed to finance a mine to produce the coal required as input for a plant of that size.

The capital cost of such a coal mine might run $40 to $50 million for a western strip mine. The economics of the operation might call for the use of a single coal supplier.

Must the coal supplier for a liquefaction plant necessarily be the petroleum company operating the liquefaction plant? That is, must it be a completely captive operation?

There is no reason that it need be as long as the oil company operating the liquefaction facility can contract for a long-term coal supply as electric utilities do now.

A more direct analogy exists in the case of the first coal gasification plants. These developments require capital investments of several hundred millions of dollars with auxiliary coal mining operations approaching the size of those required for a 50,000-barrel per day synthetic liquid fuel plant.

Each of the several gasification projects that have been announced will have the coal supplied to the gasification plant by a coal company independent of the gas company. The same situation could prevail with liquefaction projects.

In fact, there may be no economic necessity for oil companies alone to develop the liquefaction facilities either. What is to prevent companies outside of the oil industry from erecting liquefaction facilities whose output they would sell under long-term contracts to the petroleum company that would carry out some or all of the additional steps of refining, transporting, and distributing the petroleum products.

Entry of such firms would be feasible, however, only if the fruits of government-sponsored R. & D. in liquefaction are made freely available to all potential users and if government policy prevents the most desirable coal reserves from being locked up by a few large oil companies.

It is alleged that competition in coal may also be potentially harmed from the so-called deep-pocket threat posed by the oil companies.

That is, it is believed that the dominant position of coal companies acquired by the giant oil companies with their enormous financial sources will give them a competitive edge over smaller rivals in the industry.

Market conditions in many cases require that new coal mines produce several million tons of coal a year, requiring a capital outlay of perhaps $15 to $30 million.

This amount may exceed the capitalization of most independent coal companies, and, it is argued, make it impossible for the smaller firms to compete with companies controlled by oil producers.

Much the same argument could be made against the acquisition of coal companies by large noncoal producers as well and need not be restricted to acquisitions by petroleum companies.

In fact, several large noncoal mining companies have acquired leading coal producers, yet neither these firms nor the companies controlled by oil producers as a group have appreciably increased their share of the total coal market.

We have seen that the oil companies far from dominate coal production; however, their aggressive coal reserve acquisition program may pose a long term threat to effective fuel competition.

I have already noted that Humble Oil & Refining Co. has acquired billions of tons of reserves in Illinois and in several Western States.

Their vigorous coal acquisition activity in Illinois along with the coal reserve acquisition activities of other major oil companies in recent years have driven up the price of coal acreage in that state and have resulted in most of the remaining desirable coal reserves being locked up.

The oil companies also have been active in acquiring substantial reserves of low-sulfur strippable western coal. By April 1971, oil companies had acquired leases on about 25 percent of coal land then leased by the Federal Government.

They were producing on only 4 of 77 leases. Much of the unused coal reserves were undoubtedly being withheld from the market for future liquefaction.

An FTC study finds that the 15 largest coal companies control 26-1/2 billion tons of coal reserves with oil affiliated companies accounting for one-half of the total.

Control of this type may seem unimportant in view of the vastly greater quantity of available coal reserves in the country. Much of the Nation's coal reserves, however, are not economically mineable under existing conditions.

Thus the oil companies' strategically placed Western coal reserves give them a strong competitive position.

To this point we've looked at the potential damage to competition from the oil industry's entrance into coal mining. Now let's briefly analyze the record to determine its impact to date on competition.

Two indicators of industry conduct are price and output behavior. We have already seen that the oil-dominated coal companies in the few years in which they have operated in the coal industry have neither restricted output as a monopolist might be expected to do nor have they apparently gained market shares at the expense of their independent coal competitors as the deep pocket theory would suggest.

Some critics have alleged that collusion has existed in pricing and output decisions in coal, especially since petroleum companies have entered the industry.

It is impossible to speak with certainty about this matter, but a cursory examination fails to support the charges.

In fact, there is strong evidence for the belief that many coal companies, particularly those with underground mining operations in the East, have suffered losses or have had substantially reduced profit margins in the last year or two as a result of sharply lower productivity stemming from enforcement of the Coal Mine Health and Safety Act of 1969.

Furthermore, the long term coal contracts which account for a substantial share of coal sold to electric utilities lock in coal operators to a fixed price plus escalated cost increases for the duration of the contracts.

These contracts remove the coal from the open market for the life of the contract and protect the buyer from prices being pushed up during strong coal markets and the seller from depressed prices when markets are soft.

Collusion might exist when the contracts are entered into, but by their nature, both price competition and the opportunity for collusion disappear during the contracts' duration.

The coal companies controlled by oil producers possess inadequate market shares in most markets to artificially control prices.

One can even make a case for the oil-dominated coal companies increasing competition as a result of the de novo entry into coal mining of Humble in Illinois and of several other oil companies that have announced new mine openings in the West.

To this point I have sketched out the extent of oil industry penetration in coal mining and some of the implications of this entry.

What policy prescription might be appropriate in light of the situation as outlined above? The first possibility is divestiture of coal companies acquired by the major petroleum producers.

This approach appeals to a number of critics of the merger trend in the coal industry. For this to be an effective policy, however, more evidence is needed to support the view that competition has been adversely affected as a result of these mergers.

Successful use of divestiture also hinges on the outcome of two pending Supreme Court cases involving attempts by the FTC and the Justice Department to overturn the acquisitions by Kennecott Copper Co. of Peabody Coal Co. and General Dynamics Corp. of United Electric Coal Co.

A second approach might call for the ban on future acquisitions of coal companies by petroleum firms. While previous mergers may not have resulted in undue concentration we cannot be certain that future mergers would not do so.

It is hard to justify coal-oil mergers if we intend to maintain vigorous competition in the energy area. I noted earlier that several oil companies with newly acquired coal reserves have opened coal mines or plan to open them.

This development plus the drive for coal reserves by a large number of other oil companies leads one to believe that oil companies that entered the coal industry through mergers probably would have entered independently if antitrust action had barred their coal merger activity.

Another policy question has to do with control of the vast government coal reserves that are presently uncommitted. The Federal Government, through its ownership of 40 million acres of Western coal lands, is the dominant factor in the future coal reserve picture.

Currently there is a moratorium on the leasing of most of the Federal coal lands while the Bureau of Land Management, which manages the Government's mineral lands, develops a new leasing policy.

The Bureau intends to develop a policy that will achieve a fair financial return to the government, will match coal supplies with market demands in a rational way, and will assure environmental protection.

In addition the Government's leasing policy might provide for maximizing competition in the energy sector. This might require setting up procedures to encourage newcomers to enter the coal industry by mining government land and to restrict coal acreage allotments to individual firms, especially those already controlling extensive coal reserves.

Present BLM regulations limit holdings of Federal Government coal leases to 46,080 acres per state per firm. The Bureau might reduce that limit, place it on a tonnage rather than on an acreage basis if reasonable tonnage estimates can be made, and call for a competitive impact analysis in addition to an environmental impact statement before the federal lands are released for bidding.

We need to insure that firms possessing less financial power than the large oil companies are capable of entering the coal industry through the Government land bidding process.

In addition to insuring free access to Government coal lands on future leases, we need to assess the competitive effect of existing coal reserve ownership patterns.

If, for example, a firm outside of the coal industry wished to acquire substantial, desirable coal reserves in Illinois to support a coal gasification plant, it might have difficulty in doing so.

It would find the most suitable reserves locked up by several major oil companies and a handful of large coal companies.

The Bureau of Mines data on coal reserves may mislead us into believing that there are available unlimited reserves of economically minerable coal. However, not all coal reserves are equally desirable.

To determine the competitive effect of coal reserve ownership requires that we have a better understanding of who owns or controls reserves and more information about the potential availability and production costs for presently uncommitted reserves.

The Bureau of Mines and the Bureau of Land Management could fulfill the second of these needs. Currently we possess fairly crude estimates of coal reserves that classify them according to the reliability of data used in making the estimates.

Thus reserves are categorized as either "measured," "indicated" or "inferred." Within these categories reserves are grouped according to seam depth and thickness.

Obviously a seam of high quality bituminous coal 7 feet thick and found at a depth of 150 feet is more attractive than a 3 foot seam of lignite at 1,000 feet. We should make better estimates than we now have of relative mining costs for coals with different geological characteristics to put the United States reserve totals in a better perspective.

More important for the subcommittee's immediate needs is to gain access to more complete and detailed coal reserve data than we now possess. It would improve our understanding of coal reserve ownership if these data were sought not only from the petroleum companies but from coal mining companies and large coal land owning companies as well if that is possible.

[The exhibits submitted by Professor Moyer follow:]

EXHIBIT 1

OUTPUT BEHAVIOR OF MAJOR COAL COMPANIES ACQUIRED BY OIL PRODUCERS, 1966-72

[Million tons]

Coal Company	Parent company	Year						
		1972	1971	1970	1969	1968	1967	1966
Consolidation	Continental Oil	64.9	54.8	64.1	60.9	59.9	56.5	[1]51.4
Island Creek	Occidental Petroleum	22.6	22.9	29.7	30.4	[1]25.9	25.9	23.7
Old Ben	Standard Oil of Ohio	11.2	10.5	11.7	12.0	[1]1.9	10.3	9.9
Arch Mineral[2]	Ashland Oil-H. L. Hunt	11.2	2.1					
Pittsburgh & Midway	Gulf Oil	7.7	7.1	7.8	7.6	9.2	9.0	[1][3]8.9
Total U.S. bituminous coal output		595.4	552.2	602.9	560.5	545.2	552.6	[3]533.9

[1]Year company was acquired
[2]Much of Arch Mineral's increased output came in 1972 from its acquisition of Southwestern Illinois Coal Co.
[3]Control by Gulf Oil dates to 1963.
Source: Coal Mine Directory, "Keystone Coal Industry Manual," various years.

EXHIBIT 2

MAJOR ACQUIRED COAL-OIL COMPANIES' OUTPUT AS PERCENTAGE OF TOTAL COAL OUTPUT, 1966-72

Coal Company	Parent company	Year						
		1972	1971	1970	1969	1968	1967	1966
Consolidation	Continental Oil	10.9	9.9	10.6	10.9	11.0	10.2	9.6
Island Creek	Occidental Petroleum	3.8	4.1	4.9	5.4	4.8	4.7	4.4
Old Ben	Standard Oil of Ohio	1.9	1.9	1.9	2.1	1.8	1.9	1.9
Arch Mineral	Ashland Oil-H. L. Hunt	1.9	.4					
Pittsburgh & Midway	Gulf Oil	1.3	1.3	1.3	1.4	1.7	1.6	1.7
Total		19.8	17.6	18.7	19.8	19.3	18.4	17.6

Source: Exhibit 1

EXHIBIT 3

INDEX OF ACQUIRED COAL-OIL COMPANIES' OUTPUT, 1966-72
[1966 = 100]

		Year						
Coal company	Parent company	1972	1971	1970	1969	1968	1967	1966
Consolidation	Continental Oil	126	107	125	118	116	110	100
Island Creek	Occidental Petroleum	95	97	125	128	109	109	100
Old Ben	Standard Oil of Ohio	113	106	118	121	100	104	100
Arch Mineral	Ashland Oil-H. L. Hunt	(1)	(1)	(1)	(1)	(1)	(1)	(1)
Pittsburgh & Midway	Gulf Oil	86	80	88	85	103	101	100
Total U.S. bituminous coal output.		112	103	113	105	102	104	100

[1] Not applicable.

Source: Exhibit 1.

EXHIBIT 4—SMALL OIL COMPANIES WITH COAL OPERATING INTERESTS

OIL COMPANY	COAL COMPANY
Belco Petroleum,	Hawley Fuel Co.
McCulloch Oil Co.	Four small coal companies (names unavailable)
Transcontinental Oil Co.	Greer-Ellison Coal Co.
Crestmont Oil and Gas Co.	Black Lode Coal Co.
Mapco	Webster County Coal Corp.

Ray reviews the activities of oil firms in the U.S. nuclear industry. In her view, petroleum technology is readily transferable to many aspects of nuclear industry operations. Given an urgent need to develop domestic sources of energy, Ray finds it would be unwise categorically to deter oil firms from putting their resources to work in other energy areas.

15

OIL COMPANIES IN THE URANIUM INDUSTRY

STATEMENT OF HON. DIXY LEE RAY*, CHAIRMAN U.S. ATOMIC ENERGY COMMISSION, BEFORE THE SENATE INTERIOR AND INSULAR AFFAIRS SPECIAL SUBCOMMITTEE ON INTEGRATED OIL OPERATIONS—DECEMBER 6, 1973

I am pleased to be here and to have the opportunity to speak to this subject.

The Special Subcommittee on Integrated Oil Operations is interested in the "competitive implications of the entry of major petroleum companies into the nuclear power field."

While the Antitrust Division of the Department of Justice and the Federal Trade Commission have primary responsibility for enforcement of the antitrust laws, the Atomic Energy Commission does have a responsibility with respect to the competitive implications of nuclear industry developments.

The Atomic Energy Act of 1954 states, in its opening section, that, "the development, use, and control of atomic energy shall be directed," among other things to "strengthen free competition in private enterprise."

---

*Chairman, U.S. Atomic Energy Commission at the date of her testimony. Now a lecturer and writer.

We do consult with the Justice Department and the Federal Trade Commission on competition in the nuclear industry and, as I will describe later, the Atomic Energy Act requires the Justice Department's review of competitive aspects of certain nuclear licensing actions.

It should not be necessary to preface my remarks with an extensive discussion of nuclear energy, but I want to describe certain characteristics of the nuclear industry that have a direct bearing on the issue of participation by the petroleum companies. These include the development of nuclear technology by the Government and the difficulties of transferring the commercialization task to private hands; the massive investments needed to enter the nuclear business and the long delay in returns; the complex and demanding standards which must be met; the continuing requirements for surveillance of operating plants; and the laws and regulations to which the industry is subject.

The development of a commercial nuclear industry was essentially due to actions taken by the Congress and the AEC to encourage widespread participation in the peaceful uses of nuclear energy. The objective of those actions was the commercialization of nuclear technology.

Success was considered to have been achieved when private firms entered the field and the technology was used in commercial applications.

Private participation in nuclear programs is an important issue for no other sector of the energy economy has entailed the use of such vast public resources in its development. The price of participation by private parties has also been high. Entrance into the business usually involved massive inputs of capital with long delays in profitable returns.

There are high costs associated with the application of any new and complex technology, especially in the nuclear industry which levies such exacting requirements for safety and reliability. Because of the need for high standards of quality and competence, potential participants must be able to demonstrate superior capabilities in both technical and managerial fields. The demanding conditions of nuclear technology create a natural selection process which greatly limits the field.

The institutional and administrative practices surrounding nuclear operations further restrict potential participants. The lengthy licensing process and the need for continued surveillance, which are necessary for the safe use of nuclear materials, impede entry by those who cannot afford or will not tolerate involved procedures and delay. Stringent environmental regulations must also be taken into account.

The Atomic Energy Act of 1954, Public Law 83-703, provides the legal means for private participation in nuclear activities. The act recognizes the need to foster competitive conditions as the transition to private enterprise proceeds. The antitrust provisions in section 105 declare that nothing contained in the Atomic Energy Act shall relieve any person from the operation of the antitrust statutes.

Consequently, as private firms enter any phase of nuclear operations, they are subject to the antitrust laws for which the Department of Justice and the Federal Trade Commission have enforcement responsibilities.

In conjunction with the foregoing, section 105 of our act also requires the Commission to report to the Attorney General any information it may have with respect to nuclear activities which appear to violate or to tend toward the violation of the antitrust laws or to restrict free competition in private enterprise.

In addition, the Commission is required, by section 105 of the act, to obtain the advice of the Attorney General with respect to the antitrust implications of applications for licenses to construct and operate nuclear powerplants and other major nuclear facilities.

In those instances where the Attorney General believes that the granting of a license may create or maintain a situation inconsistent with the antitrust laws, a hearing and a Commission decision on this licensing aspect may be necessary.

Quite apart from these special provisions, the Commission has conducted studies and reported results to the antitrust agencies on important facets of nuclear industry development.

A major study in this area, completed in 1968, was carried out for the AEC and the Department of Justice under a joint contract with Arthur D. Little, Inc. The study report has proven to be a useful document on the nature of the nuclear industry ane the prospects of workable competition in the nuclear power supply sphere.

Beyond such special studies, interagency discussions have been held periodically on nuclear industry developments, and notices of important transactions o organization moves in the industry have been supplied to the Department of Justice.

Like the rest of the electric power industry, nuclear electric power is served by two major groups of suppliers, the manufacturers and builders of nuclear powerplants and the fuel producers and processors. Both of these areas are more complex technologically and involve greater expenditures than is the case in the nonnuclear spector of the electric power industry. The flow of materials, for example, in the nuclear fuel cycle, starting at the uranium mine and ending with the shipment of radioactive wastes to a Federal repository is decidedly different than the process of supplying coal or oil to a powerplant. While the volume of natural resource materials is much smaller for nuclear fuel, it must be concentrated in a milling process, changed to a gaseous state, UF_6, in a conversion plant, upgraded in an enrichment plant, converted back to a solid oxide and fabricated into metal-clad fuel elements before it even reaches the nuclear electric powerplant.

Relatively small amounts of material are utilized but they are subjected to complicated technological processes and utilized in facilities with huge capital costs.

To mine, process, enrich, and fabricate fuel for the rapidly expanding nuclear industry, there must be an accompanying growth in every segment of the nuclear fuel cycle.

In addition to those segments earlier described, there are complex operations for the handling of spent fuel from nuclear reactors, for its reprocessing, and for management of nuclear wastes.

The enrichment process and waste management are the only phases of the nuclear fuel cycle still in Government hands. Efforts are under way to facilitate entry of private firms into the enrichment operation. An efficient increment of new enrichment capacity using the new gas centrifuge processes is estimated to cost about $1.5 billion for an 8,750 metric ton unit. We have estimated that some $16.5 billion, in constant dollars, could be required for additional enriching capacity alone before the year 2000.

Capital investment for uranium exploration development of new mines and new mills for concentration of ores would be about $18 billion on the same basis.

Beyond this, the conversion and fabrication stages of the fuel cycle would require new investment on the order of $10 billion and the facilities for fuel reprocessing and waste management would probably need about $1 to $2 billion investment.

Investments by the equipment manufacturers, architect-engineering, and construction firms are all in addition to the investment needs for the utilities' powerplants and for the various phases of the nuclear fuel cycle.

Through December 1, 1973, the utility industry has spent or committed nearly $70 billion for nuclear power generating facilities that are now in operation, under construction, or on order. The cumulative sum of capital expenditures on all new nuclear generation facilities through the end of this century is estimated at $450 billion in terms of constant 1973 dollars.

More than 60 percent of this investment is expected to be made for nonbreeder reactor types with the remaining expenditures for breeder reactors to occur in the latter part of this period.

There are currently four U.S. equipment manufacturers offering light water reactors (LWR's). General Electric and Westinghouse are the principal vendors, but two firms with a long history of experience in the manufacture and construction of electric power facilities, Combustion Engineering and Babcock & Wilcox, also supply nuclear steam supply systems.

The record of contract awards since the first sales and the share of the total by these four firms in the last 2 years are set forth in an attachment to my prepared testimony.

I would like to turn now to the matter of oil company participation in the nuclear industry.

1. NUCLEAR REACTORS

In October 1967, the Gulf Oil Corp. acquired the general atomic division of General Dynamics Corp. They have since proceeded with the development and manufacture of a high temperature gas-cooled reactor, HTGR, to compete with the commercial LWR's now being sold by the four vendors mentioned earlier. This reactor has operated in an experimental plant at Peach Bottom in Pennsylvania and will be demonstrated in a 330-megawatt unit at Fort St. Vrain in Colorado early next year.

The company now offers the HTGR on a commercial basis and has sold a total of six additional plants, two each in Pennsylvania, Delaware, and California. Southern California Edison has, in addition, an option for two plants.

This reactor uses helium instead of water as the coolant; it operates on a thorium-uranium cycle as opposed to uranium only in the LWR and its thermal efficiency should be about 39 percent compared to 39 percent for the LWR.

In addition to potential technical advantages, the utilities should welcome the entry of an alternate supplier of nuclear power plants and equipment.

On June 4, 1973, Gulf announced that it had entered into an agreement with the Royal Dutch Shell Group for a joint venture which would encompass not only the Gulf commercial fuel fabrication capabilities and its HTGR effort, but other activities conducted by the California-based Gulf Energy & Environmental Systems.

According to *Business Week* magazine, Gulf does not expect a profit from reactor sales for another 5 years. Through Shell's participation, the venture will be infused with some $200 million in new capital and a greater potential for worldwide expansion in reactor sales.

2. URANIUM RESOURCES

Exploration for uranium by oil companies began its major growth in the 1967 to 1968 period when orders for commercial nuclear power reactors made it clear that there would be a substantial future need for uranium. Only a few oil companies were active prior to that time.

In 1972, 15 oil companies were engaged in exploratory drilling for uranium. Seventy-two other companies also explored in that year.

The oil companies performed about 53 percent of the 15.4 million feet of drilling for uranium in that year, although they constituted only 17 percent of the companies actively exploring.

As a result of these efforts, oil companies currently control about 50 percent of U.S. uranium ore reserves minable at a cutoff cost of $8 per pound of U_3O_8. Of the 10 companies with the largest uranium reserves, 4 are oil companies.

Two mills were built by oil companies in the last few years to process uranium ore into uranium concentrates. Oil companies control 4 of the 16 mills now operating. The four mills constitute 43 percent of currently operating U.S. uranium milling capacity.

The efforts of the oil companies have made a significant contribution to the expansion of U.S. uranium resources and production capability.

Uranium requirements are projected to increase from 8,000 tons of U_3O_8 this year, and a production capability of 18,000 tons, to annual production requirements of 38,000 tons in 1980 and 120,000 tons in 1990.

Since the current and near-term earnings from uranium operations will not provide large amounts of funds for reinvestment, capital investment from outside the uranium industry will have to increase considerably in the years ahead to discover the reserves needed and develop the many new mines and mills.

Ultimate potential U.S. uranium resources are as yet unclear and a significant contribution to the U.S. energy position may result from farther delineation of U.S. resources.

3. ADDITIONAL FUEL CYCLE OPERATIONS

In addition to their participation in uranium resources aspects of the nuclear fuel cycle, oil companies are also interested in fuel fabrication, processing of irradiated fuel and other parts of the fuel cycle.

There are six U.S. companies that are fabricators of replacement nuclear fuel. Two of them, Gulf and Exxon, are oil companies, and the other four are the manufacturers of light-water nuclear power reactors.

Normally, the reactor manufacturer furnishes the first core and frequently furnishes several reloads. Companies independent of the reactor manufacturer also provide reload services.

As indicated in the following summary of the leading oil companies' activities, there has been substantial initiative in several areas of the fuel cycle.

A. Gulf Oil Corp.

Gulf General Atomic announced, on May 26, 1969, that it was offering fuel fabrication services for light-water reactors and that, in conjunction with this service, it would provide fuel management services to meet individual utility needs. This activity is in addition to its HTGR work mentioned earlier.

To continue R. & D. in LWR fuel, Gulf has arranged for access to United Kingdom Atomic Energy Authority development facilities and production know-how.

In July 1971, a new, jointly owned company, Gulf United Nuclear Fuels Corp., was formed to take over essentially all of the commercial nuclear fuel facilities of United Nuclear with Gulf providing capital for the operation.

United Nuclear was the first and, for several years, the only successful independent fabricator of reload nuclear fuel.

In 1973, Gulf bought out all of the United Nuclear interests in the previously jointly owned company. It was announced, on December 3, 1973, that Gulf plans to divest itself of its UO_2 fuel fabrication activities.

Gulf, together with Allied Chemical, is building a plant in Barnwell, S.C., to process irradiated fuel from LWR's. Its capacity will be 5 metric tons of uranium, MTU, per day and is expected to begin commercial operation in 1977. The plant's estimated cost is $130 million and it will have sufficient capacity to handle the discharged fuel from approximately 50,000 MWe of nuclear capacity.

B. Kerr-McGee Corp.

Kerr-McGee Corp. has been active in nuclear fuel processing for a number of years and has not made any major acquisitions of other companies involved in nuclear activities.

Although Kerr-McGee has fabricated sizable quantities of fuel elements for use in some specialized Government reactors, so far it has not announced any plans to enter the commercial power reactor fuel reload market. The corporation also has a facility in operation at Sequoyah, Okla., that is capable of converting about 5,000 tons of uranium per year from ore concentrates, U_3O_8, to uranium hexafloride, UF_6.

The plant was designed to accommodate ready expansion to a capacity of 10,000 tons of uranium per year and the engineering design for such an expansion is underway. The only other private UF_6 conversion plant is a facility at Metropolis, Ill., owned by Allied Chemical Corp.

C. Getty Oil Corp.

In April 1968, Getty and Skelly oil companies purchased 20 percent interest in the existing stock of Nuclear Fuel Services, NFS, and agreed to purchase certain additional stock to be issued by NFS.

Nuclear Fuel Services was originally formed in 1962 as a joint venture to process irradiated fuel by W.R. Grace & Co., 80 percent ownership, and American Machine & Foundry Co., 20 percent ownership.

On February 27, 1969, Getty Oil, Skelly Oil, and W.R. Grace & Co., announced that Getty had agreed to purchase the remainder of Grace's interest in NFS, giving Getty 89 percent and Skelly 11 percent interest in JFS. Getty holds about 50 percent interest in Skelly.

In 1970, a $15 million expansion of the NFS plant at West Valley, N.Y., was undertaken to expand capacity of the irradiated fuel reprocessing plant from 1 ton to 3 tons per day.

Despite extended efforts by NFS to obtain orders for nuclear fuel reloads, it was reported in May 1973, that NFS was discontinuing its efforts as a reload fuel fabricator.

D. Exxon Corp.

In March 1969, Standard Oil of New Jersey announced plans to start construction of a nuclear fuels development and fabrication plant. The new plant was initially named Jersey Nuclear Co., but was changed to Exxon Nuclear Co., in January 1973. Located near Richland, Wash., it started operation as a nuclear fuel fabrication facility in 1971.

The plant can also fabricate mixed oxide, plutonium-uranium fuel and offers services in uranium fuel management, nondestructive testing, project construction management, plant activation and support operation, outage management, and personnel training. The total number of orders that Exxon Nuclear has under contract, including options, amounts to 105 reload batches.

In addition to the nuclear capabilities mentioned above, Exxon Nuclear is actively investigating future commercial opportunities in the field of uranium enrichment. It has participated in steps 1 and 2 of the AEC enrichment technology access program for private industry. It is considering both gaseous diffusion and gas centrifuge processes in a joint economic evaluation effort with the General Electric Co.

Apart from the AEC industrial participation program, Exxon Nuclear is also jointly sponsoring, with the Avco Corp., a research effort aimed at enrichment of uranium by means of laser excitation.

My discussion up to this point has dealt primarily with oil companies that are presently involved in nuclear activities. I think I should also say a few words about some oil company ventures into the nuclear arena that were not sufficiently rewarding to justify their continuation.

For example, in April 1967, the Atlantic Richfield Corp. acquired Nuclear Materials and Equipment Corp., NUMEC, a company that had been in existence for a number of years and which was offering a wide range of fuel fabrication capabilities.

In 1968, Atlantic Richfield planned construction of a large spent fuel reprocessing plant to be located on the east coast and also made a serious bid to obtain orders for fabrication of reload nuclear fuel. In 1971, however, Atlantic Richfield announced that it was phasing out all nuclear fuel activities at its NUMEC facilities, as well as its plans for a reprocessing plant.

In March 1969, Continental Oil announced that it had entered into a partnership with Aerojet-General to form a new organization, C/A Nuclear Fuels, to design and fabricate reload nuclear fuel. In January 1970, however, the partnership was dissolved and the plans were abandoned.

As noted above, Nuclear Fuel Services has discontinued its efforts as a reload fuel supplier and Getty Oil has considered selling Nuclear Fuel Services.

An analysis of the competitive implications of the operations of these oil companies requires study of their impact at each specific phase of the nuclear fuel cycle or other activity. In this context, unilateral entry into a market by a new firm can be favorable to competition.

On the other hand, many of the oil company moves noted above were through acquisitions. In some cases, existing firms did not have sufficient financial resources or were not inclined to sit out the long waiting periods until operations such as fuel reprocessing reached levels of activity adequate to show a profit. The competitive results in some cases may not be obvious until several years in the future.

Obviously, the degree of vertical integration evidenced by oil company ventures in various phases of the nuclear fuel cycle or in the manufacture and supply of plant and equipment also invites further study and analysis. Firms like Gulf, Exxon, Getty, and Kerr-McGee are becoming fairly well established in various phases of nuclear fuel cycle operations.

In fulfilling its obligation to strengthen free competition in private enterprise the Commission will, of course, continue to give great weight to the opinions and advice of the antitrust agencies. At the same time, however, we can guide and influence the pattern of development of the nuclear industry by persuasion and through contract mechanisms, through Commission policies in such areas as access to technology, where appropriate, by considering anticompetitive factors in exercising our authority to license.

All of these mechanisms must, of course, be used responsibly, and ventures backed by oil companies should be studied as objectively as any other undertaking. In this connection, it should be recognized that the oil companies bring a degree of experience and technical competence in many nuclear industry operations that are not readily duplicated elsewhere. Their background in geological investigations, drilling, and oil exploration obviously facilitates their diversification into uranium exploration and mining; and their experience in oil refining and chemical process industries is helpful in certain other phases of the nuclear fuel cycle.

There is now an urgent need for effective action by the Federal Government to assure both a short-term energy supply and the availability of the adequate energy for the longer term. The physical, financial, and managerial assets of the large oil companies should play an appropriate part in our planning to meet the Nation's energy needs.

Needless to say, this must be accomplished within the framework of our antitrust laws and the national policy of fostering competition.

The large multinational oil companies are undoubtedly appraising their roles at this time. Their new organizational and operational strategies may have profound impact on other energy industries.

It would not seem wise, categorically, to deter any firms from putting their resources to work in other energy areas. If prevented from participation in the domestic energy industries, they may move toward diversification outside of the energy field, or they may direct their efforts into other foreign energy operations as they are forced to relinquish control in foreign oil-producing areas.

If we are to succeed in a rapid and efficient shift to indigenous energy sources, these companies should be attracted to new energy industry opportunities within the United States.

We must continue to encourage new participants into the nuclear industry. At the same time, however, we must assure that the development of the nuclear industry is consistent with the antitrust laws and the requirement in the Atomic Energy Act that, "the development, use, and control of atomic energy shall be directed * * * to strengthen free competition in private enterprise."

Wilson addresses whether it would be desirable social policy
to restrict oil companies from operating in the coal industry.
After describing the nature of the coal market in some detail,
Wilson concludes that consumers there are well protected by
competitive market forces and could only be hurt by new
government regulation to limit entry into coal. Wilson also points
out that oil entry into coal has resulted in an infusion of capital
and technology into the industry and predicts that oil-owned coal
subsidiaries will contribute substantially to increasing national
coal output.

WHO'S MINING THE COAL?

STATEMENTS BY WALLACE W. WILSON,* CONTINENTAL ILLINOIS NATIONAL BANK AND TRUST COMPANY OF CHICAGO, BEFORE THE ANTITRUST AND MONOPOLY SUBCOMMITTEE, COMMITTEE ON THE JUDICIARY, UNITED STATES SENATE—JULY 14, 1975

Mr. Chairman, and members of the Committee: My name is Wallace
W. Wilson. I am Vice President, Energy and Mineral Resources Division,
of Continental Illinois National Bank and Trust Company of Chicago, and
have been associated with this bank for more than 19 years. My responsibilities have included account administration, financial planning and lending activity for a broad spectrum of the energy industries, including major
integrated oil companies, independent oil and gas producers, coal and metal
mining companies and joint ventures for the development of synthetic
fuels. Prior to joining Continental Bank I was employed as manager of a
headquarters engineering staff for a major international oil company, and as
Assistant Professor of Petroleum Engineering at the University of Texas. I

---

*Vice President, Continental Illinois National Bank and Trust Company of Chicago.

also served as a research group leader for another large oil company, and as a staff engineer for a consulting petroleum engineering firm. My total professional experience with the energy industries spans more than 33 years.

I belong to a number of engineering, professional and honorary organizations related to the production and utilization of energy fuels, and serve on the Energy Resources Commission for the State of Illinois.

My appearance here today is with regard to S. 489, which would amend the Clayton Act by prohibiting the ownership of assets in certain forms of energy resources by major, integrated oil companies. My remarks are based upon my lengthy experience in the energy resource field, and are not necessarily the views of my present employer.

I propose to direct my remarks principally to existing and prospective ownership of coal assets by oil companies. Since uranium, oil shale, geothermal steam and solar energy comprise, in the aggregate, only a minute share of our domestic energy supply, specific reference to them will be quite brief.

In your introductory statement to this bill on January 9, 1975, Mr. Chairman, the initial paragraph describing S. 489 included tar sands with other energy resources to which this bill applied, but I find no mention of tar sands in the body of the bill. I respectfully suggest that the record should be clarified to show that there is no Congressional intent to bar ownership of so-called tar sands by oil companies.

It is my considered belief, Mr. Chairman, that legislation which would build a fence around the coal industry and post it off limits to the free entry of other types of businesses would be economically counterproductive and potentially disastrous to the National goal of achieving greater self-sufficiency in energy fuels. To forbid integrated major oil companies from owning coal assets, merely because oil and coal are both energy fuels and ownership of more than one form of energy resource might create the potential for illegal monopolistic activity is, in my view, the very antithesis of fostering free competition throughout our economy. It is much like telling the owners of McDonald franchises that they may sell hamburgers, but not hot dogs, because both are food products competing for the free choice of consumers.

Mr. Chairman, this legislation, insofar as it relates to the coal industry, seems to be predicated upon a presumption of great opportunity for illegal, noncompetitive marketing conditions, which I do not believe exist and by all odds never could occur. I should like to expand upon this statement by showing that: (a) there are very limited numbers of present or potential consumers of coal, (b) coal is essentially a feedstock, used mainly for the production of other types of energy and to a lesser extent in making steel and chemicals, (c) the so-called retail market for coal is very small and of declining importance, (d) interfuel competition between coal and other forms of energy is quite limited although governmental actions created massive disincentives for coal consumption.

The markets for coal are quite limited, both as to the numbers of consumers and the uses for which it is bought. Currently about 66 percent of U.S. coal is sold to electric utilities, who burn it in highly sophisticated steam generating furnaces, to power turbines for the generation of electric power. With but few exceptions, electric utilities buy their coal in large volumes, pursuant to long-term, often life of mine coal sales contracts, in order to avail themselves of economies of scale in the price of the coal and the transportation costs.

About another 23 percent of U.S. coal output is used in manufacturing iron and steel, including a large part of the coal that is exported overseas. Most of this metallurgical coal is produced by so-called captive mines, or wholly-owned subsidiaries of steel companies; virtually all of their supplemental metallurgical coal needs are purchased subject to long-term contracts, in order to be assured of adequate supplies. This leaves about 11 percent of the total coal output which is used as fuel by manufacturers of cement and ceramic materials, or as a raw material for making chemicals and other industrial products, along with a very small and diminishing volume sold on the retail market for home consumption, as fuel.

It is estimated that at least 80 to 85 percent of the coal consumed in this country is bought and sold subject to long-term contracts, usually negotiated in advance of the construction of a new mine. These contracts customarily provide for price adjustments based upon changes in actual costs of production and in stipulated price index levels. Such contracts very often run for the life of the mine, or for some lesser term with options for renewals. The balance of the coal industry's output usually is referred to as "spot" coal, principally that production in excess of contract volumes from mines subject to long-term contracts, plus the total output of relatively small producers whose production either is too small or too sporadic to enable them to sell through long-term contracts. Spot coal usually is sold in relatively small volumes at negotiated prices to industrial consumers and to municipally-owned power plants; until recently, TVA characteristically bought heavily in the spot coal market.

Although coal very definitely is an energy fuel resource, it should be noted that a very high percentage of all coal produced in this country is more realisitically a *feedstock,* or a chemical, if you will permit a slight exaggeration, used mainly to produce either a higher, more useful form of energy or industrial materials such as steel, portland cement and chemicals. For the most part these heavy industrial markets for coal are only moderately available to petroleum products; coal-based coke, for example, used in manufacturing steel, is substantially cheaper than coke made from petroleum derivitives, used principally for high-purity electrodes in electric arc furnaces. On the other hand coal is used scarcely at all as a fuel for transportation equipment, or for home heating, or for any other purpose directly competitive with petroleum and natural gas, *except* the generation of electric power. It can be seen that significant interfuel competition between coal and petroleum products occurs only in the electric utility industry, comprising a relatively small number of consumers, all of which are subject to continuous regulation by state and federal agencies.

Contrast the marketing of coal with that of petroleum products. Virtually all coal is sold in large wholesale quantities, pursuant to long-term sales contracts to electric utilities, steel companies and industrial users. Petroleum products are heavily oriented toward fuel and lubricants for transportation equipment and the retail market. Whereas significant volumes of aviation fuels, industrial oils and lubricants customarily are sold subject to short or medium-term wholesale sales contracts, the retail market for various grades of motor fuel comprises a very large share of the petroleum industry's cash crop. When an automobile driver pulls into a gasoline station to fill the tank, he does so after having been subject to the competitive efforts of numerous other gasoline marketers in the area. Such competition is vigorous, continuous, and affects nearly everyone to some extent.

This type of competition within the coal industry is quite rare because retail sales are such a small part of the total market. The real competition takes place at the bargaining table, negotiating for a long-term sales contract with an electric utility, or an industrial consumer of coal.

When such a consumer decides to enter the market for coal he usually requests bids for certain volumes of coal, of a specified grade and quality, for delivery to a named delivery point, over some well-defined period of time. There is competition for this business between potential suppliers of such coal, but the number of companies which elect to bid may be quite limited; in some cases no bids may be received at all and the prospective buyer may need to revise his bid to fit the available supply. This is because the coal company, in order to compete successfully, must have an adequate reserve of coal of the desired quality, located at a point where transportation can be obtained at realistic costs, and also has or can obtain the necessary technical and supervisory manpower, the capital needed to construct the mine, and the multitude of approvals now required before construction can begin.

After coal sales contracts have been negotiated, the mine has been developed and coal deliveries are begun, the mine for all intents and purposes becomes an adjunct facility to the plant which consumes the output. Only rarely will such a mine be available to serve any other market. By the same token the plant which takes the mine's output rarely would be a potential market for a competing fuel, absent governmental interference with fuel markets or other regulatory actions. A furnace constructed to burn one type of fuel, such as coal, is a specialized facility that can be converted to burn other fuels equally efficiently only at great expense, including the economic cost of downtime.

At this point mention should be made that there were wholesale conversions of coal-fired electric utility plants, especially along the Atlantic Coast, as a result of FPC regulations that artificially held the price of natural gas at a fraction of the equivalent heat cost of coal, and later on as a result of legislation that scrapped the already leaky oil import controls on foreign residual fuel oil. It developed, of course, that artificially low natural gas prices stimulated its consumption and discouraged the development of new sources of supply adequate to serve the expanded demand. Similarly the piece of "cheap" imported fuel oil soared to several times the equivalent cost of coal, once the OPEC cartel became well established.

To summarize this part of my presentation, Mr. Chairman, I do not believe that interfuel competition between coal and petroleum products, including natural gas, is of such a nature that new legislation is either desirable or necessary to protect consumers. In the absence of governmental interference with prices, or regulations which would limit free choice among alternative fuel supplies, the consumers of virtually all coal produced in this country have opted for coal on a long-term basis and have invested their capital in specialized equipment designed only for coal. Competition among individual suppliers of coal is keen, but such factors as the availability of reserves of a specified quality, the cost of transportation and the availability of manpower and capital all tend to limit the number of potential sellers of coal to a given consumer at a given time. Once the mine is in operation and supplying coal to its ultimate consumer, both the mine and the plant usually cease to be factors in the competitive market of energy fuels. To put this into a slightly different perspective, competition among suppliers of different forms of energy fuels would be increased by establishing governmental policies that encourage the free entry of all kinds of businesses into other business activities, rather than build a wall around one industry and post off-limits signs that pertain to only one sector of our economy. At the same time, I believe that competition in the energy fuels markets would be better served by eliminating artificial price controls which long ago outlived any practical value they ever had, and now only deter the development of new sources of supply.

I would like to turn now to several other important aspects of major oil companies' investments in the coal industry. In my view this has been beneficial to the coal industry, its customers and the general economy. These benefits derive principally from major infusions of new capital for the development of new mines and to explore for new reserves, and from greatly increased research and development of new mining technology and coal conversion processes.

To put these assertions into proper perspective it is necessary to review briefly the performance of the coal industry during the last, say fifty years. A graph of annual coal output would look much like a roller coaster, as the industry experienced several complete economic cycles. During this period coal mining changed from an almost completely underground, pick and shovel operation to about a 50-50 mix of highly mechanized underground and large-scale surface mining, requiring only a fraction of the former number of employees but greatly increased amounts of capital. Coal's marketing practices also changed, from a business heavily oriented to serve the steel mills, railroads, smaller industrial loads and retail trade to the present emphasis on the electric utility industry.

In the mid 1950's, after experiencing boom conditions during and immediately following World War II, coal dipped into a prolonged major depression, caused principally by price competition from natural gas and imported residual fuels. I have already mentioned how FPC regulations of natural gas at give-away price levels, and the rapid growth in imports of once-cheap foreign fuel oils caused a major fuel conversion program involving a large percentage of formerly coal-fired electric utilities along the Atlantic seaboard and particularly in the New England states. Significant growth in coal demand did not resume until the 1960's, when it was becoming painfully apparent that the Nation was facing a growing shortfall of indigenous fuel resources, principally because of the economic disincentives to capital investment created by FPC regulation of natural gas prices and our growing dependence on foreign petroleum suppliers.

These same economic deterrents to domestic exploration and the development of new sources of crude oil and natural gas played a large role in motivating investments in coal by both large and small oil companies. They could foresee quite clearly that with national policies which perpetuated a continued drift toward growing reliance upon foreign oil, domestic petroleum operations necessarily would decline. At the same time there was significant underinvestment in coal, in industry with long-term growth potential for both primary fuels and synthetics. Further, the technology of coal mining appeared to have room for significant improvements and the research-oriented oil companies recognized additional potential in this area. In short, coal appeared to have good opportunity for growth with new capital investment, while the prospects for new investments in domestic exploration and development of petroleum were becoming poorer.

I think it realistic to assume that oil companies which made large capital investments in coal during the late 1960's and early 1970's have had second thoughts about the returns originally anticipated. The explosive growth of the environmental ethic and the enactment of the Mine Health and Safety Act in the waning days of 1969—which set the stage for three successive loss years during 1971, '72 and '73—played havoc with industry productivity and profits, particularly in underground mining.

It is my firm belief, however, that coal industry participation by oil companies—both large and small—will be critically important to the success of efforts to double coal output by 1985, which is literally the cornerstone of Project Independence and every other plan I have seen to date, intended to reduce our hazardous dependence on foreign oil.

In order for this ambitious program to succeed we necessarily must develop almost three times our present productive capacity in slightly over ten years, while during the previous twenty years the industry did little more than hold its own by replacing depleted mines with new productive capacity. The economic cost of this program has been researched by several prestigious groups, including the National Academy of Engineering, which projected a need for new capital equivalent of $21 billion in 1974 dollars. This means that annual investments in new mines over the next ten and a half years, must *average* nearly four times the average investment rate of the last five years.

Significantly, the National Academy of Engineering projects that the preponderance of new coal output will be from new mines in the Western states, and a large part of the coal must come from Federal leases. As you no doubt know there is a moratorium on new coal leasing in this area and except for relatively small blocks of private land, plans for new mines cannot go forward until this is resolved. In addition to this impediment, however, a recent Appellate Court decision, in the case of Sierra Club v. Morton, effectively has stopped all coal mine development in this area for an indefinite period of time.

This Western area, involving especially parts of Wyoming, Montana and North Dakota, includes important blocks of coal land now held by several major oil companies that had started to construct facilities for large new mines to serve a number of electric utilities, principally in the Southwestern part of the country, which are in urgent need of coal to replace dwindling supplies of natural gas. Regardless of the merits of the case involved, I think it should be noted that this shutdown occurred after many millions of dollars had been invested that will remain unproductive, at least until this case has been settled. Not only has money been invested in the mine facilities, but the utilities are well along with plans for refitting boilers to burn the coal they contracted for. In my own judgement none of the independent coal companies could long survive an indefinite deferment of income from such large investments as already have been made to develop this area.

Much of the preceding part of my statement also applies to the nuclear fuel business, with the notable caveat that the physical quantities involved and its present economic importance are minute by comparison with coal.

Uranium has only one market as a fuel resource, the electric utilities. Uranium has no foreseeable significant applications to retail trade or to land or air transportation.

At the present time nuclear energy provides less than two percent of our total supply of energy, perhaps four or five percent of the electric power generation capacity. National Academy of Engineering has forecast an increase in nuclear power to a level of about 17 percent of our total energy consumption by 1985, while others estimate that this percentage will range between 6 and 14 percent. In order to accomplish the NAE goal some 193 new, 1300-1500 megawatt reactors (or the equivalent) would need to be constructed and on line by the end of 1985. Contrast this with a 1973 nuclear power capability equivalent to only 17 such plants. To fuel the new plants about 71 new, average-sized uranium and thorium mines will be needed; there were 17 in 1973. I suggest these figures demonstrate that there is ample room for participation and competition in this business, for all who chose to enter it.

As you likely have heard, virtually all of the new nuclear power plants for which schedules had been announced by the end of 1973 have been deferred or cancelled because of spiraling costs and the financial difficulties of the electric utilities. At this time there is no immediate basis for revising the estimates, referred to above, as to the nuclear capacity which will be built during the next ten years. On the other hand if the stated objectives are to be achieved, the rate of capital investment in such plants must accelerate at a rate considerably higher than forecast to make up for delays in the program. Based on our experience with the most recently completed plants, the total elapsed time from announcement to startup is nearly ten years. To put it mildly, the nuclear power plant construction program is in great difficulty.

Here again, Mr. Chairman, the only business area where potential competition exists between uranium and petroleum is the electric utility industry, and interfuel competition would not exist after a decision has been made to construct a nuclear plant. Thus the only remaining germane question is whether one or more major oil companies could gain sufficient control of uranium resources to control pricing throughout the industry. I respectfully suggest that there is not now any basis for such a presumption. If indeed one oil company or several in combination were to announce plans for projects equivalent to a potentially illegal share of the anticipated new uranium mining capacity needed by 1985, there would be ample time for judicial relief at that time.

So far as I have been able to determine, the role of oil shale as a viable source of energy in the near future appears to be quite limited. Oil shale still appears to be only marginally economic as a substitute for natural crude oil and the huge amounts of capital needed for its development likely will deter all but the most attractive projects for a very long time. Much of the work done to date is essentially of a research character and the first one or two commercial-sized projects likely will produce no more than 50,000 barrels per day each, compared with our present crude oil producing capacity of nearly 10 million barrels per day. I certainly see nothing in this picture which offers any threat of anti-competitive actions by major oil companies.

Geothermal steam—the darling of the media—has even less long-term potential because the steam must be used in close proximity to the producing wells and economies of scale preclude small generating plants. Only one field is now in commercial operation at this time, in California, driving a very small generating plant. In my view geothermal steam is a very marginal source of energy and there is no justification for prohibiting oil company participation in this business.

Solar energy is another very marginal potential source of thermal energy, and it has received much more attention than present technology can support. The heat from the sun is characterized by having low entropy, meaning that the usable heat content is small. In point of fact, the sun's radiant energy striking the earth's surface is comparable with that of a large black body with a surface temperature of only about 450°F. This is about 50 percent less than the temperature of steam used to drive conventional turbines in electric power plants, even assuming 100 percent efficiency of conversion, which is not now possible. Present collector systems average 25-30 percent efficiency and are frightfully expensive. Of course this technology will improve and in time affluent home owners could look forward to obtaining some fraction of their home heating and cooling from solar energy. I can see no need now, or in the foreseeable future, to limit oil companies from participating in any aspect of solar energy development.

I thank you, Mr. Chairman, for the opportunity to appear here today.

INDEX